DECODING
THE LOST SYMBOL

The Unauthorized Expert Guide
to the Facts Behind the Fiction

SIMON COX

A TOUCHSTONE BOOK
Published by Simon & Schuster
New York   London   Toronto   Sydney

 Touchstone
A Division of Simon & Schuster, Inc.
1230 Avenue of the Americas
New York, NY 10020

First Touchstone trade paperback edition November 2009

TOUCHSTONE and colophon are registered trademarks of Simon & Schuster, Inc.

For information about special discounts for bulk purchases,
please contact Simon & Schuster Special Sales at 1-866-506-1949 or
business@simonandschuster.com

The Simon & Schuster Speakers Bureau can bring authors to your live event.
For more information or to book an event contact the Simon & Schuster Speakers
Bureau at 1-866-248-3049 or visit our website at www.simonspeakers.com.

Manufactured in the United States of America

10 9 8 7 6 5 4 3 2 1

Library of Congress Cataloging-in-Publication data is available.

ISBN 978-0-7432-8727-2
ISBN 978-1-4391-7261-2 (ebook)

Contents

CONTENTS

Introduction

It was April 2009, and I was just arriving at the London Book Fair at the Earls Court Exhibition Halls. I was intending on catching up with friends, my UK publisher, and having a general look at what was new in the publishing world. However, I knew that something remarkable had happened the minute I had arrived. An air of excitement and expectation filled the packed halls, and smiles were emanating from all around. Grown men were close to tears.

I instantly knew what had happened: the new Dan Brown book had been announced.

This was to be the start of nearly five months of manic preparation and debate. Clues and hints would be given out, opinions bandied about, and crazed supposition would fill thousands of web pages. However, let's wind back the clock to the publication of Brown's previous Robert Langdon thriller, *The Da Vinci Code*, in 2003.

Back then, Dan Brown was a semisuccessful author of several thrillers, one of which was the first Robert Langdon novel, *Angels & Demons*, published in 2000. Sales had been average to poor, and Brown's publisher decided to take a gamble with *The Da Vinci Code*, sending out ten thousand free copies to bookstores and their book buyers, reviewers, and trade professionals. The plan worked, and soon sales really began to take off.

At the time, I was the editor in chief of a U.S.-based newsstand magazine called *Phenomena*. *The Da Vinci Code* was starting to cause quite a stir within the alternative-history genre that I inhabited; in fact, several authors that I had worked for as a researcher had their work credited as source material for Brown's book. (*Phenomena* even ran an article "casting" the movie version of *The Da Vinci Code*, should it ever come to pass. For the record, not one of the actors we thought would be so terrific in the roles of Dr. Robert Langdon, Sir Leigh Teabing, and the book's other characters was cast for Ron Howard's 2006 film starring Tom Hanks.) Eventually a small London publisher approached me about writing a short guide to *The Da Vinci Code*. The book, *Cracking the Da Vinci Code*, went on to become an international best seller in its own right. I subsequently wrote *Illuminating Angels & Demons*, a companion to Brown's other Langdon-based novel.

Intriguingly, the dust jacket of the U.S. hardcover edition of *The Da Vinci Code* seemed to contain clues hinting at the next novel in the series. This fascinated me, and I found out all I could about these clues and the secrets that they potentially held.

Time passed, and rumors began circulating that a title had been chosen. The new book was to be called *The Solomon Key*—an apparent reference to a medieval book on magic with the same title. Impatiently, I began researching all that I could about this centuries-old text, which supposedly was written in Italy during the Renaissance but claimed a lineage that went all the way back to King Solomon himself. Perfect material for a Dan Brown thriller, I thought. Brown's publishing team registered a new website, solomonkey.com, and everything seemed poised for the new book to arrive soon.

More time passed . . . and more time passed . . . and still no definitive word about the new book, though plenty of fresh rumors abounded: Brown had scrapped the book; there would be no follow-up to *The Da Vinci Code*. Brown, exhausted from having fended off a high-profile copyright-infringement lawsuit in London, had decided to take an extended break from writing. It was even claimed that the 2004 movie *National Treasure*, starring Nicolas Cage as a treasure hunter seeking a mysterious war chest hidden by the Founding Fathers, had stolen so much of the forthcoming book's thunder that it required a complete rewrite. The unsubstantiated allegations were completely fanciful, of course, but they replicated over and over like a virus on the ever-conspiratorial internet sites that monitored the story, sending the rumor mill into overdrive.

Then came the 2009 London Book Fair. Only a couple of months before, I had predicted to my UK publisher that the announcement would indeed be made at the London event. More in hope than expectation, it has to be said, but accurate nonetheless.

A press release was handed out by Brown's publishers, and suddenly a new title presented itself: *The Lost Symbol,* to be published on

September 15, 2009. What could such an enigmatic title mean? What was lost? Which symbol? The race was on, the game was afoot, and I rushed headlong into research-and-reading mode. What you hold in your hands before you is the outcome of that labor.

Before long, a new website appeared, at www.thelostsymbol.com, though nothing but a holding page was evident for quite a while. Then, out of the blue, the site added links to a Dan Brown Facebook page and Twitter feed. Excitement grew to fever pitch, as thousands of people became Facebook and Twitter followers of Dan Brown overnight.

Steadily, these new media outlets began to reveal tantalizing clues and tidbits of story line. With each revelation, I furiously took notes and researched everything I could find. It was as if a whole new world were opening up. It was a cornucopia of material, and I started ordering more new books for my library to cover some of the subjects mentioned.

Some of the clues actually gave coordinates to several locations, such as the so-called Bimini Road. This unusual underwater structure off the island of Bimini in the Bahamas is claimed to be a man-made edifice and a remnant of the lost island of Atlantis. I had spent two summers on Bimini a number of years back as part of my research for a book about Atlantis. "Great," I thought, "now I have a head start on some of the material." Coordinates were also given for the Great Pyramid of Giza, the last standing wonder of the ancient world and another place with which I was intimately familiar. Then there were coordinates to Newgrange in Ireland, a monumental passage tomb built around five thousand years ago. The stone structure is famous for its alignment to dawn on the winter solstice, when a narrow beam of light briefly illuminates the floor of the chamber. I had just visited Newgrange with the author and Freemason Chris McClintock.

Possible adversaries and secret societies were hinted at. Ciphers, codes, and cryptograms were revealed. Historical figures were mentioned. It was all adding up to a furious game of who could be first to reveal the answers to the clues. Websites sprang up detailing the background and history of some of the people, places, and groups being mentioned. It was an internet feeding frenzy.

Then I remembered something: Bishop Manuel Aringarosa, a character from *The Da Vinci Code*, whose name had a hidden meaning. Aringa is the Italian word for "herring"; rosa means "red." Dan Brown liked to throw multiple red herrings into the mix. I began to look at the Twitter and Facebook clues in a new light. What if many of these were indeed red herrings? What if I were immersing myself in subjects that weren't included in the published book? That's when I stopped even looking at the Facebook and Twitter pages. After all, everything would be revealed on the day of publication, September 15.

Even this date, we were told, was part of the puzzle; chosen specifically for the book's release. I began to check almanacs, history books, websites, conspiracy theorist blogs, but found nothing. Then it hit me: 09.15.09; 9 plus 15 plus 9 equals 33. So it was true. The Freemasons, and specifically Scottish Rite Freemasons, would be a central theme of the book—something that had been hinted at on the dust jacket of *The Da Vinci Code* years ago.

Then, before I knew it, publication day arrived. I began reading *The Lost Symbol* furiously. When I finished some twelve hours later, I realized that my suspicions had proved correct: many of the clues leaked over the previous months on Dan Brown's Twitter and Facebook pages were indeed aringarosa—red herrings. There was no Morgan affair; no Aaron Burr; no William Wirt (and the strange story of his skull); no Knights of the Golden Circle; no substantial mentions of Albert Pike; no Benedict Arnold; no Confederate gold; no Babington plot; no Alexander Hamilton and the origins of the New York Stock Exchange; no Sons of Liberty; no Lost Colony of Roanoke; no Robert Hanssen, the U.S.-born Russian spy; no Checkpoint Charlie in Berlin.

Cleverly, there was no Key of Solomon, either. Instead we have a family with the surname of Solomon, who hold the keys to the eventual outcome. The Great Pyramid figures in the story, though not prominently and not in the context that many had thought.

Dan Brown and his publishers had managed to pull off something of a coup, keeping the plotline of *The Lost Symbol* pretty much under wraps until the day of publication (although a couple of U.S. newspapers did print reviews the day before, in defiance of the publisher's embargo). It was an amazing feat, especially considering that the book's print run exceeded five million copies, and it guaranteed Brown a huge amount of media and public attention.

So: what did we end up with? Is *The Lost Symbol* a worthy successor to *Angels & Demons* and *The Da Vinci Code*?

The Lost Symbol is, in the end, a pretty good thriller that keeps Robert Langdon on his toes and involves some big themes and historical enigmas. However, it's the deeper, more hidden elements of the book that I believe will have the most impact over time. Between the lines of the novel, Dan Brown has attempted to write something akin to a hidden Hermetic text. It's a bold and ambitious undertaking, and one that I applaud him for. Indeed, the last ten chapters of the book and the epilogue are more or less an extended treatise on Deism, Hermetic thought, and religious tolerance.

The Freemasons are the secret society of choice this time around. I'm sure that there will be those who see Freemasonry as a covert, sinister movement intent on power and blasphemy. I see it rather differently. I am not a Freemason, nor will I ever be one. But I do know many Freemasons. Indeed, Ian Robertson, one of the chief researchers for this book, is a Freemason, as is my friend Chris McClintock, author of the soon-to-be-published Sun of God book series on the origins of the Freemasonry and its symbolism. Neither of them is in any way sinister, nor are the countless other Freemasons that I know and respect. I like the stance that Dan Brown has taken with Freemasonry within *The Lost Symbol*. Many commentators thought that the Masons would, in effect, be portrayed as the "bad guys," but this is not the case. In fact, Brown makes a convincing argument for Freemasonry being a tolerant and enlightened movement with some interesting and forward-thinking ideas.

While it should be said that Freemasonry is a secretive society, it is not a secret society. Membership is easy to research and find out about, and most members are not shy about letting you know that they are within the craft, as it is called. Since the heyday of Freemasonry in the eighteenth century, it has attracted men of a certain social standing and, to an extent, still does. But the group has become more welcoming as of late, and I hope that this trend continues.

One of the things I wanted to get across within some of the entries of this book is that maybe it's not Freemasonry we should be wary of—instead maybe we should fear the real secret groups and societies of which we know very little or nothing. Then again, maybe we are simply chasing shadows, wisps of rumor and supposition that have tormented us for millennia; a fear of secret and hidden things that, in the end, may not be that secret or hidden after all. Another thing worth noting is that although many of the people mentioned in this book were not Freemasons (Pierre L'Enfant springs to mind), or at least we have no evidence that they were, they would have been intimately familiar with the society and its workings. Many of their contemporaries and peers would have been members, and the craft would have been all around. It seems likely, for instance, that Thomas Jefferson, though we have no direct evidence of his membership in a Masonic lodge, did have sympathies with the Masonic ideals of brotherhood, enlightenment, and religious tolerance.

Once again, like my previous guides to Dan Brown's books, this book is laid out in an easy-to-read A-to-Z format. There are some sixty entries in all; fewer than in previous guides. This was deliberate, as I wanted to give you a much more in-depth look at some of the themes, places, people, and groups featured in the novel.

The BBC in the United Kingdom once called me "a historian of the obscure," a title that I like very much indeed. I have aimed to bring you some of that history of obscure and hidden subjects within the pages of this book. If you feel the urge to look deeper and delve further into some of the interesting subjects highlighted here, take a look at the bibliography and start building your own library of esoteric and arcane subjects. Just make sure that you remember to sleep and eat while familiarizing yourself with the ancient mystery traditions—it's an addictive pursuit but also a very rewarding one, and one that I hope many of you will undertake.

If you want to talk about, debate, or extol any of the subjects in this book or the novel itself, head over to my website at www.decod ingthelostsymbol.com, where you will find a forum for debate and articles and blogs. If you want to contact me directly about any of the issues raised, I have my own Facebook page under my name and can be found on Twitter too (@FindSimonCox).

Writing this book was a lot of fun, and it has given me a newfound respect and admiration for the men who founded a new and fledgling nation in America, at the end of the eighteenth century. As a British writer and historian, it's a period of history that I was not that familiar with and I have really enjoyed the research and subsequent writing about this tumultuous time. The Founding Fathers really were incredibly enlightened and forward-thinking men, who guided the formation of a republic with steady hands and an unwavering resolve. I will forever look at them, and this period of time, in a brand-new light from now on.

I hope you enjoy *Decoding The Lost Symbol*, and find its contents enlightening and interesting. I pass it on to you with the hope that you will find it as fun to read as it was to write.

Simon Cox
Bedford, United Kingdom
September 2009

Nullius in verba ("Take nobody's word for it")

—MOTTO OF THE ROYAL SOCIETY

DECODING
THE LOST SYMBOL

Abaddon

One of the pseudonyms used by Mal'akh in *The Lost Symbol* is that of Dr. Christopher Abaddon. It's an interesting choice, encompassing the names of Jesus Christ and the demon Abaddon.

In ancient Hebrew, *Abaddon* means "place of destruction" and "the destroyer." According to the New Testament's book of Revelation, chapter 9, Abaddon is the angel of the Abyss, or bottomless pit. He rules over a swarm of vicious locusts. These are not just any locusts, however: they have human faces and women's hair, breastplates as strong as iron, lions' teeth, and scorpions' tails. When the fifth angel sounded his trumpet, the locusts roared out of the thick smoke of the Abyss and descended upon the earth to torment any man or women who did not have the seal of God on his or her forehead.

In Greek, Abaddon translates as *Apollyon*, which means "destroyer." Abaddon is also associated with death and hell in ancient rabbinical writings, and in the Old Testament, Abaddon refers to the realm of the dead, like Hades or hell (see Job 26:6). In these ancient texts, it's clear that Abaddon can be an individual, as in the book of Revelation, or a place of the dead and destruction. The Dead Sea Scrolls mention a place called "the Sheol of Abaddon"—*Sheol* being the Hebrew word for the underworld.

The Coptic Christian Church translates his name as Abbaton; under this guise, he is the angel of death. Within certain Coptic writings, it becomes clear that Abaddon/Abbaton is a mirror image of the Christ figure; indeed, the text known as the Apocalypse of Bartholomew mentions Abbaton as having been present in the tomb at the moment of Christ's resurrection. Interestingly, a close look at Coptic legends associated with this demon reveals the character of Christopher Abaddon/Mal'akh. It is said that anyone who venerated him might be saved at the end of days, and Abbaton plays an important role in the scenario of the Last Judgment. In this guise, Abaddon can almost be seen as the Antichrist, which perfectly fits the character in *The Lost Symbol*. In contrast to those seeking knowledge and enlightenment, Mal'akh is hell-bent on preventing the discoveries of Noetic

Science from being disseminated to the wider world. He also desires to discredit Freemasonry and have it be seen as sinister. He is the antithesis of his father.

The name Abaddon has been used extensively in modern popular culture. Even author J. K. Rowling, in her Harry Potter books, created a character named Apollyon (the Greek version of the name), a one-time Hogwarts school caretaker who used to punish the students.

Akedah

In *The Lost Symbol*, Mal'akh wields an ancient weapon with a notorious past called the Akedah knife. Not content to furnish the villain of the novel with just any old ancient knife of power, Dan Brown tells us that this is the most famous knife in existence.

We learn that Mal'akh spent a large part of his fortune obtaining this legendary weapon, crafted more than three thousand years before from an iron meteorite that had crashed into the desert of Canaan. It was said to be the very knife that Abraham had wielded in the book of Genesis, when he was prepared to sacrifice his son Isaac to obey God's command. Other illustrious and notorious owners of the knife have included Nazis, popes, and European alchemists, among others.

At the end of *The Lost Symbol*, Mal'akh places the Akedah knife in the remaining hand of his father, Peter Solomon, and attempts to coerce his estranged father into killing him. Something interesting to note here is that Mal'akh places the Akedah knife in the left hand of Peter Solomon, now his one remaining hand. We are told that "*the* left hand serves the darkness," and also that the removal of Peter Solomon's right hand had been designed with this very moment in mind; quite simply he has no choice but to use his left hand to grasp the knife. If Peter Solomon were to carry out this sacrificial killing with his left hand then, according to Mal'akh's twisted beliefs at least, the sacrifice would be perfect, and Mal'akh's would secure his place as a demon in the afterlife.

Furthermore, the scene takes place on a granite altar in the House of the Temple, leaving no doubt that this is a re-creation of the biblical story of Abraham and Isaac.

It is in the Hebrew Bible's book of Genesis that we find the story, which is called the Akedah, or "The Binding of Isaac." Abraham was being tested by God, who told him: "Take your son, your only son Isaac, whom you love, and go to the land of Moriah, and offer him there as a burnt offering upon one of the mountains of which I shall tell you."

Abraham, following God's instructions, left early in the morning for Mount Moriah. He arrived at the sacred spot three days later. There Abraham bound his son to an altar. He was about to take Isaac's life with his knife when an angel appeared and implored Abraham to stop, telling him that he had passed God's test. So it was that Isaac was spared, and a ram was sacrificed on the altar instead.

The story fits neatly into *The Lost Symbol* because we are told that Mal'akh took his name and identity from Moloch, a fearful fallen angel who appears in John Milton's *Paradise Lost*, the epic poem that describes the fall of man. We begin to see the relationship between Moloch and sacrifice in this poem:

> First Moloch, horrid king besmear'd with blood
> Of human sacrifice, and parents' tears.

There are also references to Moloch in the biblical texts that link the Deity with sacrifice. This is in accordance with the story of the Akedah and God's command that Isaac be offered up by Abraham. In the book of Leviticus, we find the following passage, as God instructs Moses, " 'You will not allow any of your children to be sacrificed to Molech, thus profaning the name of your God.' "

Dan Brown has brought together all of these elements, and the climatic scene in the House of the Temple is loaded with historical references and symbolism relating to sacrifice. Not only do we have Mal'akh, modeled on Moloch, (also spelled Molech in some versions of the Bible) but he's clutching the very knife of Abraham. Also, he asks his father to slay him beside the altar in a sacred temple. Offering oneself as a willing sacrificial victim is a recurrent theme in the ancient world. In fact, a growing body of evidence reveals that many cultures practiced human sacrifice, with the victims willingly offering themselves. To be sacrificed seems to have been considered a great honor. Even today, we can see how this motif and very real practice still influences the behavior of extremists who volunteer without reservation as suicide bombers.

Many scholars believe that Isaac was no child when he was bound to the altar. Various sources place his age somewhere between twenty-five and thirty-seven, so he would have been perfectly capable of resisting his father if he had wanted to. Flavius Josephus, the first-century Jewish historian, refers to this very concept, and in his *Antiquities of the Jews*, he states that Isaac responded to the news that he was to be sacrificed with equanimity:

> *Now Isaac was of such a generous disposition as became the son of such a father, and was pleased with his discourse; and said "that he was not worthy to be born at first, if he should reject the determination of God and of his father, and should not resign himself up readily to both their pleasures; since it would have been unjust if he had not obeyed, even if his father alone had so resolved." So he went immediately to the altar to be sacrificed.*

The Akedah is without a doubt one of the most controversial sections of the book of Genesis, and debate still rages about not just God's motives but also those of Abraham and Isaac. By ordering Abraham to kill his firstborn and beloved son—a son who came to Abraham's wife, Sarah, only after much suffering—we see God testing the absolute limits of someone's faith. Even today this test is taught as a moral lesson in several faiths, and the parable is not just contained within the Jewish sacred writings; for example, it is also found in the Islamic Qur'an.

The setting of the Akedah, on Mount Moriah, has special significance in *The Lost Symbol*. This sacred mountain, the "mount of the Lord" according to Genesis 22:14, happens to be where Solomon's Temple was later constructed. Mount Moriah is, to many scholars, the Temple Mount. I cover Solomon's Temple in further detail elsewhere in this book, but it is worth mentioning here that not only is Solomon's Temple fundamentally important within Freemasonry but it also served as a model for the Capitol building in Washington, DC.

One final intriguing attribute of the knife of Akedah in *The Lost Symbol* is its construction. We are told that it was forged of iron from a meteorite. The Bible's version of the Akedah story makes no mention of this, but Brown's invention is not a complete fabrication.

It is well known that the ancient peoples of the Middle East would construct sacred knives and powerful weapons from meteoritic iron that had fallen in the form of meteors. The metal was highly prized, not only because it was a source of iron which could be forged, but also because meteorites were often described in the ancient world as thunderbolts, probably because of the observed phenomena when a meteor descends from the skies and impacts the earth. Therefore a weapon shaped from a thunderbolt was a potent symbol indeed.

Archaeologist and historian G. A. Wainwright, in a seminal 1932 journal article titled "Iron in Egypt," states that many ancient peoples came to call this form of iron from the skies "lightning-iron." He also cites the story of Antar, the pre-Islamic Arabian warrior and poet, who came to possess a powerful sword he called Dhami:

> On discovering the stone to be a thunderbolt the man gave it to a black-smith to have a sword made of it. On two separate occasions a single stroke of this supernatural weapon clove through the armour and split horse and horseman asunder, "so that they fell apart in four pieces." On another occasion it clove a warrior "to his girdle." These magic weapons have naturally been in great demand throughout the East.

The Egyptian god of light Horus himself wielded a blade of meteoritic iron in his legendary clash with the god Seth, in which Horus defeated Seth in revenge for the death of his father, Osiris.

In addition to meteoric iron's potency, it was sought after for its profound religious significance. A sacred ritual in ancient Egypt, known as the Opening of the Mouth, called for using a sacred knife, or adze, known as *Ntrwj*-blades to pry open the mouth of a dead pharaoh. This ritual was to enable the dead king's spirit to ascend to heaven. The blades were formed from meteoritic iron, known to the Egyptians as *bja*. To complement the knives' celestial origins, their handles were shaped like the constellation Ursa Major, otherwise known as the Big Dipper or the Plough.

It is clear why in the eyes of the ancient priests, these blades made from meteoritic iron were such powerful objects. They were perfect for opening the mouth of the deceased in a religious ritual because they were actually made from thunderbolts themselves. What better way to physically and metaphorically prise open the lips of the dead.

The Ancient Egyptians also believed that the vault of heaven itself was constructed from *bja,* and that upon death, the limbs of the deceased were themselves turned into *bja.* Furthermore, the word *bja* was used to describe a "miracle" and it also could be used for "to depart from."

From this, we come to understand that iron that fell to earth was not just iron from the heavens, it was actually seen as being heaven *itself;* being nothing less than the very same material that heaven was constructed from. Since it could also mean "depart from" it is clear that the Ancient Egyptians believed that these meteors had left heaven to fall to earth.

The Muslims later held a belief that Allah's angels used meteors to drive away Satan and to fight supernatural beings called *djinns.* With such powerful concepts in play, it is no wonder that knives and weapons forged from such a material were considered weapons of the gods; thunderbolts that could be brandished by mortal hands.

Putting all of this together, we see why Mal'akh would use a knife crafted from extraterrestrial iron; there is no more potent a weapon than one shaped from such material. Abraham too would have been aware of the significance of such a knife.

Alchemy

In *The Lost Symbol*, Dan Brown has pulled together various traditions that fall under the banner of the Western mystery or esoteric tradition. The Great Library of Alexandria is mentioned, as are the ancient cultures of Egypt, Rome, and Greece. Mystery schools feature, as does the Hebrew Kabbalah, Hermeticism, the mystical Rosicrucians, tarot cards, and Freemasonry. Arguably, the most important, having influenced all of the above, is alchemy, referred to as the perennial philosophy. This is at the heart of the Western mysteries and pervades all traditions in some way, shape, or form through its exquisite language of symbols.

The origins of alchemy are completely lost in the mists of time but are extremely ancient. It was known to and practiced by the Egyptians and Chinese in antiquity. Its name means the "land of Khem," or the "black land," from the Arabic name for Egypt, *Al-Khemia* or *Kemet*. The reference to black relates to the fertile soil of the Nile Delta that spread across the Nile Valley, with the annual flooding of the river. It is from this name that alchemy is often called the "black art," and from this that the modern science of chemistry arose, but this name did not appear until the seventeenth century. Robert Boyle, an alchemist and friend of Isaac Newton's, wrote *The Sceptical Chymist* in 1661. It is widely regarded to be the first book about the new science of chemistry.

Professor Robert Langdon, in the novel, states that Newton had written letters to Boyle warning him that the mystical knowledge they were studying could not be communicated without dangerous consequences to the world. Today, however, many of Newton's alchemical texts can be viewed online, courtesy of the Newton Project in England, at www.newtonproject.sussex.ac.uk.

There exist many fabulous legends of alchemy's origins. The Egyptian god Thoth was said to be its founder. He is described as the "god man" who brought religion and learning to Egypt and was credited with having invented writing, mathematics, music, astronomy, architecture, and medicine. The similarities among Thoth, Hermes, and Mercury—being custodians of all knowledge as well as the intermediaries between heaven and earth within their respective cultures—have collectively shaped the figure known as Hermes Trismegistus, the father of alchemy.

It is Hermes Trismegistus who has given his name to the word *Hermeticism*, primarily through a collection of Hellenistic texts known as the *Corpus Hermeticum*. These texts came to the fore again during the European Renaissance and became essential reading for the esoteric-occult revival.

Hermes Trismegistus, we are told, created a fabulous emerald tablet said to contain the secrets of creation for those who can penetrate their meaning. Sir Isaac Newton made an English translation around 1680 of the alleged content of the tablet that has come down to us through ancient texts:

'Tis true without lying, certain and most true. That which is below is like that which is above and that which is above is like that which is below to do the miracles of One only Thing.

And as all things have been and arose from One by the mediation of One: so all things have their birth from this One Thing by adaptation.

The Sun is its father, the Moon its mother, the Wind hath carried it in its belly, the Earth its nurse. The father of all perfection in the whole world is here. Its force or power is entire if it be converted into earth. Separate thou the Earth from the Fire, the subtle from the gross, sweetly with great industry. It ascends from the Earth to Heaven and again it descends to the Earth and receives the force of things superior and inferior.

By this means you shall have the glory of the whole world and thereby all obscurity shall fly from you. Its force is above all force for it vanquishes every subtle thing and penetrates every solid thing. So was the world created. From this are and do come admirable adaptations whereof the means (or process) is here in this. Hence I am called Hermes Trismegistus, having the three parts of the philosophy of the whole world. That which I have said of the operation of the Sun is accomplished and ended.

The emerald tablet is the key text used in alchemy, as it maps out the seven steps of transformation required to create the elusive "philosopher's stone."

Other legendary traditions claim that the father of alchemy is Seth, the son of Adam, who apparently created the tablet in the hope that those who followed its teachings would correct the fall of Adam from the Garden of Eden, by allowing them to discover the key to perfection. In some Gnostic legends, Seth is also given the secrets of the Kabbalah from Adam. Other variants say that the tablet was saved from the great flood by Noah, who took it aboard the ark and afterward hid it in a cave near Hebron. Sarah, the wife of Abraham, later discovered the tablet, and it informed the Hebrew faith. Yet another tale is that Miriam, the daughter of Moses, was entrusted with its safekeeping; she placed it into the Ark of the Covenant along with the sacred relics.

It is also said to be one of the tablets brought down from the mount by Moses. In esoteric circles, the Ten Commandments were said to have been the exoteric teachings for the masses, while the emerald tablet was reserved for initiates of the mysteries.

In Islamic tradition, Hermes Trismegistus is paralleled with the wise man Idris, who revealed divine laws to the faithful. Some Muslim scholars have also associated Idris with Enoch. The apocryphal Book of Enoch describes the angelic wisdom, which was shared with Enoch. In some Kabbalistic traditions, Enoch is transformed into the archangel Metratron, to become the chancellor of heaven. The different names given all have one thing in common: they represent the personification of the qualities and values that seekers of true perfection—the alchemists—strive to reach.

The emerald tablet was said to have been discovered by Alexander the Great and later exhibited at the Great Library of Alexandria in Egypt. This library was reportedly a massive repository for alchemical texts that were destroyed by a great fire. Fortunately, Arab scholars had copied many of the works, thus preserving the knowledge over the following centuries. Alchemy then found its way into Europe by way of the Islamic invasion of Spain and the south of France in 711. Latin translations began to appear as early as the twelfth century and took hold from the Renaissance onward.

The influence of alchemy translated into legends of the Holy Grail as they developed in Europe. The Sacro Catino, a sacred hexagonal bowl in Genoa, Italy, has been identified by some as the Holy Grail. Legend says that it was fashioned from a solid piece of emerald and was the dish used at the Last Supper. In his epic poem *Parzival,* dating from the thirteenth century, the German poet Wolfram von Eschenbach describes the Grail as a green stone, and not as the familiar cup. Possession of the stone in the Grail tradition offered the individual eternal life in the same way that the philosopher's stone of the alchemists is said to. The emerald tablet, according to a final legendary account, was said to have been last seen in the tomb of Christian Rosenkreuz, the legendary founder of the Rosicrucians.

Alchemy, with its strange language and symbolism, can be seen as a complex subject. The purpose of alchemy is transmutation, turning figurative lead into gold. Although many alchemists of the Middle Ages claimed to have actually turned physical lead into gold, Robert Langdon was correct in his summary when he stated that spiritual alchemy is about enlightenment. It is an investigation into Hermetic philosophy to discover the interconnectedness of everything, the Macrocosm and the Microcosm, the Above and the Below, in order to utilize this knowledge in spiritual and practical ways. This would also explain why the members of the Royal Society, or "Invisible College," were fascinated by its teachings.

With the rise of the various sciences of the eighteenth century and beyond, alchemy was viewed as an outdated superstition by the masses. Today, however, alchemy is experiencing a renaissance and is viewed in a completely new light, with psychologists and quantum physicists seeing parallels between their work and alchemy. The famous analyst Carl Gustav Jung spent the latter part of his life studying the rich symbolism of alchemy; this inspired his groundbreaking work on archetypes, to help clients bring about inner transformation. Today there is an array of websites and groups dedicated to the study of alchemy and alchemical texts and drawings, possibly making the black art the most accessible that it has ever been.

The figurative process of change is characterized in a number of ways that correspond to seven steps. For example, with metals, lead to gold is lead to tin, tin to iron, iron to copper, copper to mercury, mercury to silver, and, finally, silver to gold. They were chosen in this order because each metal is viewed as being superior to the one before it, with gold the most perfect. Each step has a range of other correspondences, such as to the planets: Saturn, Jupiter, Mars, Venus, Mercury, the Moon, and then the Sun. In terms of alchemical elements (not to be confused with the chemical elements of the periodic table), the sequence is fire, water, air, earth, sulfur, mercury, and salt. When you think of the old expression of someone being the "salt of the earth," it possibly now begins to make more sense than it once did.

Alchemical elements are used very much as descriptions of the characteristics or nature of things. For example, acid is a mixture of the elements fire and water; water, obviously, because acid is liquid, but also fire because of its ability to burn. The names for each of the steps are described as calcination, dissolution, separation, conjunction, fermentation, distillation, and coagulation.

Using the language of symbols, alchemical diagrams are filled with strange images. For those who understand what the images represent, however, it will map out one of the stages of the alchemical process as described on the emerald tablet, the key text in alchemy. The diagrams also need to be studied carefully as to what is at the top and bottom of the picture or on either side. This is because alchemy works to bring together opposites, to create a union of all things; the philosopher's stone, often depicted as an androgynous character, is described as the chemical wedding.

In the symbolism of Freemasonry, the steps to enlightenment are symbolically illustrated as the rough ashlar (stone) and the polished ashlar. The new candidate is the base material lead or the rough ashlar, and he or she is transformed into an enlightened master Mason, or the polished ashlar or gold. Freemasonry describes this in the third degree, as the point within a circle, which has no circumference, from which no master Mason can err. This process is by way of entering the porch-way or entrance to King Solomon's Temple, past the great pillars of Boaz and Jachin, and journeying up the winding staircase in order to reach the holy of holies, or sanctum sanctorum. Other

Masonic allegories discuss the "lost word" and the "all-seeing eye" of God, which are similar metaphors for the philosopher's stone. In Scottish Rite Freemasonry, the double-headed eagle of the thirty-third degree serves a similar purpose.

In *The Lost Symbol*, Robert Langdon gives a lecture describing "the most hidden of all hidden things." He explains that the circle with a round dot in the middle is called the circumpunct. This is the alchemical symbol for gold, and it was the symbol of the Egyptian sun god, Ra: the ouroboros symbol of a snake eating its own tail. He offers more examples but finishes by saying that what it really stands for is the mind and soul being at one.

Langdon also focuses on the imagery of the pyramid and the symbolism of stones when he discusses the actual alchemical motto *VITRIOL*, an acronym for *Visita interiora terrae rectificando invenies occultum lapidem*. Dennis William Hauck's excellent book *The Complete Idiot's Guide to Alchemy* offers the following explanation: "Vista Interiora Terra Rectificando Invenies Occultum Lapidem (Visit the innermost parts of the earth; and by setting things right [rectifying], you will find the hidden stone). The first letters of these seven Latin words spell out *VITRIOL*, which is a natural form of sulfuric acid. This liquid fire is the fundamental agent of change in most alchemical experiments and also symbolic of the Secret Fire that drives the spiritual perfection of the alchemist."

Using this to describe the seven steps as set out in the emerald tablet, here is what we find:

Vista represents what is called the black phase of the work, and the word means "to visit or start a journey." The alchemical process is called calcination, its element is that of fire, and the corresponding verse from the emerald tablet is "The Sun is its father."

Interiora refers to our own interior work, whereby we dissolve our old self. This step is called dissolution, and its element is water. The corresponding verse from the tablet is "its Moon its mother."

Terra, meaning "of the earth," alludes to a person's essences being separated from the dregs of matter in preparation for a more spiritual life. This phase of the work is called separation, its element is air, and the associated verse from the tablet is "the Wind hath carried it in its belly."

Rectificando, the fourth phase of the work, means "setting things right." Its element is earth, and the operation represents the soul and the spirit leaving the earth together toward the Above. This represents the quintessence, or fifth element, recovered from the previous operations. This alchemical operation is called conjunction, described by the emerald tablet as "the Earth its nurse."

Invenies means that you will discover. This is the "red phase" of the alchemist's work, where the soul and spirit of the alchemist nurture the alchemical egg. This step is called fermentation, its element is sulfur, and its verse is "Separate thou the Earth from the Fire, the subtle from the gross, sweetly with great industry."

Occultum means "secret or hidden" and applies to the stage of distillation. Its element is alchemical mercury, and the verse is "It ascends from the Earth to Heaven and again it descends to the Earth and receives the force of things superior and inferior."

Lapidem means "stone"—the philosopher's stone—and is the ultimate aim of the alchemist. This phase, coagulation, brings together the purest essences from our body, soul, and spirit. Its element is salt, and the emerald tablet describes this final transmutation as "By this means you shall have the glory of the whole world and thereby all obscurity shall fly from you. Its force is above all force for it vanquishes every subtle thing and penetrates every solid thing. So was the world created."

The quest to find God (the One Mind in the language of the emerald tablet) or our own higher self is the ultimate goal. Alchemists explain that this is achieved by means of discovering the One Thing, or First Matter. This then gives the alchemist the ability to create the philosopher's stone and the elixir of life. The emerald tablet states: "And as all things have been and arose from One by the mediation of One: so all things have their birth from this One Thing by adaptation."

The quest of the alchemist and of mystics of all ages is therefore this: to change the world for the better, the work starts and finishes with you!

See also: *Freemasonry, Hermetica, Sir Isaac Newton, Philosopher's Stone, Rosicrucians.*

All Seeing Eye

The All Seeing Eye is a part of the Great Seal of the United States of America, the mysterious symbol depicted on the dollar bill.

The symbol of an eye radiating light has been used as a visual metaphor for God for many centuries. This idea of divine watchfulness over everything is a very potent image of an omnipotent deity.

To Freemasons, this eye is known as the Eye of Providence. It is usually not connected with a pyramid when used in Masonic regalia and either floats on its own or in the clouds.

An eye within a triangle can be found in artwork at least as far back as medieval times, but here the triangle represents the Holy Trinity of Christian faith; it is not an eye in a pyramid.

Going back much further in history, we find the powerful symbol known as the Eye of Horus. In ancient Egypt, the Eye of Horus was often used as a protective amulet, and pharaohs would go to their tombs with Eye of Horus amulets placed within the many wrappings that encased their mummified bodies.

The first document to bear the Great Seal, in 1782, appears to mark the debut of the Eye of Providence used in conjunction with a pyramid. Pierre Eugène du Simitière, a Swiss-born artist and philosopher, was asked to design an emblem that might be used as the seal of the nation. He accompanied the original sketch with the following description: "The Eye of Providence in a radiant Triangle whose Glory extends over the Shield and beyond the Figures."

Simitière's design was rejected twice. However, some six years later, it was suggested that the eye could be used on the reverse. That is how it came to float above the unfinished pyramid, seeming to complete the ancient structure. This is a very clever allegory, suggesting that only by the Providence of God will the nation of man be made perfect. But as Dan Brown suggests in *The Lost Symbol*, it could also be a metaphor for a more personal transformation: the apotheosis of the human mind into that of the Divine—the shaping of the rough block of stone that is the human spirit into a more perfect form.

Interestingly, in the book's final chapter, Peter Solomon's only living relative, his sister, Katherine, explains to Robert Langdon that the pineal gland in the human brain can be compared to the All Seeing Eye. According to the Western mystery tradition, the tiny, cone-shaped organ is the part of the human body often considered to be the mythical "third eye." This leads us to Buddhism and Hinduism, in which the concept of the third eye and the sixth chakra (located behind the brow) is widely accepted. In the Hindu tradition, this third eye is known as the powerful "eye of knowledge" and is believed to act rather like an internal guru, teaching us all we need to know if only we would listen. This, of course, dovetails neatly with the concepts of *The Lost Symbol*, which states quite clearly that "God is within."

Finally, we shouldn't leave the discussion of the All Seeing Eye without mentioning Manly P. Hall. The occult mystic and philosopher, whom Dan Brown quotes in *The Lost Symbol*, published his own monthly magazine called *The All Seeing Eye*. It covered various esoteric subjects, including Atlantis, tarot, I Ching, Freemasonry, ancient Egypt, and Mesoamerican mysteries.

See also: *Great Seal of the United States, Manly P. Hall, Pineal Gland.*

The Ancient Mysteries

In *The Lost Symbol*, Robert Langdon tells us that the Ancient Mysteries are the combined wisdom of the ages; a collection of the greatest mysteries known to man gathered in one place and kept secret. We learn that the Hand of the Mysteries is an invitation to an initiate to access and discover the Ancient Mysteries.

In effect, the Ancient Mysteries are the key to the whole novel. They are ultimately what Robert Langdon is searching for; the final reward for the whole quest. The clues on the granite pyramid, the search for the lost word—it is all said to lead to uncovering the Ancient Mysteries and the assumption is that they are hidden somewhere in Washington, DC.

The way they are presented in Dan Brown's book suggests that the Ancient Mysteries are the collected knowledge of many disciplines, something that could be thought of as an encyclopedia of the teachings of all the mystery schools. There is, in fact, no evidence that such a collection of writings does exist; rather, we have disparate works of ancient wisdom from the various strands of the Mysteries. While these are all of inestimable value to mankind, there is not one all-encompassing work that could be said to contain the whole truth.

Some of the earliest mystery schools we find were in ancient Greece. Many of them were well known, so their existence was not a secret. However, the actual knowledge from within the schools was fiercely guarded, and initiates were expected to guard the secrets and rites of the fraternities with their lives. Just as in Freemasonry today, the initiates of the Ancient Mysteries schools took sacred oaths, and they vowed that death should seal their lips before revealing any of the secret knowledge.

The mystery schools in ancient Greece were born from the disciplines of philosophy and mysticism, and the exploration of both subjects led naturally to the Mysteries. Sacred dramas would be performed that were connected with the Mysteries, the most prominent of these concerning Isis, the goddess whose cult began in ancient Egypt; Cybele, the great oracle of the ancient Asiatic world; and Demeter and Persephone, the Greek goddesses who gave birth to the Eleusinian mysteries.

The latter was probably the most important of the mystery schools in ancient Greece, thought to have begun in 1600 BC. It concerned itself with the recurring theme of the immortality of the human soul, known as psyche, whose true home is in the spirit world, free of the cage or tomb of the human form. As far as the Eleusinians were concerned, birth in human form was death itself for the soul, and only through death could the soul be finally reborn.

Later in Rome, there were mystery schools such as the cult of Mithras, which had imported much of the knowledge of the Persians, and so it was that the ancient knowledge was passed down through the generations. The mystery schools themselves may have evolved and changed, but the secrets that were passed down were the same.

The mystery schools of the Western world were finally forced underground between the fifth and sixth centuries when paganism was banned from the Roman Empire. It is said that the final decisive act in the destruction of the Ancient Mysteries was the closure of Plato's Academy in Athens in AD 529 by the Byzantine emperor Justinian I.

However, the Ancient Mysteries did not die. They were kept safe and simply lay dormant, waiting to flourish again. Gnostics kept safe many of the Mysteries that had become embedded within the new religion of Christianity. In the Middle Ages, the Knights Templar certainly kept alive some of the Ancient Mysteries, as did the Hermeticists and the alchemists, and the founding of the Rosicrucians and other secret orders during the Renaissance led to a resurgence in the knowledge of the ancients.

The Lost Symbol tells us quite clearly that Freemasonry not only has access to the Ancient Mysteries but acts as a guardian, keeping safe a huge body of ancient knowledge and passing it down through the various degrees of the craft. Whether or not the secrets that Freemasonry clings to are understood in the modern era is open to debate, but there is no doubt that Freemasonry is a modern mystery school that serves to keep alive the Ancient Mysteries.

In *The Secret Teachings of All Ages*, Manly P. Hall quotes Robert

Macoy, a thirty-third degree Freemason, in relaying how important the Ancient Mysteries have been in shaping human society:

> It appears that all the perfection of civilization, and all the advancement made in philosophy, science, and art among the ancients are due to those institutions which, under the veil of mystery, sought to illustrate the sublimest truths of religion, morality, and virtue, and impress them on the hearts of their disciples. Their chief object was to teach the doctrine of one God, the resurrection of man to eternal life, the dignity of the human soul, and to lead the people to see the shadow of the deity, in the beauty, magnificence, and splendor of the universe.

We glimpse from this the idea that many of the world's religions could also be classified as guardians of the Ancient Mysteries. Christianity, Islam, Judaism, Zoroastrianism, Buddhism, and countless others all contain the germ of the Ancient Mysteries, passing down sacred and ancient traditions concerning the rebirth of the human soul.

The conclusion of *The Lost Symbol* certainly alludes to this possibility. By describing the Bible as a possible collection of the Ancient Mysteries, we start to realize that ancient knowledge could have been encoded within the chapters of this religious book.

The Lost Symbol begins with a quote from Manly P. Hall, and his writings influence the novel beyond any shadow of a doubt. In *The Secret Teachings of All Ages*, he summed up the hidden wisdom of the ancients and suggested that it will rise again one day.

See also: *Manly P. Hall, Hermetica.*

The Apotheosis of Washington

Apotheosis is an ancient Greek word meaning "to change into a god," derived from *apo* ("change") and *theos* ("god"). Many ancient cultures embraced this idea, and man being raised to divinity is a common theme throughout history and myth. Though we don't find the term until after the rule of the Macedonian king Alexander the Great (336–323 BC), there is no doubt that the concept existed long before that. Kings in ancient Egypt were thought to be transformed into gods after they died, with some of the earliest writings detailing this sacred process dating back to 2400 BC, in the form of the Pyramid Texts, the earliest known religious writing, found on the inside of some fifth and sixth dynasty pyramids in Egypt. The ancient Greek religion of Orphism, based on the writings of the mythical poet Orpheus, went so far as to state that not only did the human soul become divine at death but also that it was *already* part divine.

The concept of apotheosis was also popular in ancient Rome, where deification of Roman emperors became a standard religious practice. An example is found on the Arch of Titus, which can still be seen in Rome today. The monument, raised shortly after the death of the Emperor Titus in AD 81, features scenes of him ascending to heaven on the wings of eagles.

Similar depictions of famous leaders from history continued into modern times, including Jean-Auguste-Dominique Ingres's painting *Apotheosis of Napoléon I*. And so it was that George Washington came to receive the same treatment.

The Apotheosis of Washington, painted in 1865 by Constantino Brumidi, is the crowning glory of the Capitol building: a vast, 4,664-square-foot fresco that decorates the inside of the dome itself, suspended some 180 feet above the rotunda floor. The original wood-and-copper dome had been replaced after Congress commissioned famed architect Thomas Walter to construct a much grander structure made of iron in 1855.

Interestingly, the fresco sits between the high outer shell of the dome and a lower inner shell. There is a circular opening, more than sixty feet across, and it is in this space that a plaster canopy is suspended by the aid of iron supports. This was to be the blank canvas that was afforded the artist Brumidi. Because of this peculiar construction, the oculus of the inner dome is actually smaller than the fresco itself, so it is impossible to see the entire fresco from any one vantage point inside the rotunda.

The commission for the fresco was finally given in August 1862. General George Washington, the first president of the United States, had died in 1799, and over the years, his reputation continued to grow. This fresco was to be painted in his honor. Washington was seen as the father of the nation, and as early as 1802, an engraving by the artist John James Barralet depicted Washington's ascent to heaven.

Barralet chose to portray the general ascending to Washington State's Mount Olympus, echoing some of the earliest accounts of apotheosis in ancient Greece. He also chose symbolic figures to surround Washington, such as Liberty, Father Time, Faith, Hope, Charity, and even an American Indian. Later, in 1860, we find a colored engraving illustrating the apotheosis of Washington, this time by German artist H. Weishaupt. All of these artworks reinforced the idea of the divinity of George Washington and paved the way for Brumidi's commission.

So it was that in 1862 Brumidi received a letter from Thomas Walter describing the work he was to create:

> It is intended to have a picture 65 feet in diameter, painted in fresco, on the concave canopy over the eye of the New Dome of the U.S. Capitol. I would thank you to furnish me with a design for the said picture, at your earliest convenience.

After providing preliminary sketches, both parties agreed to terms: Brumidi was to receive monthly installments of $2,000, the total amount not to exceed $40,000. The Italian-American artist began the fresco in 1865, and the scaffolding came down in 1866. When the public was finally allowed in to view the incredible painting, the reviews were very favorable. Brumidi had created what is still considered to be one of the best examples of academic painting in America.

As for the theme of *The Apotheosis of Washington*, what we see when we look up at that vast fresco is George Washington sitting in the heavens in glory, with Liberty, Victory, and Fame at his side. Thirteen maidens, representing the thirteen original colonies that formed the United States, surround him. Also shown is the United States, prospering under the guidance and protection of Roman gods: winged Mercury passes a bag of gold to Robert Morris, often referred to as the financier of the Revolutionary War; Minerva, goddess of wisdom, offers instruction to Benjamin Franklin; Ceres, goddess of agriculture, harvests along with the goddesses Flora and Pomona, who offer assistance to Young America, who in turn wears a red liberty cap; Neptune clears a path through the ocean in preparation for laying a cable along the seafloor. Finally, Freedom, who also stands on the top of the dome in the form of a large statue, is seen routing the enemies of America.

Brumidi's masterpiece drew upon many classical paintings and frescoes, yet he blended these influences with images of the modern world, creating a new vision of George Washington as *god* of the new, progressive United States.

In *The Lost Symbol*, the fresco lies at the heart of the story, and one of its underlying themes is that God is within us all; that we are ourselves god. Dan Brown tells us that this concept of man transforming into god is central to the symbolism displayed in the rotunda of the Capitol. We learn that it is not just about George Washington becoming a god; the symbolism aims to help us realize that in order to access God, all we really need is to look inside ourselves.

William Henry and Dr. Mark Gray's book *Freedom's Gate: The Lost Symbols in the U.S. Capitol* sheds new light on *The Apotheosis of Washington*. One of the many curious details it reveals concerns the circle of seventy-two stars that surrounds the artwork:

> *The fresco depicts the first President of the United States rising into the clouds in glory. Floating in the center of the painting, the deified Washington sits enthroned on a rainbow—the judgment seat of Heaven—in a circle, or "gate," of 72 stars.*

It is intriguing to discover that this ring of 72 stars actually sits at the outer rim of the opening at the top of a dome (oculus), allowing the fresco beyond to be seen. Upon closer inspection, we find that the stars are five-pointed stars. This seems significant because five-pointed stars in ancient Egypt signified the *Duat*—quite simply, heaven— quite literally a celestial underworld. It was the place where the soul of the deceased pharaoh traveled to become a god among the stars. The symbol of the *Duat* was a five-pointed star in a circle and we often see it painted onto ceilings of the tombs of the ancient Egyptians. Because we find the earliest accounts of apotheosis in ancient Egypt, it seems fitting that this ring of stars is found surrounding *The Apotheosis of Washington* in the Capitol dome. Also, the stars in *The Apotheosis of Washington* are enclosed in a long chain of intertwined figure eights, the symbol for infinity. George Washington literally sits in a ring of infinity, a very appropriate visual metaphor considering the subject matter of the painting within.

Another intriguing detail is the rainbow that runs through the cloud that Washington sits upon. *Freedom's Gate*, by William Henry and Dr. Mark Gray, highlights the significance of this, explaining that rainbows have often been used to signify the very idea of apotheosis:

> *In Last Judgment scenes, Jesus is frequently seen on or in a rainbow. Hence, the rainbow is associated with glory. This makes sense. Symbolically, rainbows are intermediaries between heaven and earth. They are bridges the gods use to toggle between the worlds*
>
> *. . . In the Great Perfection or Rainbow Body, teaching the human body is considered an intermediate phase, a bridge. Our next phase, putting on the Light Body, is referred to as putting on the whole armor of God in Ephesians 6:10–20. This Light Body (or Star Body, Rainbow Body) is our hidden, inner "spiritual" body referenced in numerous traditions. In Sufism it is called "the most sacred body" and "supracelestial body." Taoists call it "the diamond body," and those who have attained it are called "the immortals" and "the cloudwalkers." The ancient Egyptians called it "the luminous body or being."*
>
> *From this perspective, the meaning behind the symbolism of George Washington sitting on the rainbow is clear. Washington is a perfected human, not only an enlightened Grand Master, but also an "American Christ," in tune with his divine nature. He is now*

*somewhere over the rainbow, and his image is a bridge between
Heaven and Earth.*

It seems that Brumidi was well versed in the symbolism of transformation, and he went to great lengths to encode many of these elements within *The Apotheosis of Washington*. What at first glance
appears to be nothing more than a very well-executed fresco venerat-
ing the first U.S. president turns out to be a painting that is literally
bursting with symbolism. Considering the links between the Capitol
building and Freemasonry, this is not at all surprising.

Toward the end of *The Lost Symbol*, Robert Langdon—while viewing *The Apotheosis of Washington*—quotes the words of Manly P. Hall,
taken from the incredibly dense and brilliantly written *The Secret
Teachings of All Ages*, written in 1928: "If the infinite had not desired
man to become wise, he would not have bestowed upon him the faculty of knowing."

It's a very fitting quote, because many of the ancient secret teachings are literally embedded within *The Apotheosis of Washington*. It
takes eyes to read the signs, but when we study the fresco in detail, we
start to realize that Brumidi was fully conversant with the heady and
intoxicating language of symbolism.

See also: *Constantino Brumidi, Capitol Building, George Washington*.

Sir Francis Bacon

Sir Francis Bacon was a man who cast a long shadow over the philosophical thinking of the Western world. He is one of Dan Brown's
"brain trust of the world's most enlightened minds," along with Sir
Isaac Newton, Robert Boyle, and Benjamin Franklin, and is referred
to as such in *The Lost Symbol*. He appears again as the author of *New
Atlantis*, the book describing a utopian vision of a society said to have
influenced the Founding Fathers in establishing the United States of
America.

The Bacon Society of America, founded in 1922, paid tribute to Sir Francis by stating, "It should be of particular concern to Americans to become better acquainted with Bacon's part in the planting and promoting of the earliest British colonies in North America, because, although not generally known, he assisted in preparing the 1609 and 1612 charters of the Virginia Company."

This contribution is perhaps one of the reasons he is acknowledged in the main reading room of the Library of Congress, where above a statue representing Philosophy is an abbreviated quote from Bacon's essay "Of Truth": "The inquiry, knowledge, and belief of truth is the sovereign good of human nature."

Bacon (1561–1626) was the author of *The Wisdom of the Ancients*, in which he explained the hidden meaning that he thought was revealed in ancient myths, and he was the man apparently chosen by King James I of England and Ireland (he also held the title of King James VI of Scotland) to mastermind the authorized version of the Bible known as the King James Version. In *Sir Francis Bacon: Poet, Philosopher, Statesman, Lawyer, Wit*, author Parker Woodward writes, "It has been suggested that the Authorized Version of the Bible printed 1610/11, was submitted for final editing to Francis, but that could only have been for rounding off its English, the translation having been made by a special commission of scholarly clergymen."

American occultist and philosopher Manly P. Hall was more convinced of Bacon's role in producing the King James Bible. In a lecture called "Rosicrucian and Masonic Origins," he contended, "The first edition of the King James Bible, which was edited by Francis Bacon and prepared under Masonic supervision, bears more Mason's marks than the Cathedral of Strasburg."

Francis Bacon studied at Trinity College, Cambridge, then spent three years in France in the service of the English ambassador. He worked as a barrister, eventually becoming solicitor general and attorney general. His own claim was that his interests lay in gaining knowledge of everything, and his written work displays a wonderful command of the English language.

Bacon became a member of parliament in 1584. A few years later, the Earl of Essex, an ambitious favorite of Queen Elizabeth I, recognized his talents and became his patron. However, the rebellious Essex attempted to seize power; he was subsequently tried and executed. It was Bacon who produced the official report on the matter. He successfully gained the favor of King James and was knighted by him in 1603. In 1618 Sir Francis became lord chancellor as well as the first Baron Verulam, and, in 1621, Viscount St. Albans. However, he soon fell from grace after being convicted of corruption. With his political career over, Bacon spent his last years occupied mainly with his literary work.

The manner of Bacon's supposed death (there are some who claim he died at a later date, faking his death at this point) is perhaps indicative of his inquisitive nature. He'd been giving thought to the idea of preserving meat by freezing it. To test his theory, one snowy day he bought a fowl and stuffed it with snow. Sadly, the exposure to the cold brought about pneumonia, and he died just a few days later. But before he expired, Bacon did write a letter in which he explained cheerfully, "As for the experiment itself, it succeeded excellently well . . ."

In one scene from The Lost Symbol, Katherine Solomon and Robert Langdon dash through the streets of Washington, desperately trying to evade the CIA. They duck behind the graceful Folger Shakespeare Library, a repository for many valuable and rare manuscripts dating from the time of William Shakespeare, including the original Latin copy of Bacon's New Atlantis. William and Sir Francis were contemporaries, of course, but maybe more.

Many experts simply cannot believe that Shakespeare, a small-town boy from Stratford-upon-Avon, England, could possibly have acquired the knowledge and background to write the famous plays that bear his name. If he did not, then naturally the question arises, who did? There are a number of possible candidates, among them Christopher Marlowe, the Earl of Oxford, the Earl of Derby—and Bacon. According to some, Sir Francis is a strong contender due to his extensive travel on the continent, which exposed him to many of the political intrigues and courtly rituals present in Shakespeare's plays. It has also been commented on that, based on the legal details and procedures in some of the plays, the author must have had legal training, as Bacon did, and possessed the diplomatic, philosophical, and linguistic skills of the playwright.

In the nineteenth century, one of the most enthusiastic supporters of the theory that Sir Francis Bacon had authored Shakespeare's works was a Minnesota politician named Ignatius Donnelly. During his five years in the House of Representatives, from 1863 to 1868, Congressman Donnelly made use of the facilities at the Library of Congress to advance his studies. Donnelly later served as a Minnesota state senator. After leaving politics, he pursued his literary interests. Specifically, he set out to decipher the body of Shakespeare's work and determine whether or not it belonged to the Bard of Avon. The key that Donnelly tried to apply was the Bacon cipher, a method of concealing a message within a text that Bacon had described and illustrated in his book *The Advancement of Learning.* That Sir Francis Bacon was the inventor of a cipher was perhaps not surprising, given his role in government, which presumably required messages to be sent securely.

In 1888 Donnelly published the fruit of his exhaustive study: *The Great Cryptogram,* a book of more than one thousand pages. He claimed to have found number patterns that, when combined, provided this decoded message: "Seas ill said that More low or Shak'st spur never writ a word of them." The convoluted method he used to come up with this supposed admission within the texts, that Shakespeare was not the author, detracted from some of his more cogent evidence.

Today Ignatius Donnelly is better remembered for his work *Atlantis: The Antidiluvian World,* a favorite among historical revisionists, conspiracy theorists, and alternative historians. Like Sir Francis Bacon, whom he admired so much, Donnelly was convinced that Plato had been correct when writing about the mythical land of Atlantis.

For those who enjoy number symbolism—and of course this would include Robert Langdon—there is a well-documented "coincidence" to be found in the King James translation of the Bible, the one that Bacon supposedly worked on. The holy book was completed in 1611, when Shakespeare was forty-six years old. If you turn to Psalm 46, you'll find that the forty-sixth word from the beginning is *shake* and the forty-sixth word from the end is *spear*. It is delightful to think that William Shakespeare's "ghostwriter" could have inserted this little joke.

In *The Lost Symbol*, Dean Colin Galloway of the Washington National Cathedral credits Sir Francis with being able to "write in clear language," in the context of anticipating human enlightenment, while Robert Langdon knows him to have been a Rosicrucian. The Rosicrucian symbol was a flowering rose on a cross. Dean Galloway suggests that Bacon may have even been the legendary Christian Rosenkreuz, founder of the Rosicrucian movement. The renowned scholar Frances Yates, in *The Occult Philosophy of the Elizabethan Age*, presents this argument: "I have argued in *The Rosicrucian Enlightenment* [one of her earlier books] that Francis Bacon's movement for the advancement of learning was closely connected with the German Rosicrucian movement, having a similar mystical and millennial outlook. . . . I emphasized that Bacon's *New Atlantis*, published in 1627, a year after his death, is full of echoes of the Rosicrucian manifestos."

Sir Francis Bacon himself described a movement or group with Rosicrucian ideals in his *The Advancement of Learning*, when he says: "so in learning there cannot but be a fraternity in learning and illumination, relating to that paternity which is attributed to God, who is called the father of illumination or lights."

Sir Francis was well aware that merely to conduct and observe scientific experiments was not enough. To be worthwhile, these observations require careful analysis. In *New Atlantis*, he tells the story that enhanced his reputation among the men who went on to form the Royal Society. They took inspiration from Bacon's vision of "Salomon's House" on his "Island of Bensalem." This was a kind of research college (its name derived from the biblical King Solomon) where scientific inquiries into the creations of God were pursued.

Bacon's *New Atlantis* is set on a utopian island, Bensalem, in the South Pacific. Considering that it was written in the early seventeenth century, the year is probably around 1623, a paradise of enlightenment. It is in sharp contrast with the Europe of the time, when various forms of Protestantism and Roman Catholicism were in sharp and sometimes deadly conflict. The name Atlantis is taken from the mysterious civilization, which, according to legend, was inhabited by advanced people in very ancient times. Its disappearance and its original whereabouts have been argued about for millennia.

Bacon's influence in the development of science was not that he made great discoveries or set up elaborate experiments. He did, however, outline the principle of modern scientific investigation, in that we should be open-minded about the possible conclusion of an experiment until proof is obtained. In *The Advancement of Learning,* he states, "If we begin with certainties, we shall end in doubts, but if we begin with doubts, and are patient in them, we shall end in certainties."

Sir Francis Bacon authored many books and propagated many big ideas. He was, undoubtedly, a multifaceted genius. Alexander Pope (1688–1744), the British poet and literary scholar, said of him, "Lord Bacon was the greatest genius that England, or perhaps any country, ever produced."

See also: *Manly P. Hall, Rosicrucians, the Royal Society and the "Invisible College."*

Boaz and Jachin

In *The Lost Symbol*, the character Mal'akh is revealed to have numerous tattoos all over his body. The two designs that adorn his legs are said to represent Boaz and Jachin, the mysterious pillars that it is believed stood in the porch of the eastern entrance to Solomon's Temple in Jerusalem, with Jachin standing on the right and Boaz on the left. These pillars have two distinct sets of mythologies associated with them: a biblical one and, interestingly, a Masonic one.

Etymologically, it would seem that *Jachin* means "establish," and *Boaz*, though this is somewhat disputed, may mean "strength." Some scholars see a relationship, metaphorically, between King Solomon, as represented by Jachin, and King David, as represented by Boaz. Others see Boaz as representing the grandfather of King David and Jachin as representing a certain high priest. Both pillars seem to symbolically represent the priesthood (Jachin) and the royal line (Boaz).

What is certain, though, is that these two pillars were thought to stand in the porch of Solomon's Temple, with Jachin standing on the right and Boaz on the left of the eastern entrance. Some editions of the Bible say that the pillars were made of copper; other versions say bronze or brass for the material used. These pillars may well have been influenced by the use in Egypt of pillars guarding the entrances to temples, and the use of pillars in Roman temples of the Levant.

In 2 Chronicles 3:15–17, its is said of the pillars: "In the front of the hall he made two pillars thirty-five cubits high, and on the top of each, a capital measuring five cubits. He made festoons [decorative chains], in the Debir, to go at the top of the pillars, and made a hundred pomegranates to go on the festoons. He erected the pillars in front of the temple, one on the right, the other on the left; the one on the right he called Jachin, and the one on the left, Boaz."

2 Chronicles 4:13–17 describes how the pillars are decorated: "the four hundred pomegranates for the two sets of filigree—two rows of pomegranates for each set of filigree; the ten stands and the ten basins on the stands; the one Sea and the twelve bulls oxen beneath it; the ash containers, scoops, and forks. All the utensils made by Huram-Abi made for King Solomon for the Temple of Yahweh were of burnished bronze. The King made them by the process of sand casting, in the plain of the Jordan between Succoth and Zeredah."

However, in 2 Kings 25:17, there is a discrepancy in the size of the pillars: "The height of one pillar was eighteen cubits, and on it stood a capital of bronze, the height of the capital being five cubits; round the capital were filigree and pomegranates, all in bronze. So also for the second pillar."

The Bible's last reference to the pillars comes in Jeremiah 52:17, when they are broken up and carried off to Babylon.

Boaz and Jachin have literally become the pillars that Freemasonry is built upon. The role they play in the ceremonies, mystery, and rituals of Masonic lodges cannot be understated, and the symbolism attached to them is seen as very important. The two pillars are to be found in every Masonic hall in the world, though their placement is not uniform within the Masonic craft.

In *The Lost Symbol*, Mal'akh's leg tattoos of Boaz and Jachin are described as follows: "his left leg spiraled and his right vertically striated. *Boaz and Jachin*." What is meant by this? Here we seem to have a nod to Scotland's Rosslyn Chapel, a location explored at length in Dan Brown's previous book, *The Da Vinci Code*. The chapel, built in 1446, is thought to symbolically represent Solomon's Temple. Mal'akh's tattoos depict two pillars at Rosslyn Chapel: the so-called Apprentice pillar, with its beautifully spiraled carving, which many Masons believe represents the pillar of Boaz in Solomon's Temple; and the Masons pillar, with its straight, striated carvings, which is claimed to be an image of Jachin from Solomon's Temple. These highly decorated pillars form the centerpiece of one of Rosslyn Chapel's most enduring myths and are believed by many Masons to symbolically represent these twin pillars, within a chapel that itself is thought to symbolically represent Solomon's Temple.

In some Masonic imagery, the pillars are said to be the "pillar of fire" and the "pillar of cloud."

See also: *Freemasonry, Solomon's Temple*.

Constantino Brumidi

Constantino Brumidi was the Italian-born artist responsible for painting the pivotal artwork in the Capitol building, the fresco that adorns the ceiling of the dome, known as *The Apotheosis of Washington*. This vast fresco remains one of the best examples of academic painting in America.

Little is known of Brumidi's life before he came to the United States. Born in Rome on July 26, 1805, his father was Greek, from the Peloponnese, while his mother was Italian. Brumidi studied at the illustrious Accademia di San Luca after showing a great aptitude for art as a youth. The academy was named after Saint Luke, who was supposed to have painted the Virgin Mary, and was adopted as the patron saint of painters' guilds. Founded in 1593, Accademia di San Luca had a long history of training fine artists, including painters, sculptors, and architects.

After graduating from the academy, Brumidi set about building a career for himself in Rome. His prodigious talent was recognized, and he received the patronage of Pope Gregory XVI. The young artist was given the task of working on frescoes within the Vatican and restoring the loggia of Raphael (a beautiful colonnaded porch on the second story of the Apostolic Palace in the Vatican). But a conflict with the papal secretary of state over political matters saw the end of Brumidi's work there, and his next assignment would be for Prince Alessandro Torlonia, then the eighth richest man in the world. Later, in 1847, he worked for Pope Pius IX, painting a full-length portrait of the Pontiff, again cementing Brumidi's status as one of Rome's finest painters.

Brumidi's course seemed set. He had carved a niche for himself and continued to attract the patronage of the city's wealthy aristocracy. Suddenly, revolutionary fever gripped Rome, and his world was turned upside down. On November 15, 1848, Pellegrino Rossi, the minister of justice of the Papal States, was assassinated, prompting rioting in the streets and demands for a democratic government. The pope himself fled the city, and the Roman Republic was established.

Brumidi's decision to side with the revolutionaries was to be his downfall, however. The pope, with the help of several European powers, soon wrested control back from the upstart republic. Brumidi was arrested in 1851, accused of being a part of the uprising, and was sentenced to eighteen years in prison.

Soon after, Pope Pius IX, whom Brumidi had become acquainted with when he had painted his portrait just a few years before, granted Brumidi a pardon on the condition that he leave Italy for good. So it was that Brumidi, his wife, Anna, and their two children, left Italy for New York.

Brumidi became a U.S. citizen and began a new career for himself. He carried on where he had left off in Rome, completing a fresco behind the altar in St. Stephen's Church in New York, before working in Baltimore and then Mexico.

It was on the way home to New York from Mexico in 1854 that Brumidi stopped off in Washington, DC. Greatly impressed by the grand architecture of the city, and especially the U.S. Capitol, he arranged a meeting with Captain Montgomery C. Meigs, the supervising engineer of the Capitol, and suggested that he would be available to decorate the building's many empty spaces.

Meigs was a controversial figure at the time; many did not agree with the appointment of a military man to such an important position within the Capitol. He succeeded in upsetting many of the artists of the day, and petitions requesting his removal were submitted to Congress. However, Meigs had a strong vision of his own. He set out to ensure that the Capitol would become the single greatest national monument of the republic, and he wanted it brimming with all the skill and invention that the greatest American artists could muster.

At the time, the Washington volume of the American Guide Series listed Brumidi as "a decorative painter of mediocre talent, [who] worked in what was left of the tradition of Raphael and Correggio." This seems an amusing description in the light of what we now know Brumidi would go on to create. Kent Ahrens, in "Nineteenth Century History Painting and the United States Capitol," from *Records of the Columbia Historical Society of Washington, D.C.*, comments on how Brumidi went on to establish himself in Washington:

> *However mediocre, Brumidi was a frescoist and as such possessed a skill which no contemporary American artist shared. Perhaps he also possessed already the beginnings of a dream, that as Michelangelo had dedicated his later life to the glorification of St. Peter's, so he, Brumidi, would dedicate himself to the new cathedral of human freedom, the Capitol of the United States. He asked Meigs for employment as an artist, and he suggested that the task suitable for him was to adorn the walls and ceilings with frescoes.*

Brumidi was first asked to contribute a series of frescoes in the House Committee Room on Agriculture in 1855. Meigs wrote, "This will enable Congress to see a specimen of this the highest style of architectural decoration." The results attracted much attention and ensured that Brumidi would work in the Capitol for the next twenty-five years.

In 1856 Brumidi began sketching designs for what we now call the Brumidi Corridors. The architect of the Capitol, Thomas Walter, had originally conceived the corridors to be decorated simply and then hung with oil paintings. However, Captain Meigs had other ideas. Because of Brumidi's experience restoring Raphael's loggia at the Vatican, he asked the artist to attempt a much more elaborate design. Working with a team of artists and assistants from the 1850s through the 1870s, Brumidi made the corridors his own, and the finished design can still be appreciated today. Brumidi worked in the corridors during the 1850s, 60s, and 70s.

Constantino Brumidi seems to have always wanted to paint a grand fresco within the dome of the Capitol, and there is evidence that he made an oil sketch for what became known as *The Apotheosis of Washington* as early as 1859. (He wasn't officially offered the commission until four years later.) When Brumidi finally completed his crowning achievement, he had ensured that his name would forever be remembered among those of the great American artists.

Long after *The Apotheosis of Washington* was completed, in 1866, Brumidi continued to work inside the Capitol, adding to the decoration of the corridors and many rooms of the Senate wing. The final project he would tackle was the frieze that surrounds the base of the dome, fifty-eight feet above the rotunda floor.

However, the long years had taken their toll, and by 1879, at age seventy-four, Brumidi's health was frail. He was often afflicted by bouts of asthma as well as severe diarrhea. On top of this, his working conditions were strenuous, to say the least. Barbara A. Wolanin, author of *Constantino Brumidi: Artist of the Capitol,* offers this firsthand account of what Brumidi had to endure: "this wonderful old man has daily to climb up to an elevation of fully eighty feet, enter a window and then descend a ladder at least twenty five feet long to the little pent up crib where he toils. He is so aged and feeble that he requires help to reach the place, and you can easily imagine the fatigue attendant upon the mere labor of getting to and away from his work. Besides in stormy wet tempestuous weather he cannot get there at all."

To give the artist some comfort, a chair was provided and set atop the precarious scaffold. In October 1879, Brumidi fell from this chair, with nearly fatal consequences. Again, from *Constantino Brumidi: Artist of the Capitol:* "while sitting upon a temporary scaffold, and near its edge the chair turned from under him and threw him over; he caught the round of a ladder and remained suspended by the strength of his arms for the space of fifteen minutes, till officer Lammon descended from the top of the Dome to the scaffold and called two men from the floor of the Rotunda to assist in the rescue of your petitioner."

While Brumidi did recover—in fact, he worked the very next day on the same scaffold—his increasingly ill health prevented him from seeing the frieze finished. He became confined to his house at the outset of that season's cold weather and died in February 1880.

Today a bust of Brumidi sits in the Brumidi Corridors, a memorial to the long years he dedicated to the beautification of the numerous halls and spaces of the Capitol. He completed more works of art in the Capitol than any other artist, and his name is stamped firmly across the building.

Brumidi himself would proudly sign his name "C. Brumidi: Artist Citizen of the U.S." His adopted country is surely as proud of him and his achievements as he was to be an American.

See also: *The Apotheosis of George Washington, Capitol Building.*

Capitol Building

Across the world, the United States is often represented by the image of the Capitol building, its perfect, pure white dome set against the sky. It is as iconic an image of America as the red, white, and blue flag.

Yet most people have never seen past that glorious façade. They have no idea what wonders lie inside the dome, or just how large and complex the Capitol building is. Not only is it a museum filled with fine art and treasures, but it is where Congress conducts the business of the U.S. federal government.

Today it is hard to imagine the seat of government not being in Washington and the Capitol building, but it took extraordinary efforts to create what would become the heart of the nation. While victory in the American Revolutionary War was achieved in 1781, it took until 1789 to form what is today known as the U.S. Congress. The newly formed Congress sat first in New York but moved to Philadelphia after just two sessions. The Residence Act of 1790 set out a detailed plan for establishing a new capital city. After much debate, it was agreed that a site on the Potomac River in the region known as the District of Columbia be selected. Both New York and Philadelphia protested at the creation of this new city, each hoping to secure the seat of government for itself. The compromise that was brokered designated Philadelphia as the temporary seat of government until the new capital in Washington was completed. The Residence Act stated that the president, George Washington, had to ensure that the new Capitol building would be completed and ready for Congress to move into by December 1800.

Design of the new capital began in earnest, with George Washington taking an active role in its execution. Pierre Charles L'Enfant, a French-born architect and veteran of the American Revolutionary War, was appointed the task of designing the new city. The final layout and design of what would become Washington, DC, was presented and accepted on August 19, 1791, with the location of the Capitol and other federal buildings, including the White House, marked out.

Just as a fine painting sits in a frame befitting its artistry, the Capitol was set within a grand arrangement of vistas and avenues that swept toward what was at the time Jenkins Hill. In a letter to George Washington, L'Enfant wrote that the virgin hill was like "a pedestal waiting for a monument."

However, despite having agreed upon the location of the Capitol, there was no design for the building itself. The name of the new seat of government had been decided, with "Capitol" chosen over "Congress House," and Jenkins Hill was to be renamed Capitol Hill, after the famous hill in ancient Rome known as the Capitoline Hill—but there was no design for the Capitol. By 1792, L'Enfant had fallen out with George Washington, ending his tenure as chief designer. So the search was on to finalize a design for what would be the most important building in the United States.

Remarkably, what would end up as one of the world's most famous and recognizable buildings began with a $500 design competition in 1792. Looking back at some of the contenders, one wonders what might have happened if one of the other designs had been chosen instead. We could very well be looking up at a curious giant stone eagle perched on a pedestal!

The design that won the day was that of Dr. William Thornton, a physician and amateur architect. Thornton was handed the prize money as well as a plot of land in the city. Although his design was modified considerably over the years, the building we see today was born from the plans he submitted. The famous dome, however, was not a part of the original design. The first incarnation of the Capitol design featured a far less grand wood and copper dome designed by Charles Bullfinch that was only half the height of today's stately design. But the Capitol was to be without a dome for a long time yet.

After the Jenkins Hill site was laid out, and the foundation constructed, the cornerstone of the Capitol was laid on September 18, 1793. It was accompanied by a grand ceremony, the first in the new federal city, and presided over by none other than the president of the United States, George Washington, who came dressed in full Masonic regalia. After the pomp and ceremony, a silver plate was placed in a trench over which the cornerstone would be laid. The plaque read:

This South East corner stone, of the Capitol of the United States of America in the City of Washington, was laid on the 18th day of September, in the thirteenth year of American Independence, in the first year of the second term of the Presidency of George Washington, whose virtues in the civil administration of his country have been as conspicuous and beneficial, as his Military valor and prudence have been useful in establishing her liberties, and in the year of Masonry 5793, by the Grand Lodge of Maryland, several lodges under its jurisdiction, and Lodge 22, from Alexandria, Virginia.

Despite ongoing problems with sourcing sufficient labor for the construction of the Capitol, as well as continuing funding shortages, the Senate wing of the building was completed in 1800. Congress held its first session there in November. Unfortunately George Washington didn't live to see the day, having died the previous year. It fell to the second U.S. president, John Adams, to make the first speech in the still unfinished building:

It would be unbecoming the representatives of this nation to assemble, for the first time, in this solemn temple, without looking up to the Supreme Ruler of the universe, and imploring his blessing. May

37

this territory be the residence of virtue and happiness! In this city may that piety and virtue, that wisdom and magnanimity, that constancy and self-government, which adorned the great character whose name it bears, be forever held in veneration! Here, and through-out our country, may simple manners, pure morals, and true religion, flourish for ever!

It was a speech full of the promise of what the Capitol and the nation itself might become, but the truth was, the Capitol wasn't anywhere near finished. In fact, it wasn't until 1811 that the wing intended for the House of Representatives was completed. Meanwhile, the central section that would one day house the dome had not been touched since the foundations had been laid almost twenty years earlier.

The year 1812 was fateful for the Capitol. Benjamin Latrobe was by now in charge of building work, having become the fourth architect in charge of the construction. His designs were proceeding favorably, but the outbreak of the War of 1812 threatened to destroy all the progress made. The British army took control of Washington in August 1814, with disastrous consequences for the United States, and many federal buildings were ordered to be burned down by the British admiral George Cockburn. This act is known as the Burning of Washington and although the interior of the Capitol was almost completely destroyed, the outer construction remained. Still, much of the work of the preceding two decades was undone and one wonders what George Washington would have thought had he still been alive.

After the war ended in 1815, Latrobe returned to Washington with a new mandate to rebuild the Capitol. This time he had been given more freedom and was able to introduce his own ideas into the design. He came up with a new design for the dome, to replace the original envisaged by Thornton, but he was destined not to see it built. The architect-engineer, deeply frustrated by reports that he was responsible for the slow progress at the Capitol, resigned in 1817 after an outburst in front of President James Monroe.

Charles Bullfinch took over as architect of the Capitol. Under his stewardship, the Capitol was finally completed in 1829, thirty-six years after George Washington had laid the cornerstone. The Capitol finally had its wood and copper dome, redesigned by Bullfinch. Within the dome, he'd created a rotunda that replicated the dimensions and the grandeur of the Pantheon in Rome, complete with its own oculus, a hole through which the sun could stream through and the heavens glimpsed.

From 1830 to 1850, work continued inside the Capitol, but the building's exterior remained as Bullfinch had left it. Construction began on a tomb for George Washington below the lower rotunda, or crypt, in anticipation of the centennial of his birth in 1832. However, at the last minute, one of Washington's heirs refused permission to move his remains, in deference to the late president's will and instructions regarding his burial. So it was that the proposed tomb in the Capitol became a storeroom.

Disappointed by this turn of events, Congress discussed other ways that Washington might be honored. It was decided that a marble statue should be carved and placed in pride of place in the rotunda itself. Sculptor Horatio Greenough was given the task and the result depicted George Washington as Zeus, seated with bare chest, pointing at the heavens with one hand, and holding forth a sheathed sword in the other.

The completed statue, a truly epic piece of sculpture, weighing some twenty tons, was placed in the rotunda in 1841, but it was to remain there for two years. Public outrage over Greenough's portrayal forced officials to move it to the Capitol grounds. The statue was eventually donated to the Smithsonian National Museum of American History, where it still resides today.

While people were happy to consider the deceased George Washington as divine, it seems that they did not want to see their first president *literally* as a god—at least not close up. In *History of the United States Capitol*, William C. Allen states that Charles Bullfinch summed up the public mood at the time—a strange mix of outrage and amusement—in a letter to his son:

I fear that it will cause much disappointment—it may be an exquisite piece of work, but our people will hardly be satisfied with looking on well developed muscles, when they wish to see the great man as their imagination has painted him . . . [I] am not convinced the sculpture is suited for modern subjects; the dress presents insuperable difficulties . . . And now I fear that this will only give the idea of entering or leaving a bath.

In *The Lost Symbol*, Robert Langdon refers to this very statue, making the point that Peter Solomon's severed hand pointing upward is not the first hand to have graced the rotunda, and that for at least two years, Washington's upraised hand had pointed in the same direction. However, it must be stated that when the statue of Washington was installed in the rotunda, the famous fresco, *The Apotheosis of Washington*—toward which Peter Solomon's hand was directed—had not even been conceived.

So it was that the first chapter of the Capitol's history came to an end. Due to the United States's rapid growth during the 1850s, the building had to be expanded. The Senate proposed another competition and placed an advertisement in local Washington newspapers: "It is required that these plans and estimates shall provide for the extension of the Capitol, either by additional wings, to be placed on the north and south of the present building, or by the erection of a separate and distinct building within the enclosure to the east of the building."

After an extensive review, Thomas U. Walter became the new architect of the Capitol in May 1851. His designs would change the Capitol forever and create one of the modern world's most memorable buildings. During Walter's reign, the building would triple in size. In addition, he replaced Bullfinch's wood and copper dome with the one that we see today: a grandiose structure made of iron and stone, and twice as tall as Bullfinch's design.

The earliest date that Walter mentions working on the design for the new dome was May 1854. We know that he was inspired by the dome of St. Paul's Cathedral in London, along with St. Peter's Cathedral in Rome and the Panthéon in Paris. Walter was not in charge of the construction, however. Captain M. C. Meigs was brought in as engineer in charge of the whole Capitol refurbishment in 1853, and, despite many differences and quarrels, the two men worked together to construct the dome. Meigs had a tremendous flair for administration and an eye for fine detail, and drove the project forward, often with the sheer force of his will alone.

Under Meigs's watchful eye, the Capitol was transformed into a work of incredible beauty, both inside and out. The interiors received as much lavish attention to detail as the exterior. He supervised the most fantastic iron and glass ceilings, installed exquisite marble carvings, and hired the most talented artists to create breathtaking rooms and corridors—including Constantino Brumidi, who began painting frescoes in the Capitol and then went on to complete *The Apotheosis of Washington*, which adorned the interior of the new dome.

It would take many volumes to describe accurately all the Capitol's many features and rooms, every inch of which is covered in wondrous decoration and the most exquisite craftsmanship. Yet the Capitol is still evolving.

In 2000 the Capitol Visitor Center was added, and we see this featured in *The Lost Symbol* as Langdon arrives, expecting to present his lecture. The new visitor center provides a much-needed separate entrance for tourists and contains many of the modern facilities required of a building attracting the numbers of visitors that flock to the Capitol.

One thing that does seem to be an invention in *The Lost Symbol* is the statement that there once was an eternal flame in the crypt. While it is true that, for a time, the rotunda floor was open to allow a view into the crypt, this feature had been created to allow visitors to peer down at the tomb of George Washington. When the plans to bring his remains to the Capitol were scrapped, the hole in the floor was left open for a time. Vivien Green Fryd describes its closing in her book *Art and Empire: The Politics of Ethnicity in the United States Capitol, 1815–1860*:

In preparation for the eventual transfer of Washington's remains to the basement of the Capitol, however, the builders left a circular opening about ten feet in diameter in the center of the Rotunda floor, enabling visitors to view in the crypt a statue of Washington that was eventually to be placed above his tomb. In 1828, Congress ordered the closing of the aperture, because dampness emanating from it adversely affected John Trumbull's paintings on the walls of the Rotunda.

There is no evidence of the eternal flame that Dan Brown cites, and the star on the floor of the crypt below the rotunda actually marks the point from which the city of Washington's streets are laid out.

At the end of *The Lost Symbol*, we see Robert Langdon and Katherine Solomon lying on their backs meditating on the meaning of *The Apotheosis of Washington* and the phrase painted on the curved surface, *E pluribus unum:* "Out of many, one." We start to wonder, not for the first time, what exactly was in the minds of the great men who raised this stone edifice on this hill.

In *Freedom's Gate: The Lost Symbols in the U.S. Capitol*, William Henry and Dr. Mark Gray put forward the idea that the Capitol, as well as being the seat of government for the United States, is actually a temple of the people, a place of enlightenment that anyone can experience and that everyone can access:

Is the U.S. Capitol actually a temple? In our quest to answer this question, we discovered that indeed it is. At the core of this living and continually evolving civic temple is Jefferson's Enlightened vision of Liberty as the new secular religion of Light. The mighty Capitol Hill is a great High Hill, in the tradition of all holy hills. The temple atop this mount emerges as a Temple of Enlightenment and Transformation that uses sacred architectural principles and spiritual symbolism to create a magnificent space or place where Heaven and Earth unite. By definition it is a gateway, a stargate, to use a 21st century term.

There is little doubt that the Capitol was constructed with as much purpose and vision as the finest cathedrals of the Middle Ages. Many find it a truly spiritual place and are greatly moved by the experience of being in the rotunda. Some would say that this is just the effect of the weight of history pressing down on the visitor, but it surely is much more. The Capitol has been carefully sculpted into a solemn place of transcendence. Henry and Gray highlight what the Capitol really represents and the long lineage of holy buildings, such as Jerusalem's Solomon's Temple and Rome's Pantheon, in whose shadow the Capitol truly lies:

America was the place where religious and political refugees from Ireland, France, Germany, Italy, and other parts of Europe came for safety and better lives free of tyranny, religious and civil persecution. They came seeking religious freedom and liberty. Many enthusiastically supported their leaders who sought to create a "city on a hill" or a "holy experiment," the fulfilment of the New Jerusalem. The Puritans who came to America in 1630 brought with them a copy of the King James Version of the Bible. Translated in 1610 by a team of scholars led by Sir Francis Bacon it established English as the new literary language. English would be the language of the New Atlantis.

When we look up at the imposing structure of the Capitol, we are not looking at a modern building, we are looking at the past, the present, and the future melded into a monument to mankind's enduring love of the mysteries of the universe and the unknown.

See also: *The Apotheosis of Washington, Sir Francis Bacon, Constantino Brumidi, Pierre L'Enfant.*

Cerneau Rite

In the prologue to *The Lost Symbol*, Dan Brown writes about a Masonic ritual in which Mal'akh is receiving the thirty-third degree. This evocative scene plays out like a stereotypical idea of what a layperson might think such a ritual entails. However, it is not an accurate depiction of modern-day Masonic practice and is one of the only places in the novel where Brown casts a shadow upon the rituals and symbolism of Freemasonry.

What we are actually witnessing in the prologue of *The Lost Symbol* is indeed a real, and well-documented ritual of initiation, but not for the regular Scottish Rite order that it is supposed to depict. The ceremony, in fact, dates back to the nineteenth century, when a renegade group of alternative Scottish Rite Masons formed what was to become the Cerneau Rite. The Cerneau Supreme Council was never properly chartered by the either the northern or southern jurisdictions of Scottish Rite Freemasonry and remained outside mainstream Freemasonry, establishing early power bases in New York and New Jersey. Albert Pike, head of the Southern Jurisdiction of the Scottish Rite, was especially vocal in his opposition to the group and refused to issue it a charter.

In the ritual, Mal'akh raises a human skull to his lips and drinks bloodlike red wine from it. The Cerneau ritual for the thirty-third degree did indeed incorporate a human skull, as well as an entire skeleton. And much of the invocation that Mal'akh utters is also accurate for the Cerneau ritual. In the actual ritual, the member who is receiving the thirty-third degree utters the words:

> *I furthermore solemnly swear that I will hold true allegiance to the Supreme Council of the United States of America, its territories and dependencies. And that I will never acknowledge any body or bodies of men as belonging to the Ancient and Accepted Scottish Rite, claiming to be such, except such as hold allegiance to this Supreme Council, or those who recognize this Council. To all these I do most solemnly swear, calling upon the Most High God to ratify my oath.*
>
> *And should I knowingly or willfully violate the same, may this wine I now drink, become a deadly poison to me, as the hemlock juice drunk by Socrates. [Initiate drinks wine out of the skull.] And may these cold arms forever encircle me. Amen. [Skeleton's arms enfold the initiate.]*

Some of the above words are spoken by Mal'akh in the rite as described in the book.

In 1807, Joseph Cerneau established a Grand Consistory of the Rite of Heredom in New York City, claiming a right to organize and charter bodies as the "Ancient and Accepted Scottish Rite." By 1813, he had established a Supreme Council in New York and, by 1816, had established branches in Maryland and Baltimore. In 1889, however, an edict was issued by the Grand Master of Masons of the District of Columbia against the Cerneau Rite followers, stating that alleged members of the Cerneau Rite had entered into fraternal relations with members of the Grand Orient of France. A second edict was also issued, as reported in the *New York Times* of April 23, 1890, thus:

A second edict on the subject has just been issued by the present Grand Master annulling the former edict and declaring it no longer in force. It directs that Masters of lodges under its jurisdiction cease to include in the recognized and imperative test to be administered to visitors to their lodges the statement by such visitors that that they are not members of any body acknowledging allegiance to the said Gorgas-Cerneau rite.

However, their rehabilitation within the craft was short-lived, and by the early twentieth century, the Cerneau Rite was all but snuffed out and lost.

Aleister Crowley was said to have been initiated into the thirty-third degree of Scottish Rite Freemasonry in Mexico, within a Cerneau ritual.

See also: *Aleister Crowley, Freemasonry, House of the Temple, Scottish Rite Freemasonry.*

CIA—Office of Security

In *The Lost Symbol,* an assault on the U.S. Capitol's director of security turns Robert Langdon into a fugitive. He flees the building's basement for the streets of Washington, DC, trying to remain one step ahead of the CIA. The agency, with all of its manpower and technological resources, is trying just as hard to apprehend Langdon and the mysterious pyramid he is carrying.

The Central Intelligence Agency (CIA), an independent agency of the U.S. government, is responsible for providing national security intelligence to the senior levels of federal policymakers. Within the CIA is the Office of Security, which is responsible for upholding the internal security of all agency personnel, operations, and facilities. In addition, the Office of Security runs the CIA's security-clearance program and investigates breeches in procedure. It also handles protection for defectors to the United States from other countries. In a nutshell, the men and women of the Office of Security are the spies that spy on the spies.

The Office of Security launches investigations within the United States in response to alleged actions that jeopardize intelligence sources and methods. In a small number of these cases, it has been alleged that intrusive methods of investigation were employed, such as surveillance, unauthorized entry, intercepting mail, and illegally reviewing tax returns. There has been much debate over the questionable nature of these methods and whether or not it was proper for the CIA to use these techniques, regardless of the dangers at hand. A subdivision of the Office of Security is the Technical Security Division, charged with seeing to it that all security systems used by the CIA are state-of-the-art. This includes everything from debugging CIA facilities and setting up white-noise machines to installing locks, safes, and alarms in CIA facilities. It has been alleged that the Technical Security Division even plays bug-planting games where two teams, working independently, test their methods. One team hides the bugs and the other tries to find them. It should be noted that there is no evidence of a non-CIA bug ever having been found in agency headquarters.

The Lost Symbol's Katherine Solomon tells Langdon and Dr. Colin Galloway of a controversial espionage technique that the CIA had experimented with for more than twenty years: remote viewing. This involves "viewers" who claim to be able to see distant events remotely. Some claim not only distant geographical viewing, but also future and past events. From the early 1970s to the mid-1990s, an agency project known as Stargate tried using psychics and intuitives to ascertain the validity and effectiveness of remote viewing for potential military and political advantage. The program has been extensively written about and speculated upon by serious authors and conspiracy theorists alike, and many of the remote viewers involved have been named. Some of the more famous names include Ingo Swann, Pat Price, Lyn Buchanan, and Joseph McMoneagle. In an article on remote viewing in the January-February 2004 issue of *Phenomena* magazine, author and researcher Richard Dolan has this to say: "Are remote viewers accurate all the time, is their information complete? Of course not, but there is compelling evidence that, in many cases, something is going on that, by the standards of current science, should not be going on. In other words, there is good reason to believe that remote viewing is for real."

Although the CIA officially terminated Stargate and other remote-viewing programs in the mid-1990s, speculation is rife that projects of this type and others investigating the possible application of myriad psychic and occultic phenomena for security purposes may still be in operation and funded by the CIA.

Since 2009, Leon E. Panetta has been the agency's nineteenth director in its history. Previously, he served as President Bill Clinton's chief of staff from 1994 to 1997. Before that, Panetta was a California congressman for sixteen years.

His predecessor at the CIA was Porter Johnston Goss. There is some evidence that when Goss attended Yale University, he belonged to a secret society known as Book and Snake (B&S). Other members have included future journalist Bob Woodward, U.S. Treasury Secretary Nicholas Brady, and Congressman Les Aspin Jr. It is thought that Book and Snake had connections to another famous secret society, Skull and Bones (S&B). Two future chief executives have belonged to the latter organization: George H. W. Bush (director of the CIA for one year under President Gerald Ford) and his son George W. Bush. Many members of Skull and Bones have been Freemasons. Conspiracy theorists have speculated that the elder Bush is a member of the Freemasons, but he has never publicly confirmed this.

The Office of Security is headquartered in the main CIA offices in McLean, Virginia. The 225-acre facility sits on the west bank of the Potomac River and is approximately seven miles from downtown Washington. Since 1999, the complex has been officially named the George Bush Center for Intelligence, but it is more popularly known as Langley, after the estate that formerly occupied the location. With more than 22,000 employees, the facility is large enough to warrant its own zip code: 20505.

In 1990 a sculpture called *Kryptos*, by artist Jim Sanborn, was installed in an inner courtyard on the Langley campus. The ten-foot-high S-shaped copper piece, which resembles a scroll, is covered in ciphered messages (made up of 865 letters, to be exact) that have been the subject of considerable energy to decode them. At present, as two CIA staff members refer to in *The Lost Symbol*, the mystery is still intact, though a portion of the code has been broken.

The lobby of the main building sports a biblical quote etched into the wall: "And ye shall know the truth, and the truth shall make you free" (John 8:32). Also included in the facility is a museum, a 7,000-seat auditorium, and, of course, the CIA library. The museum, called the National Historical Collection, houses the CIA's collection of spy gadgets and materials accumulated over the years. Much of it is still classified, and so the collection is closed to the public. The CIA Library is the world's best collection of materials about intelligence, with more than 125,000 books and 1,500 periodicals. It also is home to the Historical Intelligence Collection, reported to exceed 25,000 volumes.

One of the main characters in *The Lost Symbol* is Inoue Sato, director of the Office of Security in the CIA. She seems to embody all the most evident traits of the CIA: knowledgeable, authoritative, intelligent, suspicious, and strong.

See also: *Kryptos*.

Circumpunct

The circumpunct is one of the oldest symbols known to mankind, essentially a circle with a dot in the center. Its name is derived from the Latin *circum*, or "around on all sides"—in other words, a circle and a punct, or point. Even the least artistic person could draw it. Certainly our ancient ancestors liked the circumpunct's pleasing simplicity and often took it to symbolize something of significance. Importantly, it was probably the most symmetrical shape they could create.

Here's how to construct a circumpunct outdoors, without pencil or paper: Take a piece of string—say, about two feet long—and tie a stick or a rock to one end. Next, place the other end of the string on the ground and hold it firmly in place while you stretch out the string until it is taut. Now, with your other hand, move the outer end of the string (with the stick or rock attached) in a circle, as you would a compass, inscribing a circle in the ground (or ice, or sand, or a rock, or some other surface). That's all there is to it.

In *The Lost Symbol*, Robert Langdon discovers the circumpunct impressed upon his fingertip after withdrawing his hand from a stone box that housed the pyramid. The Reverend Dr. Colin Galloway, dean of Washington National Cathedral, links its appearance with alchemy. Alchemists used the circumpunct as a symbol for gold, since the sun is, of course, similarly colored to the precious metal some of them claimed to have the power to create.

The universality of the image is illustrated by some of the diverse cultures that have left images of the circumpunct in their inscriptions, such as the Native American Chippewa or Ojibwe tribes of the United States and Canada, whose rich cultural heritage is being passed on to new generations. The circle circumscribing a point was used to represent our word *spirit* in their pictorials of their religious practices, scratched onto birch bark rolls. In Mexico, the Huichol tribe, remnants of the Aztecs, believe the circumpunct to symbolize the Eye of God, as did some early Christians.

To two of the world's oldest civilizations, the point within a circle represented the sun. An ancient Chinese script used it to symbolize the solar disk (the sun) or a day, while to the ancient Egyptians, it stood for their great deity and sun god, Ra, and for the sun itself. The Egyptians sometimes referred to themselves as "the cattle of Ra," since a legend described how the tears and sweat of the god were formed into the first people. You might find it strange that the Egyptian people would consider a god's sweat a suitable ingredient for creating humankind. However, the blue lotus (*Nymphaea caerulea*) was greatly loved in Egypt for its beauty and its scent, which was equated with the divine essence and thought to contain the perfume of Ra's sweat. Many examples of Egyptian art show people sniffing the lotus. The ancient word for Ra's tears, *remyt*, also used to create mankind, is intriguingly similar: *remeth*.

Egyptian obelisks were seen by their builders as a metaphorical connection between heaven and earth, with their topmost pyramidions symbolizing the rays of the sun as they fall to earth. The Washington Monument, the obelisk structure that holds the key to the lost word in *The Lost Symbol*, is revealed to be a circumpunct: the circular plaza surrounding the monument provides the physical setting for the symbol.

Astrologers and astronomers recognize the circumpunct as representing the sun. Medieval astrologers, who were also astronomers, used the sign for the earth, since they believed that it was God's special creation and therefore was the center of the universe. The space circling the earth was equivalent to a great ocean surrounding an island.

On Salisbury Plain, Wiltshire, in southern England, sits a massive and mysterious circumpunct: the ancient monument Stonehenge. It is believed to be around 4,500 years old, although some of its huge stones may have been erected hundreds of years before that. Outside of its stone structures runs an earth bank and ditch (the henge), which archaeologists suggest dates to around 3100 BC. Thus, the henge forms the outer circle and the stone inner ring forms the remainder of the design. The countryside for miles around had been a cemetery for a long period of prehistory, being covered with burial mounds. While this part of England was regarded by ancient people as very special, it is by no means agreed as to *why*. The debate about the function and purpose of Stonehenge has theorists touting it as an ancient calendar, an astrolaboratory, a temple, or a place of sacrifice.

In the Kabbalah, which has its own interpretation of Hebrew Scriptures, the circumpunct symbolizes Kether in Sephirot, for those who follow its mystical precepts. Kether (Keter) is the crown at the top of the Sephirot of the Tree of Life. The Tree of Life is a diagram to illustrate the creation of the universe.

In Freemasonry, it is a symbol for the control of emotions. Freemasonry is absolutely full of symbolism. One of the objects most closely linked with the Brotherhood is the compass, which would be the most useful instrument, of course, in drawing a circumpunct.

Pythagorean philosophers referred to God, or the Primary Being, as Monad, from whom all else ultimately sprang. God himself is the Monad of Monads. Monad was represented by the circle with a point at its center. When the word is used for a single indivisible unit, it takes on the meaning of an atom. To Taoists, it symbolizes the divine creative spark.

Dan Brown's last mention of the circumpunct in *The Lost Symbol* is

Robert Langdon's realization that the painting of *The Apotheosis of Washington* on the ceiling of the Capitol building has the characters arranged in two concentric rings.

What is most fascinating, perhaps, is that for so many centuries and across so many beliefs and philosophies, the point within a circle symbol has been regarded as having a special significance, often representing aspects of God. Could it be something more than its simple design that holds the circumpunct's appeal?

See also: *Alchemy, The Apotheosis of Washington, Freemasonry.*

Aleister Crowley

The Lost Symbol describes Aleister Crowley as someone who greatly inspired Mal'akh at a time when he was still calling himself Andros Dareios and living New York. We are told that it was through Crowley's writings that Mal'akh learned about ritual magic and incantation.

So who was Aleister Crowley? Some may know him by his popular title of "the Wickedest Man in the World." Sections of the popular press labeled him "the most evil man who ever lived." Rather than reject these titles, Crowley seemed to flourish in the air of notoriety that followed him, and he did nothing to try changing people's opinions of him. In fact, one of the titles that he gave himself was "the Beast Whose Number Is 666."

Should there remain any doubt as to the public perception of this man, we need only look at a transcript of a 1934 libel case involving Crowley. While summing up, the judge said to the London jury: "I thought that I knew of every conceivable form of wickedness. I thought that everything which was vicious and bad had been produced at one time or another before me. I have learned in this case that we can always learn something more . . . I have never heard such dreadful, horrible, blasphemous, and abominable stuff as that which has been produced by the man who describes himself to you as the greatest living poet."

He was born in 1875 in Royal Leamington Spa in Warwickshire, England, the son of a successful, retired brewer turned itinerant preacher. Both of his parents were very strict Christians, being of the ultraconservative Plymouth Brethren sect. Throughout Crowley's childhood, signs abounded that all was not well, especially after his father died of cancer in 1887. Young "Alicks" rejected what he considered to be the religious dogma of his parents' faith, causing a rift within the family. His mother, distraught at his rebellious ways, began calling him "the Beast"—in reference to the figure of the Antichrist found in the Bible's book of Revelation. Rather than take offense, Crowley reveled in it; he proudly referred to himself as the Beast until his death.

Things did not improve for Crowley until he turned twenty-one years of age and he inherited his father's fortune. Finally free, of the religious background that he loathed, Crowley went to the University of Cambridge, where he took the first steps toward what would become a lifetime devoted to the occult.

He devoured books on magic and alchemy, and by 1898 he had been initiated into an esoteric society called the Hermetic Order of the Golden Dawn. Among its members at one time or another were the poet William Butler Yeats and occultist Dion Fortune. Group activities included communing with angelic spirits from the "other side." Crowley, however, was more interested in attracting devils to the room he'd set up specifically for practicing black magic. He left the order a few years later and acquired an estate known as Boleskine House, on the shores of Scotland's infamous Loch Ness. There he established his own temple.

Over the next few years, Crowley, by then married, would attempt to make sense of magical ritual. He describes the ultimate aim of his great work in his book *Magick in Theory and Practice*, which, strangely enough, contains glimpses of the Noetic Sciences mentioned in *The Lost Symbol:* "There is a single main definition of the object of all magical Ritual. It is the uniting of the Microcosm with the Macrocosm. The Supreme and Complete Ritual is therefore the Invocation of the Holy Guardian Angel; or, in the language of Mysticism, Union with God."

Despite Crowley's sordid reputation, there is no firm evidence to suggest that he was a practitioner of the dark arts. He seems to have been strongly opposed to the notion that he was somehow a black magician, and he went on public record to make his opposition to black magic clear, saying in a 1933 British newspaper article:

To practice black magic, you have to violate every principle of science, decency, and intelligence. You must be obsessed with an insane idea of the importance of the petty object or your wretched and selfish desires.

I have been accused of being a "black magician." No more foolish statement was ever made about me. I despise the thing to such an extent that I can hardly believe in the existence of people so debased and idiotic as to practice it.

Crowley's most enduring work is his study of the Law of Thelema, which he discovered while honeymooning in Cairo. There, he claimed, a spirit guide named Aiwass—a messenger of the Egyptian god Horus—dictated to him the final text of the book he was writing: *The Book of the Law*, or *Liber AL vel Legis*. It contains Crowley's succinct and oft-quoted explanation of the Law of Thelema: "The word of the Law is Thelema. Who calls us Thelemites will do no wrong, if he look but close into the word. For there are therein Three Grades, the Hermit, and the Lover, and the man of Earth. Do what thou wilt shall be the whole of the Law."

Meaning? That we are all free to live as we choose. However, Crowley proposed that before we exercise this free will, we must look deeply within ourselves and come to know ourselves and uncover the true nature of our will. Free will is to be interpreted as an individual's destiny or purpose in life, and with it comes great responsibility and self-discipline. *The Book of the Law* could be said to be a treatise *against* black magic; in fact, the principles that Crowley penned and lived by forbade its practice.

Despite the vast body of work he left behind, it was probably Crowley's fondness for sex magic that earned him his wicked reputation. He routinely participated in magic rituals that involved sex with both men and women. History probably would have been kinder to him had he not outraged polite society of the early 1900s with some of his more salacious antics.

Returning to *The Lost Symbol*, it is relevant to note that Crowley's studies of the occult also introduced him to Freemasonry. By his own accounts, he was initiated up to the thirty-third degree in 1904 at a lodge in Paris and continued to press for entry into lodge meetings in London but was refused. Crowley also confessed in his autobiography that he had been initiated as a thirty-third degree Mason through the Ancient and Accepted Rite of Masonry, at a lodge in Mexico. All of these facts are hard to verify outside of his own claims; further complicating matters, he later received entry to the thirty-third degree, among other honors, via postal contact with a controversial British-born Mason and occultist named John Yarker.

Crowley was also associated with Freemasonry through an order known as the Ordo Templi Orientis (OTO), which modeled itself on Freemasonry, becoming a member in 1912. In 1923 Crowley went on to proclaim himself Outer Head of the Order, and after no one disputed his position, he went on to lead the organization for many years.

Whether he was seriously interested in Freemasonry will never be known, but one thing is certain: with his many connections, Crowley would have been privy to many of the secrets of the Brotherhood. He seems to have been keen to assimilate the knowledge he had gained from Freemasonry with that from his occult studies. In his book *The Confessions of Aleister Crowley: An Autohagiography*, he offers the following:

> I proposed to define freemasonry as a system of communicating truth—religious, philosophical, magical, and mystical; and indicating

the proper means of developing human faculty by means of a peculiar language whose alphabet is the symbolism of ritual. Universal brotherhood and the great moral principles, independent of personal, racial, climatic, and other prejudices, naturally formed a background which would assure individual security and social stability for each and all.

The truth is that today Crowley is still an enigma. One thing is certain, though: if he were here today, reading *The Lost Symbol*, he would appreciate the persistent thread of the book, that God is within us all. That would have been familiar territory for him. Furthermore, he would have warmly embraced the concept of Noetic Science and practical applications such as *The Intention Experiment*. For what is magic ritual if not the application of human will over the physical environment around us? We may label them differently now, but to Crowley there would be no difference; the basis of the magic he practiced and that of Noetic Science are identical. "Do what thou wilt shall be the whole of the Law."

See also: *Freemasonry, Institute of Noetic Sciences.*

Dollar Bill Symbolism

The dollar bill is a magical thing. This everyday item for millions of Americans is replete with sacred and mystical symbolism. For those who have eyes to see, the dollar bill is a cornucopia of the mysterious and strange, chock-full of symbols and hints at a deeper meaning.

In *The Lost Symbol*, Katherine Solomon and Robert Langdon are trying to evade the CIA in the back of a cab. Katherine suddenly takes out a dollar bill and a pen and proceeds to outline a Star of David over the pyramid of the Great Seal on the back of the bill. She also highlights the letters M, A, S, O, and N.

The dollar bill's cameo appearance in the book hints at its much greater—and largely untold—role in the mysterious symbolism of the founding and creation of the fledgling United States. Let's take a close look it and try to glean meaning from the myriad symbols and magic on display. But first, what are the origins of the dollar bill as we see it today?

Strangely enough, we don't need to go back through the mists of distant time to find the origins of the present dollar bill. The birth date for the cloth, paper, and ink that make up the dollar bill was 1935, in the administration of President Franklin Delano Roosevelt, in the years after the worst economic recession the world had ever seen. However, its the cast of characters involved that prove to be the mysterious secret ingredient in this recipe.

One of these shadowy occultist figures was a man named Nicholas Roerich. A striking-looking man, Roerich sported a shaven head and a long white beard. His piercing eyes were said to be able to look into your soul. Nicholas Roerich was a Russian émigré to the United States who became renowned as a painter, peace activist, and philosopher. He traveled extensively throughout the Far East and Europe and was nominated a number of times for the Nobel Peace Prize. Roerich was also a great friend of U.S. Secretary of Agriculture Henry Wallace.

Henry Agard Wallace, a close confidant of Roosevelt's, was a thirty-third degree Freemason, as was the president. Wallace would go on to become the thirty-third vice president of the United States under Roosevelt, and came close to being nominated to run for office as the thirty-third U.S. president. In the end, that honor went to Harry S Truman, who was also a high-ranking Freemason.

There was another side to Henry Wallace. He was interested in the occult and associated with some notorious occultists of the time. These associations would ultimately lead to Wallace being deemed naïve and easily impressionable, and untrustworthy as a politician.

Wallace was a Theosophist (a follower of the writings and doctrine of Helena Blavatsky), through which he became acquainted with Nicholas Roerich. The two men also shared an interest in Rosicrucian ideas and philosophies. Many researchers and conspiracy theorists see the connection between Roerich and Wallace as pivotal in the decision to place both sides of the Great Seal of the United States on the dollar bill. Wallace later claimed that he first saw the truncated pyramid motif of the Great Seal in a small government-published booklet and showed the image to FDR. Both men, being Freemasons, instantly recognized its symbolic significance.

It has been said, however, that it was Roerich who influenced Wallace on the matter of the dollar bill's design. The two men certainly met on occasion and corresponded frequently. Indeed, it was their correspondence that was to nearly bring Wallace's career crashing down. The "guru letters," as they become known, ended up in the hands of some Republican politicians and journalists. Wallace's letters were headed "Dear Guru . . ." and signed with the letter G, supposedly standing for Galahad, Roerich's pet name for him. The letters revealed that Wallace was a much more devoted follower of Roerich's than had been previously thought, and made the connection between the two men even stronger.

Roerich was undoubtedly familiar with the motif of the unfinished pyramid and the All Seeing Eye above it, believing it to represent, among other things, the Holy Grail and the Stone of Destiny. Roerich's influence should not be understated. Many of the Washington and New York elite of the time regarded him as a genuine enlightened guru, and his influence ran far and wide.

Some saw the eye above the pyramid differently. In the Masonic view, it is the Eye of Providence, looking down with favor upon the new nation. Others see a trace of the ancient Egyptian Eye of Horus, while still others associate the eye with the star Sirius. What is clear, though, is that the motif of the eye floating above the unfinished pyramid is both symbolic and occultic in nature. Whether or not it was intended to be so, however, is a hotly debated topic.

The cast of characters involved in the modern dollar bill also included the fascinating Manly P. Hall, a Freemason, writer, and philosopher who was also greatly influenced by the doctrines of Theosophy's Helena Blavatsky. He too was a friend of the Roerich family, and for a while attended meetings with Roerich in New York. FDR was a fan of Hall's, going so far as to have Hall's extensive library of occult, philosophy, history, and archaic books transferred to microfiche in 1942.

To what extent each of these men was involved in the dollar bill's creation isn't known, but it can be said that the design of the dollar bill was championed and brought to life by Freemasons and Theosophists. Roosevelt approved the new design in 1935, and the U.S. Treasury began printing the dollar that we use today. Now on to a discussion of its symbolic elements.

Number symbolism plays a role, with the number 13 being prominent. On the back of the bill are 13 stars above the head of the eagle, arranged in such a way that if you drew lines between them, you would form the seal of Solomon, also known as the Star of David. The eagle holds 13 arrows in one talon and 13 olive branch leaves in the other—signifying America's ability to wage war and bring about peace, to defend itself and to be a leader of peace in the world. Thirteen feathers make up each wing. Supported on the eagle's breast is a shield with 13 stripes, and its beak holds a banner bearing *E pluribus unum* ("out of many, one"). Add up the number of letters making up the Latin phrase, and you get—wild guess, anyone?—13.

On the left side, we see that the unfinished pyramid has 13 layers of masonry (incidentally, the same number of levels as the pyramid that tops the Washington Monument). Above the pyramid is the Latin motto *Annuit coeptis*, meaning "God has favored our undertaking"—also 13 letters.

Commentators have explained this as representing the 13 original colonies of the republic; hence the 13 red and white stripes on the American flag. The 13 original colonies were (from north to south): New Hampshire, Massachusetts, Rhode Island, Connecticut, New York, New Jersey, Pennsylvania, Delaware, Maryland, Virginia, North Carolina, South Carolina, Georgia.

The number 13 has many mysterious and symbolic meanings. It is seen as an unlucky number by many, after Friday the thirteenth, a day that commemorates the attack on the Order of the Knights Templar by the king of France, on Friday, October 13, 1307. This belief, though, seems to be a relatively modern occurrence. The number 13 is also associated with Christ: for example, 13 people attended the Last Supper. There are also 13 apostles.

Thirteen is also the age at which children enter their teenage years. In Jewish tradition, it is when a boy becomes a Bar Mitzvah; this is his coming of age. This could also be highly symbolic of the new republic and nation of the United States.

Interestingly, in the absolute center of the front of the dollar bill is George Washington's right eye, as seen in his portrait. This theme seems to mimic the Eye of Providence on the reverse of the note. As author David Ovason notes in *The Secret Symbols of the Dollar Bill*, "The symbolism is obvious: these associations are intended to suggest that Washington should be regarded symbolically as a kind of demigod. In spirit, he looks down over the destiny of the American nation, in much the same way as the Eye of Providence overlooks the destiny of the world. . . ."

The dollar bill is so chock-full of esoteric meaning and symbolism that it would take an entire book to cover it all. However, there is one "small" detail that is often overlooked:

Look at the front of a dollar bill. Notice that the number 1 in the top right-hand corner is placed in a shield. Now zero in on the top left corner of the shield. There, almost too tiny to notice, is a shape that almost seems to sit in the indentation. What is this tiny speck?

If you were to scan the dollar bill and enlarge the image, you would find something that resembles a miniature owl. Some say that it more resembles a spider, but this author is of the opinion that it's an owl. The image has stirred much controversy and debate, especially among conspiracy theorists who see in the owl the semblance of the god Moloch, the Canaanite deity that has come to be represented by the owl. Of course, this small shape resembling an owl may just be a slip of the original engraver's hand, which is the orthodox explanation commonly given for the mysterious appearance.

In an interesting side note, the owl happens to be the main "mascot" and motif at an elite gentleman's club called Bohemian Grove, in Monte Rio, California. This exclusive men-only club has counted many U.S. presidents as members, as well as various powerful heads of industry and finance. Once a year at Bohemian Grove, members take part in a ceremony called "Cremation of Care," in which offerings are made to a giant forty-foot owl shrine that stands at one end of a lake. The ceremony culminates in a lighting of fires around the owl and was captured on video by conspiracy theorist and radio-show host Alex Jones in 2000. Jones claimed that the ceremony was satanic in nature and proved that the United States was run by a cabal of Satan worshippers and black magicians. In *The Lost Symbol*, one of the major characters is named Mal'akh—very close in pronunciation to Moloch. Perhaps Dan Brown is making a clever, oblique reference to this controversy?

The next time you take a one dollar bill out of your pocket, take the time to really have a good look at this amazing piece of paper and ink. It has hidden meanings, sacred symbolism, and mysterious elements in equal measure. It truly is a thing of magic and wonder.

See also: *Freemasonry, Great Seal of the United States, Manly P. Hall, George Washington.*

Albrecht Dürer

Following the theme established by Dan Brown in his previous Robert Langdon novels, there is a world-renowned artist at the heart of his code breaking. From the chase around Rome led by the breathtaking marble sculptures of Bernini in *Angels and Demons* and the genius of Leonardo da Vinci in *The Da Vinci Code*, we now have the formidable figure of Albrecht Dürer, greatest of the German Renaissance artists.

Dürer, an artist and a draftsman, left a legacy of over 950 drawings, but he also authored books on measurement, the human body, and fortifications. In this respect, he was a true Renaissance man, a polymath. Five centuries after his death, at least sixty of his oil paintings still survive, as do thousands of drawings and watercolors. Painting in oil took up too much of his valuable time and brought in too little money, Dürer complained, so his workshop mainly produced prints. However, his engravings and woodcuts were to achieve an especially high standard.

Among Dürer's watercolors are landscapes. Early examples include a series depicting his journeys through the Alps of France and Italy. What he learned in Renaissance-period Italy came to moderate the Gothic style that had previously informed his art. Frances Amelia Yates, in her book *The Occult Philosophy of the Elizabethan Age*, states that Dürer "had absorbed the Italian art theory based on harmony of macrocosm and microcosm, understood in subtle geometrical terms, on the proportions of the human body as related to laws governing the cosmos, as laid down by the Architect of the Universe."

Born in Nuremberg, Germany, in 1471, Dürer was originally trained in his father's profession as a goldsmith. As he later explained in an account of his life, "When I could work neatly, my liking drew me more to painting than to goldsmith's work." Despite any reservations Albrecht Dürer the Elder may have had about his son's choice of career, he arranged an apprenticeship with the painter Michael Wolgemut, whose portrait Albrecht the Younger would render in oil and tempera years later.

Dürer's godfather, Hartmann Schedel, was a former goldsmith turned printer who produced the *Nuremberg Chronicle,* an illustrated world history, in 1493. It is tempting to think that perhaps he in some way influenced young Albrecht's decision to quit as a goldsmith, since Schedel did so himself. Wolgemut's workshop produced more than 1,800 illustrations for the *Chronicle,* so it is possible that Dürer worked on some of them during his apprenticeship.

After three years of studying under Wolgemut, in 1489 Dürer set off for a few years of travel and exploration, finally returning to Nuremberg in 1495. One of his closest friends was Willibald Pirckheimer, a scholar who was influential in the development of Dürer's interest in humanist thinking. It was Pirckheimer to whom he wrote a series of letters while working in Venice between 1505 and 1507. Among his works in Venice was a painting of the *Feast of the Garlands* commissioned by group of German merchants for the Church of San Bartolomeo.

As was common for major artists of the time, religious themes dominated Dürer's work. In 1511 a series of woodcuts of the *Life of the Virgin* and the *Great Passion* were published. Yet, on a slightly more secular note, *Knight, Death, and the Devil* was engraved on a copper plate in 1513. The knight is Christ's follower; the skull at the feet of the sturdy charger represents death, which is also personified as a decomposing corpse holding an hourglass to remind the knight that his days are numbered. The devil is left in the warrior's wake, powerless since his temptations have obviously been ignored. This artwork presaged the trend among northern European artists of depicting everyday scenes rather than drawing on religious and biblical themes. The genre style, as it came to be known, increased in popularity as Protestant forms of worship spread and the Roman Catholic tradition weakened in some states.

The character Katherine Solomon in Dan Brown's novel ascribes to Dürer a belief in Mystic Christianity, a fusion of astrology, alchemy, and science with Christianity. Certainly Dürer was influenced by Martin Luther, the reformist preacher, and he became a Lutheran Protestant.

In 1524 Dürer wrote that "because of our Christian faith we have to stand in scorn and danger, for we are reviled and called heretics," suggesting that he knew his beliefs were at odds with standard Catholic teaching.

Dürer produced two more copperplate engravings by the end of 1514: *St. Jerome in His Study* and *Melencolia*. Both are considered to be unparalleled masterpieces, and Dan Brown has chosen to highlight the latter in *The Lost Symbol*.

Raymond Klibansky, Erwin Panofsky, and Fritz Saxl, in their book *Saturn and Melancholy: Studies in the History of Natural Philosophy, Re-*

ligion, and Art, describe the conception of inspired melancholy in Dürer's *Melencolia* as being directly influenced by the book *De occulta philosophia* by the Cabalist Heinrich Cornelius Agrippa. The influence of Agrippa's work (written by 1510, though not published until 1533) suggests that Dürer had seen an early copy by this master of occult studies. Agrippa had also published a series of magic squares in his work that is mirrored within the *Melencolia.*

Dürer clearly had an interest in mathematics. This is evidenced in the number square in the *Melencolia* work. Immediately below the bell and above the predominant figure is a magic square. The sum of the numbers in each of the four rows and four columns of squares is 34, in all directions. He has cleverly ensured that the year in which he engraved the picture appears in the two central squares in the bottom row: 1514.

A series of fifteen illustrations of the Apocalypse, taken from the book of Revelation, was very successful. Cut into wooden blocks, they were made available as prints, and within a few years, the name Albrecht Dürer was recognized throughout Europe. He was indebted to Dr. Johannes Pirckheimer, father of the aforementioned Willibald, who advised him about the religious themes he was depicting. Johannes was an Episcopal councillor and a highly respected lawyer, useful qualifications in times of religious upheaval.

The Holy Roman emperor Maximilian I, a patron of Dürer's, commissioned a series of woodcuts that would be joined together to form one of the largest prints ever produced, *The Triumphal Arch.* In all, Dürer and some of his pupils designed 192 blocks depicting the huge triumphal structure envisaged to illustrate the emperor's power. The design, influenced by Johannes Pirckheimer, included Egyptian hieroglyphs.

It was perhaps inevitable that an artist as successful and influential as Dürer would attempt to influence others by writing on aspects of his craft. His *Instructions in Measurement, Treatise on Fortification,* and *The Four Books on Human Proportions* (published posthumously) displayed his broad range of knowledge.

After the artist's death in 1528, Martin Luther wrote in a letter to a mutual friend, "As for Dürer, assuredly affection bids us mourn for one who was the best of men, yet you may well hold him happy that he has made so good an end, that Christ has taken him from the midst of this time of trouble and from greater troubles in store, lest he, that deserved to behold nothing but the best should be compelled to behold nothing but the worst."

See also: *Alchemy*, *Great Architect of the Universe*, *Magic Squares*, *Melencolia I*.

The Eastern Star

Unlike Freemasonry, its more famous counterpart, the Order of the Eastern Star and its Masonic links are relatively unknown by the general public. Indeed, this is the common feeling when Professor Robert Langdon is questioned by one of his Harvard students about the exclusion of women from Freemasonry. Langdon points out that the Order of the Eastern Star (OES) is the women's branch of Masonry. While it is true that the majority of members are women, the OES is actually open to men *and* women, and has both a Worthy Matron and Worthy Patron as its highest officers.

Each OES chapter has eighteen officers, of which two are male (the Worthy Patron and the Worthy Associate Patron), with at least one having to be present for the Order to convene. Its international headquarters is located on Dupont Circle in Washington, DC, and there are some ten thousand chapters in twenty countries, claiming one million members worldwide.

To join the OES, you must either be a Mason or a female relative of a Mason: wife, daughter, niece, stepmother, sister-in-law, or mother-in-law. Strangely enough, aunts are not eligible. Women can join directly if they've belonged to the International Order of Job's Daughters and International Order of the Rainbow for Girls, a Masons-sponsored youth organization for girls; once they turn eighteen, they can graduate to the Order of the Eastern Star.

The OES is a "social order" for people of all faiths who believe in a Supreme Being (atheists are not allowed to join) and wish to advance the well-being of others. Its central tenets and lessons taught through the degrees are fidelity, constancy, loyalty, faith, and love. To this end, members raise a great deal of money for their local community and international charities.

As Langdon observes, it has been suggested that the OES was founded in France as early as 1703, although this is not certain. However, what is known is that by 1850, Dr. Rob Morris, an American lawyer and master Mason, instigated the Eastern Star degrees in its present form to enable women to join a similar, Masonic fraternity so that they too could answer the same philanthropic impulse that inspired their male relations to become Masons. Morris wrote the ritual for the Order, published in 1865 under the title *The Rosary of the Eastern Star*, detailing the degrees of the Order, names, signs, symbols, colors, and principles. Why he chose the specific symbols and emblems that he did, their deeper meaning, and the character-building lessons associated with them, is guarded closely by the Order, although the symbols are stated to relate to the stories associated with five biblical women who are held up as heroines that OED members should seek to emulate: Adah, Ruth, Esther, Martha, and Electa.

The five heroines are symbolized by an inverted, five-pointed star, and each woman is associated with a specific role, color, and symbol. Hence, Adah is a daughter; her color is blue, for fidelity; and her symbol is a sword and veil, signifying how she sacrificed her life to save her father's honor. This represents the first degree in the Eastern Star ritual and is the top-right point of the star. Moving clockwise, the second degree is Ruth, the widow, represented by yellow (constancy), and a barley sheaf, the emblem of plenty—alluding to how Ruth gathered leftover barley stalks to provide for her in her widowhood. The heroine of the third degree is Esther, the wife. Depicted as white (loyalty), she is the downward point of the star, with the crown and scepter representing both Esther's standing as queen and her noble spirit in her willingness to sacrifice herself for her people.

The fourth point is green (faith), representing Martha, the sister.

The star point contains a depiction of a broken column, symbolizing the uncertainties of life. The fifth degree is red (love) for Electa, the mother. She represents forbearance and acceptance of God's will despite harsh treatment and persecution. Her symbol is the cup, signifying her charity and hospitality.

The middle of the five-pointed star features a pentagon with an altar inside of it. The altar holds an open book, signifying obedience to the Word of God. Around the pentagram is the word FATAL, an acronym for Fairest Among Thousands, Altogether Lovely.

While it is easy to see why a five-pointed star was chosen, given the five roles generally assigned to women back in the nineteenth century, it is harder to understand why an inverted pentagram was chosen as their emblem, considering the satanic connotations often attributed to this symbol today. The explanation often given is that the inverted pentagram represents the star of Bethlehem that pointed down from heaven to earth and showed the way to Jesus Christ and his teachings. Indeed, the star of Bethlehem would appear to be the reason for the Order's name, especially considering the OED motto, "We have seen his star in the east, and are come to worship him" (Matthew 2:2). According to *History of the Order of the Eastern Star* by Willis D. Engle, Dr. Rob Morris made this connection in 1886 when he wrote: "The Eastern Star: The Star of Bethlehem once guided three wise men to the place where the infant Jesus lay. But the Eastern Star is this hour guiding fifty thousand wise women to the highest plane of earthly merit and usefulness."

However, some commentators have noted that the Eastern Star could not be the star of Bethlehem, which is traditionally represented as a six-pointed star. They contend that based on ancient Egyptian texts and iconography, a five-pointed star related specifically to the star Sirius. In ancient Egypt, Sirius was symbolized by the goddess Sopdet, who was described as having given birth to the morning star.

Others have noted that the inverted pentagram is closely associated with Baphomet, an imaginary pagan figure that has incorrectly become synonymous with the devil and Satanism. However, biblical scholar and author Dr. Hugh Schonfield has shown that by employing the sixth century BC Atbash cipher, the name Baphomet becomes Sophia—Greek for "wisdom," and closely linked to the sacred feminine.

Famous members of the OED include First Lady Eleanor Roosevelt, the author Laura Ingalls Wilder, and the author and poet Maya Angelou.

See also: *Freemasonry.*

Elohim

In *The Lost Symbol,* there is a point of revelation toward the end of the book when the main character, Robert Langdon, has one of his many eureka moments. He suddenly realizes that the Latin phrase *E pluribus unum* can in fact be applied to the early Hebrew idea of God. Langdon and Katherine Solomon go on to boldly proclaim that the God of the opening passages of the book of Genesis, *Elohim,* is in fact a plural and not a singular.

Was the God of Genesis actually thought of as not one but many?

This question has vexed biblical scholars and theologians for centuries and is still the source of much heated debate between religious scholars and agnostic historians. What is certain, however, is that the word *Elohim* is used multiple times within the Bible to denote a grouping of gods. Scholars agree on this, but some see the opening lines of Genesis as standing apart from these later instances of *Elohim* used in the plural. This points to the fact that a plural designation— probably along the lines of "divine entities"—was in use in the ancient Levant (the countries of the eastern Mediterranean) at the time of the Prophets.

What is certain is that the word *Elohim,* is related to the Hebrew word, *El* and in turn this is then used with a plural suffix, seemingly meaning gods, rather than the singular god. However, as with most things theological, there are several other sides to the story. Within Genesis itself there appear to be two accounts of the creation. Two creation myths as it were. In the first account, (Genesis 1:1–2) Elohim is the main name for God, or the gods. In the second account, (Genesis 2:5–25), the sacred name of God, Yahweh is used in the singular to denote the creator of all things. These two accounts are at odds with each other in several places and conflict in their description of the creator.

To many scholars, Elohim is indeed a plural form. However, far from denoting a plurality of gods, they see it as meaning a plurality of power, presence, majesty, and rank. In other words, a single God, with power and presence so awesome, that only a plurality can adequately describe It. To some orthodox Christians, its plural form signifies the reality of the Holy Trinity, where God is seen as Father, Son, and the Holy Spirit in one.

What is certain, however, is that the word Elohim, is used within the Bible itself to actually denote a grouping of gods in many places. Scholars agree on this, but some see the opening lines of Genesis as standing apart from these later instances of the use of Elohim in the plural. In 1 Samuel 28:13, a witch tells Saul that she sees many "gods," or Elohim, coming out of the earth, so pointing to the fact that a plural designation, probably along the lines of "divine entities," was in use in the ancient Levant at the time of the Prophets.

The word Elohim is found over 2,500 times in the Old Testament, with Yahweh occurring more than 6,000 times. A singular form of the name Elohim, Eloah, is used 57 times in the Old Testament, mainly in the book of Job. Scholars now recognize that this word was added as a singular form much later and that Elohim is the earlier rendition of the word and stem. Indeed, it is agreed that the word Elohim is the earliest name of God in biblical use—older than the Yahweh form—used by Semitic tribes and early races of the Near East.

In modern Judaism, Orthodox Jews are forbidden from using the word Elohim, as it is seen as one of the sacred names of God. The Arabic name of God, Allah, has an etymological relationship with the word Elohim too.

The word Elohim may well point to the early polytheism practiced by the tribes of the Levant before the advent of Abraham's monotheistic doctrine. It may also simply be a vestige, left over from those times, but used in a singular manner by the writers and subsequent editors of the Old Testament. But clearly the word can be interpreted in a myriad of ways, and has been through the ages. The complexity of the argument, as shown here, albeit briefly, is impossible to dismiss with a simple declaration that *Elohim* "must" be plural and therefore means many gods. In the end, the Latin phrase *E pluribus unum* (meaning "out of many, one") can actually be applied to both sides of the argument very convincingly, with many theologians and religious scholars seeing one God with a plurality of presence and power, and other writers and scholars seeing a host of gods that symbolically and metaphorically become as one.

See also: *One True God.*

Benjamin Franklin

Benjamin Franklin was another of history's brilliant, largely self-educated men who were unconstrained by modern education and fortunate enough to be able to develop their own interests and talents. Although born in Boston, he made Philadelphia his home, a town where there was more religious freedom than in Puritan Boston. He is buried in Philadelphia, and his national memorial is there, yet his family had lived in the English village of Ecton, Northampton-shire, for centuries. Benjamin Franklin was curious enough to visit the place, feeling the ties of ancestry, during his time in England. His loyalties lay ultimately, though, with America.

One of Franklin's many talents was a dexterity with numbers that is amply demonstrated by his ability to construct magic squares: grids with numbers arranged to provide a constant sum for all columns and rows. In *The Lost Symbol*, it is the 8 × 8 Franklin square that provides the sequence for deciphering a series of mystical symbols.

At the age of twelve, Benjamin Franklin began apprenticing in his older brother James's Boston printing shop. He was his father's tenth son (of seventeen children) and loved reading, although his formal education ended when he was ten. Josiah Franklin had hoped that young Benjamin might become a clergyman, but he couldn't afford to pay for the necessary education. He made the connection between words and printing and decided that printing was the life for Benjamin. James Franklin had begun to publish the *New England Courant*, and Benjamin wanted to write for the newspaper. He submitted pieces under the nom de plume Silence Dogood that were enormously popular, but the brothers fell out, and seventeen-year-old Benjamin left both the paper and Boston.

Settling in Philadelphia, Franklin found employment as a printer with the Read family, where he met his future wife, Deborah. In 1724 he traveled to London, England, and continued training to be a printer while enjoying a lively social life. He published a pamphlet in London called A *Dissertation on Liberty and Necessity, Pleasure and Pain*, in which he explained that man was not responsible for his actions, since he had no real freedom of choice. (Franklin later disavowed *Dissertation*, burning all but one of the copies he owned.) He returned to Philadelphia in 1726 and within three years had opened his own printing shop and become the owner-publisher of the *Pennsylvania Gazette*.

He "married" Deborah Read in 1730, despite the fact that she was already married, to a husband who had run off, while Franklin had an illegitimate son named William. During their partnership, she remained in Philadelphia with William and later their own two children, Francis, who died young, and Sarah, while he traveled to Europe for extended periods.

The movement of Deism was influential in the United States during the eighteenth century, and Franklin was undoubtedly a Deist. The concept of individual freedom and the introduction of reason into religion was in many ways linked to the current ideas of inquiry. Franklin published a popular almanac titled *Poor Richard's*, penned under his pseudonym Richard Saunders. In the 1753 edition, he wrote, "Serving God is doing good to man, but praying is thought an easier service and therefore is more generally chosen." Franklin's discomfort with religious pretension accounts for his being an infrequent churchgoer. According to David L. Holmes, author of *The Faiths of the Founding Fathers*, when Franklin's grandson was denied permission to wed a young woman because her parents objected to her marrying a Protestant, "Franklin's view was that religious differences did not matter in marriage, in that all religions were basically the same." The Masonic concept of a singular God that can be worshipped by all people is encompassed by this quote and is referred to in *The Lost Symbol*.

Franklin was deeply involved in establishing America's first subscription library as well as the American Philosophical Society. This society evolved from the Leather Apron Club, which Franklin had founded after returning from London. In the book *America's Invisible Guidance*, Corinne Heline describes how "In a deeply mystical ceremony, closely resembling the Masonic in form, the members of this club dedicated themselves 'to build a universe of peace, devoid of fear and based on love.' "

He was instrumental in persuading those of influence that Philadelphia ought to become a healthy, safe, and attractive place to live. Recognition of Benjamin's talents led to his being appointed deputy postmaster of Philadelphia and later deputy postmaster of North America, during which time he organized a twenty-four-hour service serving New York, Philadelphia, and Boston.

As Franklin widened his social circle, he joined the Freemasons (although taking his vows of secrecy seriously, he did not divulge this fact in his autobiography). It appears that Franklin was a dedicated Freemason, attending lodge meetings regularly and serving as Grand Master of Pennsylvania.

Successful in business, Franklin was able to retire in 1748 from hands-on involvement in his printing business and become a silent partner. Now a gentleman with time to pursue his interests and inventions, Franklin turned his mind toward inventing. Among his creations: a safer, more heat-efficient stove; bifocal spectacles; and the armonica, a musical instrument composed of thirty-seven spinning glass bowls. Touching one's moistened fingertips to the rims produces a series of ethereal notes. In the 1737 edition of *Poor Richard—An Almanack*, he included this philosophy: "The noblest question in the world is, what good may I do in it?"

Franklin dabbled with the fascination of electricity. At the age of forty-four, in the midst of a thunderstorm, he famously and dangerously flew a kite, which taught him that lightning is electrified air carrying an electric charge. He then developed the lightning rod. Franklin's scientific prowess was recognized in England by his election to the Royal Society, which awarded him its highest honor, the Copley Medal, for his discoveries in electricity. In *The Lost Symbol*, the Royal Society is linked to the Invisible College, which over the centuries was reputed to have included such illustrious figures as Isaac Newton, Francis Bacon, and Robert Boyle.

Benjamin Franklin returned to England in 1757 to try to talk sense into the Penn family, which regarded parts of America as a personal fiefdom. The Pennsylvania Assembly wanted to be able to tax ungranted lands to raise much-needed funds. Although he was unsuccessful, Franklin gained a great deal of respect in high places among the British establishment. During his time in England, however, his political position shifted, and he became convinced of the necessity for America to break away from its Colonial position.

Back in America, in 1775 he was active in the cause of independence, realizing that the King of England and his ministers were most unlikely ever to come to an amicable agreement with the colonists who opposed them. To Franklin's great disapproval, his son, William, who became the final governor of New Jersey to be appointed by King George III, remained loyal to the Crown. Benjamin Franklin was one of the men who drafted the Declaration of Independence in 1776, ensuring his place as one of the Founding Fathers of the United States. He was also on a committee established to design the Great Seal of the United States, although his suggestion for the inscription, "Rebellion to Tyrants Is Obedience to God," was not adopted.

Franklin spent 1776 to 1778 in France as part of a three-man team trying to enlist the support of England's old enemy in the cause of American independence. They were highly successful, and Franklin's personal popularity with the French savants and nobility was overwhelming. At this tumultuous point in French history, with riot and revolution and with growing interest in philosophy and a burgeoning number of Masonic lodges, it was fascinating to be in Paris. Franklin is credited with membership in the Masonic lodge, Les Neuf Sœurs, which proved to be extremely helpful in generating French support for the Americans.

Franklin negotiated a crucial treaty between France and the thirteen states in 1778. The following year, he became American minister (ambassador) to the burgeoning nation's new ally. Famously, when the great Thomas Jefferson succeeded him in the post in 1785, Jefferson was asked whether he was replacing Franklin. He replied that no one could replace him. "I am only his successor."

In the year before his death, Franklin wrote a treatise opposing slavery. As a young man, he had owned and traded in slaves, but as a Pennsylvania delegate to the Constitutional Convention and president of that state's Anti-Slavery Society, he had dared to change his views. By 1790, he was petitioning Congress for its abolition. When Franklin died at age eighty-four, some twenty thousand people attended his funeral.

The epitaph he wrote for himself as a young man, after the death of his close friend and mentor Thomas Denham, stands as a fitting tribute: "The body of B Franklin Printer like the cover of an old book, its contents torn out and stript of its lettering and gilding, lies here, food for worms, but the work shall not be lost; for it will, as he believ'd appear once more, in a new and more elegant Edition Revised and corrected by the author."

See also: *Freemasonry, Magic Squares, the Royal Society and the "Invisible College."*

Freedom Plaza

Freedom Plaza, in Washington, DC, is located on Pennsylvania Avenue between Thirteenth and Fourteenth streets, not far from the White House.

For Robert Langdon and Katherine Solomon, the plaza provides a useful diversion when they realize that their taxi driver is broadcasting their whereabouts to the CIA. The convenient location of a Metro Center station and an intersection of three Metro subway lines enable them to confuse and throw off their pursuers en route to their next destination.

The actual location of the subway station is two substantial blocks northeast of Freedom Plaza, an impression not conveyed by the novel. No doubt Langdon's vigorous daily swimming routine afforded him the stamina required to run all the way to the Metro entrance. The Blue Line Metros do run to Alexandria, Virginia, as the decoy set up by Langdon and Solomon suggests, as does the northbound Red Line to Tenleytown, their stop for Washington National Cathedral. Anybody planning to follow in Langdon's footsteps should be aware that the cathedral website suggests taking a bus from the Metro stop and estimates the walk at a mile and a half—again, a distance not hinted at in *The Lost Symbol*.

The square was originally known as Western Plaza but was renamed Freedom Plaza in 1980 to honor Dr. Martin Luther King Jr., who wrote his famous "I Have a Dream" speech at the nearby Willard Hotel in 1963. Following in the tradition attested to in *The Lost Symbol* of various groups burying things at the foundations of historic sites, a time capsule has been buried in the plaza. The contents, due to be retrieved in 2088, include a Bible and other items belonging to Dr. King.

On the floor of the plaza is a reproduction of part of Pierre L'Enfant's 1791 original design for the city of Washington, DC, showing the geometric patterns of the major routes and buildings. Pennsylvania Avenue was envisaged by L'Enfant as a ceremonial street linking the Capitol (then called Congress House) with the White House (originally known as the President's House). The now traditional post-inaugural parade down Pennsylvania Avenue, from the Capitol to the White House, gives full vent to the ceremonial possibilities of the street.

A husband-and-wife team of architects, Robert Venturi and Denise Scott Brown, designed the plaza to consist mainly of a raised platform, on which L'Enfant's layout plan is displayed in black-and-white stone. There is also a bronze plaque displaying a copy of the Great Seal of the United States, complete with the mottos *Annuit coeptis* and *Novus ordo seclorum*. It is this bronze seal that Robert Langdon and Katherine Solomon exploit in conjunction with the dollar bill to elude the clutches of the CIA.

The plaza has a statue at one end, dedicated to the dashing Casimir (Kazimierz in Polish) Pulaski. This Polish army officer met Benjamin Franklin in Paris in 1776, and, following Franklin's recommendation to George Washington, went to America. As a cavalry general, he fought with Washington at the Battle of Brandywine on September 11, 1777, where he is credited with saving Washington's life—hence the statue dedicated to his memory. Pulaski died two years later from wounds received at the Battle of Savannah. Sculptor Casimir Chodzinski and architect Albert Ross designed the statue and its base, which were erected in 1910.

See also: *Great Seal of the United States, Pierre L'Enfant.*

Freemasonry

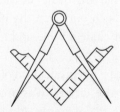

In *The Lost Symbol*, one of Professor Robert Langdon's college students asks him to explain Freemasonry. "Well," he replies, "if you were to ask a Mason, he would offer the following definition: Masonry is a system of morality, veiled in allegory and illustrated by symbols."

Freemasons' secretive rites and ceremonies are for initiates only, which is why Freemasonry is often called a secret society. However, its members typically respond to such statements in much the same way that Professor Langdon does, insisting to his class that the Masons are not a secret society, "they are a society with secrets."

These so-called secrets are veiled within the ceremonies and the symbolism of each part of the ritual dramas. Symbols are in great abundance throughout the plethora of Orders and rites that fall under the banner of Freemasonry, all of which would no doubt keep a professor of symbology gainfully employed for countless years.

These strange-looking symbols often have multiple meanings and always represent a philosophical interpretation of the stonemason's tools featured alongside biblical images. In the early eighteenth century, these were originally drawn out in chalk within the meeting room and then rubbed out to safeguard Freemasonic secrets. Over time, they became painted artworks known as "tracing boards," which are used to illustrate the educational lectures given to candidates regarding the moral principles they should adopt.

The square-and-compass emblem, the most visually symbolic sign of Freemasonry, is akin to its Star of David, representing the mundane and the Divine working together. Solomon's Temple is a central theme throughout its rituals, and significance is given to the two great pillars at the temple entrance, known as Boaz and Jachin. As a candidate progresses through the ceremonies (also referred to as degrees), the symbol of the winding staircase is presented as an allusion to Jacob's ladder, which is said mystically to lead from earth to heaven. In *The Lost Symbol*, the winding staircase within the Washington Monument seems to be its physical manifestation.

According to Kenneth Mackenzie in *The Royal Masonic Cyclopaedia* (1877), the Bible contains only one reference to winding stairs, in 1 Kings 6:8: "the door for the middle chamber was in the right side of the house; and they went up with winding stairs into the middle chamber, and out of the middle into the third."

The adoption of a winding stair in the second degree is found upon this fragmentary allusion. The symbolism of the winding stairs may be summarized thusly: The temple of Solomon represents the world purified by divine presence, or, in Hebrew, *Shekinah*; to enter the porch of the temple is therefore to be initiated a Mason; and the entered apprentice represents a child. The winding stairs do not begin until the initiate has passed between the pillars of strength and establishment, and there, as a fellow craft, he commences the ascent. As a master Mason, he receives in the middle chamber the wages, or a knowledge of the Truth.

Masonic ceremonies are said to be akin to the medieval mystery plays, whereby participants act out different roles to impart moral lessons to others. Themes of going on a great journey and searching for "that which was lost," or "the lost word," are another aspect of the ritual dramas performed throughout Freemasonry.

"The craft," as it is also often called, has included many illustrious members, from presidents, to kings, to celebrities. Mozart, Louis Armstrong, Buzz Aldrin, Harry Houdini, Harpo Marx, Henry Ford, King Hussein I of Jordan, and King George VI of Great Britain are a few examples. Of the forty-four U.S. presidents, fourteen have been confirmed as Freemasons: George Washington, James Monroe, Andrew Jackson, James Polk, James Buchanan, Andrew Johnson, James Garfield, William McKinley, Theodore Roosevelt, William Taft, Warren G. Harding, Franklin D. Roosevelt, Harry Truman, and Gerald Ford.

It is estimated that there are over two million Freemasons in North America alone and four million worldwide. Of the fifty-six signatories to the Declaration of Independence, it is rumored that many were Freemasons; this has led to speculation by some that the whole fabric of American society is based on Freemasonic principles. It is fair to say that Dan Brown, who was criticized for offending Opus Dei (a conservative Catholic group) and the Vatican in *The Da Vinci Code*, has given Freemasons an easier time. Early reports are even suggesting that the book may be encouraging a positive interest in Freemasonry, which has experienced falling numbers over the last few decades.

In an interview with the Associated Press, Dan Brown said: "I have enormous respect for the Masons. . . . With different cultures killing each other over whose version of God is correct, here is a worldwide organization that essentially says, 'We don't care what you call God, or what you think about God, only that you believe in a god, and let's all stand together as brothers and look in the same direction.' "

For others, however, Freemasonry is, at best, an odd and unorthodox movement with strange outfits and bizarre ceremonies, and, at worst, a society with sinister and subversive motives. Anti-Masonic groups and conspiracy theorists assert that the movement was responsible for the French Revolution, the P2 Lodge affair of the 1980s (which had links to the Vatican and the Mafia and nearly brought down the Italian government), and they assert that today Freemasonry is attempting to bring about a New World Order. It is therefore worth exploring what is meant by the word *Freemasonry* and why there is such a differing range of views. Can they all be right?

At the outset, the first difficulty we find is that the origins of Freemasonry are obscure, partly because of the mythological descriptions stating that it all began with Adam of the Bible, or with the builders of the Tower of Babel, or with those of Solomon's Temple, or with the ancient Egyptians who erected the pyramids. Further complicating matters, in ancient times the rituals were transmitted orally; there were no ritual books, as they have now. The organization's secrecy demanded that its members pledge on their honor to "conceal and never reveal any part or parts, point or points, of the secrets or mysteries of, or belonging to free and accepted Masons in Masonry."

For dramatic effect, during the initiation ceremonies a bloodcurdling penalty is often threatened, highlighting what will befall new members if they betray the secrets. As Dan Brown reveals in a scene that takes place in a Masonic Temple in Washington, DC, just blocks from the White House, the consequences of violating the code include having one's throat cut "from ear to ear . . . tongue torn out by its roots . . . bowels taken out and burned . . . scattered to the four winds of heaven . . . heart plucked out and given to the beasts of the field."

What Brown omitted, presumably because it lessens the effect, are the additional words explaining that these penalties were given to "Brethren" in ancient times to protect the Order from persecution, whereas today Freemasons would never inflict such harsh penalties. Rather, members who fail to live up to their oath will be treated as willfully perjured individuals, void of all moral worth and not fit to be part of such a noble society. Incidentally, most, if not all, of the Masons' "secrets" have been exposed and published over the centuries—today they even appear online.

The first actual use of the term *Free Mason* was recorded in 1376, but this was purely associated with the building fraternity in England. Scotland, however, has the earliest evidence of old medieval operative trade lodges that accepted gentlemen as members and held lodge ceremonies. For example, in Aberdeen, by around 1680, three-quarters of the lodge members were nonworkers; they became known as "speculative" Freemasons.

The earliest examples of "gentlemen masons" or "philosophical masons" include Sir Robert Moray (1641) and Elias Ashmole (1646), two of the founders of the Royal Society of London (see entry on the Royal Society for more on these characters). Over the centuries, the society's members have been known to blend the study of science with pursuits such as Hermeticism and alchemy. This period saw an increased interest in alchemy and Rosicrucianism. Although no tangible proof exists, it has been widely speculated that the ideas of the famous scientists and alchemists Robert Fludd and Sir Isaac Newton strongly influenced the development of Freemasonry.

According to the Freemasons' traditional account of their origins, the movement developed out of the operative masons' craft of the Middle Ages. As those masons were employed in building the great Gothic cathedrals of Europe, their ceremonies were specifically adopted because of the applied metaphor reflecting the human desire to strive toward divine perfection through their work. An example of one such Masonic metaphor is the taking of a rough stone and perfecting it into a perfect ashlar, or prepared stone. This apparently points out that, similarly, the Freemason, through education and diligence, can gain enlightenment when properly prepared.

Whatever the influences of the craft actually were, a defining point for the emergence of Freemasonry was the creation of the world's first Grand Lodge in London, on St. John's Day, June 24, 1717. Four lodges initially met in an alehouse called the Goose and Gridiron, but thereafter growth was rapid and soon spread around the world. By 1723, a Scottish pastor had written the first book of *Constitutions of the Freemasons*. In this work, James Anderson outlined the practices of the craft. He married ancient operative masons' codes of practice, known as the old charges, to new elements reflecting the codes of many other fraternal societies of the day.

At that time, Freemasonry used a two-grade, or two-degree, system similar to those of the operative stone masons. These were called entered apprentice and fellow of craft. The term *master Mason* was used exclusively to describe the overseer of a building project. By 1738, a revised book of constitutions contained a third degree. These initial three degrees of Freemasonry became known as Blue Masonry.

What was to follow throughout the eighteenth and nineteenth centuries was an explosion of new rites and ceremonies: Templar Rites, Scottish Rites, the York Rite, the Royal Order of Scotland, the Eastern Star, the Royal Arch, Egyptian Rites, and others more mystical in nature. Collectively these gave the eighteenth century Enlightenment another name: the Age of Freemasonry. In addition, new constitutions arose across Europe and America—not all of which recognized one another.

More sinister organizations that are not Freemasonic have also borrowed the structure of Freemasonry but have altered its ceremonies for their own aims, such as the Ku Klux Klan. It should also be noted that *Freemasonry* is a broad term; all the various groups that adopt or are conferred this title are not part of a homogenous group with a single ruling body. One of the many misconceptions about Freemasonry insists that women are excluded. The Eastern Star is a form of Freemasonry that initiates women but not in the "Blue" degrees. There are, however, a number of Grand Lodges that accept both men and women, although it is fair to say that "accepted" Freemasonry, which includes most of the American Grand Lodges, views these groups as "irregular" and doesn't enter into relationships with them.

In the prologue of *The Lost Symbol*, the initiate is prepared for a ceremony. Brown appears to have gleaned some of this from standard Freemasonic rituals and has added in a dramatic element of drinking wine from a human skull. For those readers with Masonic uncles or dads, don't worry, they actually don't do this! Or at least not now: the practice did turn up in some Templar Rites early in the eighteenth century and seems to have been taken directly from the so-called Cerneau Rite. There is also a certain Buddhist rite known as the Kapala, in which a human skull is used as a drinking vessel.

Skulls often appear in Masonic symbolism, as the character Robert Langdon explains to Inoue Sato as they inspect an eerie room called a Chamber of Reflection. The practice of staring at a skull and bones, also called *caput mortuum*, or "the emblems of mortality," while alone in a room is for initiates to contemplate that all must die; therefore each person should consider how he or she has chosen to live. A medieval parallel can be found with the invitation to contemplate the seven virtues and the seven cardinal sins. One path brings the keys to the kingdom of heaven; the other, purgatory.

Some details that Dan Brown got right: the baring of a breast, a rolled-up trouser leg, the right sleeve rolled up, and a noose or cable tow around the candidate's neck. To the layman, these practices do seem odd. What's more, a newly entered apprentice Freemason is also blindfolded, or "hoodwinked," as it is called. Each element is highly symbolic. According to the Masonic ritual:

You were neither naked nor clothed because Masonry regards no man on account of his worldly wealth or honors. . . . You were hoodwinked and with a cable tow about your neck for three reasons; first, that your heart might conceive before your eyes beheld the beauties of Freemasonry; second, that as you were in darkness, it was to teach you to keep the whole world so respecting the secrets of Freemasonry, except to such as were justly entitled to receive the same as you were about to become; and third, had you not conformed to the ceremony of your initiation, thereby rendering yourself unworthy to be taken by the hand as a Mason, you might, by aid of the cable tow, have been led out of the Lodge without having beheld even the form thereof.

You were received on the point of a sharp instrument piercing your naked left breast, to teach you that as it was an instrument of torture to the flesh, so should the recollection thereof be to your mind and conscience should you ever reveal the secrets of Freemasonry unlawfully.

You were conducted to the center of the Lodge and caused to kneel for the benefit of prayer, for before entering upon any great or important undertaking, we ought always to invoke the aid of Deity.

You were asked in whom you put your trust, agreeably to our ancient laws, as no atheist can be made a Mason; it was therefore necessary that you express a belief in Deity, otherwise no obligation would have been regarded as binding.

Much has been made of the symbolism of the Great Seal of the United States, on the one-dollar bill, and the words "In God We Trust" as allegedly being Masonic. President Theodore Roosevelt, who is known to have been a Freemason, actually wanted these words removed. In 1907 he wrote: "It seems to me eminently unwise to cheapen such a motto by use on coins, just as it would be to cheapen it by use on postage stamps, or in advertisements."

As we have discovered, Freemasonry is not at all straightforward. Over the time of its intriguing development, countless ceremonies have been invented and hundreds if not thousands of different "Freemasonic" groups have emerged. There are most certainly "good guys" and "bad guys"; there are indeed groups with noble motives and others obviously less so. In the final analysis, the Freemasons seem to be just like the rest of us—but with aprons!

See also: *Alchemy, Boaz and Jachin, Cerneau Rite, Dollar Bill Symbolism, the Eastern Star, Great Seal of the United States, Sir Isaac Newton, Rosicrucians, Scottish Rite Freemasonry.*

SIMON COX

Freemason's Cipher

A message in *The Lost Symbol* is displayed as a series of signs that the character Robert Langdon is quickly able to decipher, identifying it as a Freemason's cipher. Freemasons began to use the cipher—originally called the pigpen cipher—which was to encrypt documents around the early 1700s. During the American Civil War, Confederate officers were reputed to have used this cipher as well.

The cipher is a substitution system in which each letter of a word or phrase is exchanged for a symbol. The twenty-six letters of the English alphabet are written into four grids. Then the portion of the grid into which the letter has been placed forms the shape of that letter in the code. An example of how this looks can be found in the pages of *The Lost Symbol*.

An organization such as the Freemasons, with members who wanted to keep their affairs secret, needed a coded method for sending messages between different lodges or individual members. The minutes of a 1769 meeting of Royal Arch Masons in Portsmouth, England, contain an early mention of this code. Thomas Dunckerley delivered the charter authorizing the meeting, and the minutes record that "He also told up of this mann'r of writing which is to be used in the degree."

The minutes are all encoded in the geometric form of the Masonic cipher. Compared to other ciphers then and now, the Freemason's cipher is simple—quite crude, actually—and easily decoded. Not surprisingly, it soon fell out of use. The cipher is said to have been developed in the early 1600s by Giambattista della Porta, a scholar and occultist who lived in Naples, Italy. Della Porta wrote extensively on the occult, philosophy, alchemy, mathematics, and astrology, and was also a prolific playwright. In 1563 he published *De Furtivis Literarum Notis*, a book about secret codes and cryptography.

On the back cover of the American edition of *The Lost Symbol*, a column of Freemason's cipher symbols runs down either side. This is deciphered by turning the book ninety degrees and reading the cipher as two lines. When you apply the cipher to this code, you get the phrase "All Great Truths Begin as Blasphemies." This cipher and the answer to it are part of the Symbol Quest that Dan Brown's publisher was running as a competition upon the book's publication.

See also: *Freemasonry*.

Great Architect of the Universe

Early in *The Lost Symbol*, Professor Robert Langdon is giving a lecture on occult symbols. He explains to his class that "rather than definitive theological identities like God, Allah, Buddha, or Jesus, the Masons use more general terms like Supreme Being or Great Architect of the Universe. This enables Masons of different faiths to gather together."

Various groups, many of them Christian, have pointed to the term *Great Architect of the Universe* as proof that Freemasonry is an anti-Christian society. Yet it is very much Christian in origin, found in writings by Christian scholars. For instance, the French church reformer John Calvin used the term extensively in his brilliant work on theological issues, *Institutes of the Christian Religion*, in 1536, though he was not the first Christian writer to do so. This work would later form the basis of worship for most Presbyterian and Reformed churches. In the book, Calvin calls God by the composite name "Architect of the Universe," referring to his works within nature as architecture of the universe some ten times in total. Calvin also wrote a separate commentary on Psalm 19 in which he calls God "the Great Architect of the Universe." Calvin's ideas influenced many people over the next few hundred years, one of whom was the Reverend James Anderson.

Anderson was a Scottish Presbyterian minister who led a congregation on London's Swallow Street from 1710 until 1734. He was also a prominent Freemason of the Grand Lodge of England. In 1723 Anderson wrote the first *Book of Constitutions*, one of the most important early guides on the craft of Freemasonry and a set of rules and guide-lines that mostly remain in place today.

Anderson had studied to become a minister at the University of Aberdeen, where the curriculum was based upon Calvin's *Institutes of the Christian Religion*. This is where he most probably first heard the phrase "Great Architect of the Universe," which he incorporated into his *Book of Constitutions*. Dan Brown has possibly taken the name of Trent Anderson, the U.S. Capitol police chief in *The Lost Symbol*, from this influential Masonic figure.

Masonic tradition states that Great Architect of the Universe is meant to portray the Deity Most High in a nondenominational way, so that men of all creeds, races, and religions can become members of the craft. Freemasonry, as Robert Langdon mentions in *The Lost Symbol*, requires one to believe in a higher spiritual power: a great Deity who is seen as the master architect and master Mason, in effect. Many Christians complain that this rendering of God actually makes Him seem more abstract and distant.

Martin L. Wagner, in *Freemasonry: An Interpretation*, writes:

> In its doctrines concerning the divine immanence, Freemasonry is decidedly pantheistic, partaking of the various shades of that view of the divine. God (the Great Architect) is the "soul" of the universe and the universe is the garment in which he is clothed. . . . The Masonic view of the revelation of God, in the lower degrees, is deistic, but in the higher degrees it becomes pantheistic. The writings of Garrison, Buck, Pike, and other eminent Masons show this unmistakably. It is this particular pantheistic conception of deity, which has passed from India through the secret doctrines of the Kabbalah into modern speculative Freemasonry. . . . In Masonry, a God distinct from the life of nature has no existence.

Certain Rosicrucian groups also use the title to denote the Supreme Being of their spiritual belief system. Hermeticism also alludes to this concept of the One in its teachings. To followers of the Hermetica, each of us has the potential to be God. In Hermeticism, God is an ideal that is internal, not external—radically different from the Christian realization of God. We inhabit an observer-created universe, creating our own reality and creating God within us. This description of God is the closest to the Masonic ideal of the Great Architect of the Universe.

See also: *Freemasonry, Hermetica, Rosicrucians*.

Great Pyramid

Pyramids play a significant role in *The Lost Symbol*. A small, truncated pyramid is revealed as a major visual clue, along with its miniature pyramidion. Throughout the book, the quest to find the Masonic pyramid becomes a central theme, as the characters visit many of the mysterious and symbolic sites of Washington, DC.

The so-called Masonic pyramid, along with its pyramidion and, indeed, the pyramid as rendered on the Great Seal of the United States and the dollar bill, all trace their origins and undeniable source to the Great Pyramid at Giza, Egypt.

Of the seven wonders of the ancient world, only this one remains, standing majestically on the Giza Plateau, on the outskirts of Egypt's rapidly expanding capital, Cairo. Dwarfing mere mortals who approach it, the mass of over ninety-five million cubic feet cannot fail to impress. The great majority of Egyptologists have little hesitation in ascribing ownership and construction of it to the Pharaoh Khnum-Khufu, better known as Khufu, although some dissonant voices argue that hard evidence is lacking or even misleading. Nearby stand two other huge pyramids—Khafre and Menkaure—as well as the huge, brooding Sphinx. Authors Robert and Olivia Temple, in their brilliant book *The Sphinx Mystery*, argue that the mysterious structure with the body of a lion and the head of a king was in fact originally a representation of the god Anubis, in the form of a crouching dog. In addition, there are many smaller pyramids on the Giza Plateau—some for royal queens, one for the *ka* (spirit body) of the king—and still other structures that tend to be overlooked by visitors, who are usually drawn toward the main attraction like iron fragments toward a magnet.

The chief servants were buried near their masters in mastaba tombs, constructed so that even in the afterlife, they would be able to cluster faithfully around the master's monument. Standing 481 feet high and built of over 2.3 million stone blocks, each said to weigh an average of two and a half tons, the mastabas resemble giant benches. Yet they too are dwarfed by the Great Pyramid.

Khufu is usually credited with having ascended to the throne around 2609 BC and reigning for twenty-five years, but some sources claim that he ruled for perhaps twice that long. When completed, his pyramid must have dazzled the eyes, since the core of soft limestone seen today was encased in polished hard limestone, resembling marble. It is said that in the thirteenth century, an earthquake loosened some of the casing stones, which local inhabitants carted off to use in their own buildings. Cairo's Mosque of Sultan Hassan benefited from this scavenging, as did other mosques and fine buildings.

From the outside, the Great Pyramid gives the impression of a solid structure, but the interior resembles an ant colony, with long passageways and large chambers that may or may not have been burial chambers. The Greek historian Herodotus, writing very much later, clearly states that Cheops (the Greek name for Khufu) was not buried in the Great Pyramid.

Other mysteries associated with the Great Pyramid include the purpose of the so-called star, or air, shafts leading from the king's and queen's chambers. The basic questions of how they were built, and its design, are still inconclusive. The Great Pyramid has been studied and measured minutely and has inspired countless theories and prophesies, prompting some to coin a word for the more bizarre theorists: *pyramidiots*.

One thing that has always fascinated researchers, myself included, is the fact that no bodies have ever been found in any of the pyramids of the Old Kingdom, or third millennium BC. This has led to speculation that the pyramids in general, and the Great Pyramid specifically, were in fact not tombs but temples of initiation of some kind. It has also been theorized that the layout of the pyramids formed a map of the heavens, aligned to specific stars and constellations. This idea is referred to within the pages of *The Lost Symbol*.

The book *The Orion Mystery*, by Robert Bauval and Adrian Gilbert, advances a theory that the three great pyramids of Giza were aligned to the three stars of Orion's belt in the constellation Orion. This theory gained equal acclaim and criticism, with Egyptologists defending the traditional theories about the use and origins of the pyramids, and modern researchers and New Age followers championing the authors' claims.

In another book on the subject, *Secret Chamber,* Bauval points out how various esoteric and secret groups have long had a serious interest in the monuments of the Giza Plateau. These groups included Masonic orders and associations. Indeed, one group, known as the Millennium Project, intended to coordinate a major show at the pyramids on Millennium Eve, 1999. At this show, it intended to lower a symbolic golden capstone onto the Great Pyramid and produce a celebration of human achievement and prospects for the future via many images rapidly displayed, culminating in the spectacular lighting of the "Eye in the Sun," or "Ain Shams," as it is known in Arabic, on top of the pyramids. (In the end, the event never took place.)

This "eye in the sun" motif is, in fact, the same blazing eye of Masonic symbolic lore—sometimes known as the Eye of Providence or the All Seeing Eye—and can be seen on the dollar bill and the Great Seal of the United States. Conspicuously missing from the Great Pyramid is its benben, or capstone; the top is not pointed as is normal. Amid growing excitement, a prophecy made by Edgar Cayce (1877–1945) was recalled: according to the American psychic and healer, placing such a capstone on the pyramid would usher in a New World Order based on Masonic principles. The Edgar Cayce Foundation undertook research at Giza in hopes of discovering a hall of records under the paws of the Sphinx, as was also prophesied by Cayce.

The Millennium Project organizers were plainly trying to herald in the year 2000 with an esoteric ritual that would see the Great Pyramid once again whole, leading to a new age of enlightenment and reason.

Sadly the event failed to materialize as some Egyptians charged that the ceremony was something of a Masonic plot and un-Islamic, putting pressure on the Egyptian government to cancel this part of the celebrations. The supposed Masonic connections to the prophecy caused a great deal of bad feeling, and almost at the last minute the Egyptian Culture Ministry announced that to avoid damage to the pyramid and in deference to public resentment the ceremony would not take place.

See also: *All Seeing Eye, Dollar Bill Symbolism, Freemasonry, Great Seal of the United States.*

Great Seal of the United States

In *The Lost Symbol*, Robert Langdon and Katherine Solomon discuss conspiracy theories surrounding the Great Seal of the United States. They also visit Freedom Plaza in Washington, DC, where they inspect the huge bronze representation of the Great Seal that is laid into the pavement there. In their conversations, it is intimated that elements of the Great Seal are Masonic in nature and may well symbolize more mysterious and esoteric ideas concerning the founding of the United Sates.

On July 4, 1776, the Continental Congress began the process of creating a national emblem: a Great Seal symbolizing independence and sovereignty; a signature that would be recognized by all other nations. Early on, Benjamin Franklin suggested that the back of the seal should be adorned with the motto "Rebellion to Tyrants Is Obedience to God." However, this idea was rejected. (Franklin later used it for his own personal seal.)

It took six years and several committees to settle upon the design elements for the Great Seal. Finally, in 1782, the task of overseeing its design and implementation was entrusted to Charles Thomson, secretary of the Continental Congress. In a matter of months, the metal die had been cut, and on September 16, 1782, the official Great Seal was being used for the first time on a document. The design has remained largely unchanged.

Thomson's design for the front of the Great Seal consisted of an American bald eagle, wings splayed and upward, holding a laurel leaf in its right talon and a bundle of arrows in its left. A constellation of thirteen stars was placed above the eagle's head, and in its beak, a scroll with the motto *E pluribus unum* ("Out of many, one") in Latin. Upon the chest of the eagle was a shield, or escutcheon, with red and white alternating stripes.

For the reverse of the Great Seal, Thomson used a design element that the third Great Seal committee had decided upon: the truncated pyramid with the Eye of Providence hovering above it. A triangle, or pyramidion, was added around the eye at this stage by Thomson, as suggested by the first committee back in 1776. Two mottos, both in Latin, appear: *Novus ordo seclorum* ("A new order of the ages") and *Annuit coeptis* ("Providence has favored our undertaking").

Charles Thomson himself explained the symbolism of the various design elements in a memo to Congress:

Remarks and Explanation—June 20, 1782
The Escutcheon is composed of the chief & pale, the two most honorable ordinaries. The Pieces, paly, represent the several states all joined in one solid compact entire, supporting a Chief, which unites the whole & represents Congress. The Motto alludes to this union. The pales in the arms are kept closely united by the chief and the

Chief depends upon that union & the strength resulting from it for its support, to denote the Confederacy of the United States of America & the preservation of their union through Congress.

The colours of the pales are those used in the flag of the United States of America; White signifies purity and innocence, Red, hardiness & valor, and Blue, the colour of the Chief signifies vigilance, perseverance & justice. The Olive branch and arrows denote the power of peace & war which is exclusively vested in Congress. The Constellation denotes a new State taking its place and rank among other sovereign powers. The Escutcheon is born on the breast of an American Eagle without any other supporters to denote that the United States of America ought to rely on their own Virtue.

Reverse. The pyramid signifies Strength and Duration: The Eye over it & the Motto allude to the many signal interpositions of providence in favour of the American cause. The date underneath is that of the Declaration of Independence and the words under it signify the beginning of the new American Era, which commences from that date.

Interestingly, Charles Thomson was not a Freemason, as far as any researchers can show. Furthermore, one of the only Freemasons involved in the design of the Great Seal was Benjamin Franklin, whose ideas were not used in the end. That is not to say, however, that Thomson and other members of the Continental Congress didn't belong to *other* clandestine groups or didn't have Masonic leanings. It could well be that in this tumultuous time of revolution and war and the founding of a new nation, sacred symbolism and profane meaning found their way into the Great Seal.

Upon closer inspection, the so-called Masonic symbolism of the Great Seal can be seen in a different light. There are certainly mysterious and symbolic meanings to the design of the Great Seal, but none is overtly Masonic. In 1935, U.S. Secretary of Agriculture Henry A. Wallace, who was to go on to become the thirty-third vice president of the United States under Franklin Roosevelt, encouraged and championed the inclusion of both sides of the Great Seal upon the newly designed dollar bill. Wallace and Roosevelt were both prominent Masons, and many of the Masonic conspiracy theories about the design of the original design if the Great Seal undoubtedly emanate from this period.

However, the symbols and elements used on the Great Seal need not be originally Masonic in nature to be part of a conspiracy of symbolism. It is certainly true that the eye hovering above the unfinished pyramid has been adopted since the design of the Great Seal as a quasi-Masonic symbol, and that the pyramid in general can be seen as mysterious and symbolic. But neither of these symbols was exclusive to Freemasonry at the time that Thomson and his colleagues were designing the Great Seal.

In *The Lost Symbol*, Katherine Solomon draws a Star of David over the unfinished pyramid on the dollar bill while sitting in the back of a taxicab. This is then used as a diversion so that she and Robert Langdon can escape into the Washington, DC, subway system and away from the CIA. The scene highlights an interesting conspiratorial charge that many critics of the Masons and conspiracy theorists have brought up: namely, that there is a hidden and esoteric meaning within the Great Seal, and that it is essentially Masonic in nature. Based on all the evidence, this simply is not true.

See also: *Dollar Bill Symbolism, Freemasonry.*

Manly P. Hall

Mystic, sage, esotericist, historian, philosopher, seeker—Manly P. Hall was all of these things, and a lot more besides. Gracing the front of *The Lost Symbol* is a Manly P. Hall quote from his amazing magnum opus of a book, *The Secret Teachings of All Ages:* "To live in the world without becoming aware of the meaning of the world is like wandering about in a great library without touching the books."

Who was Manly P. Hall? Why does Dan Brown use his quote as the book's epigraph? And just what is a sage, anyway?

Manly Palmer Hall was born in Ontario, Canada, on March 18,

1901. Raised by his maternal grandmother, Hall was brought to the United States while still a young child. Through his youth and into adulthood, Hall read voraciously and studied texts about the Ancient Mystery traditions, philosophy, and the occult. He had a formidable IQ and believed that no single religion had all the answers; instead one had to look at all wisdom traditions—and add science and philosophy into the mix too. Hall was soon a regular lecturer in the Los Angeles area, attracting large audiences eager to hear his belief that universal wisdom could be attained through the myths, legends, and symbols of the ancient world.

At the age of twenty-five, Manly P. Hall authored his greatest book, the incredible *The Secret Teachings of All Ages*; this book soon became one of the most influential works on the esoteric and the occult ever written. It still stands today as a shining beacon of knowledge and philosophy within the genre. The book took some six years to complete, during which time Hall traveled extensively throughout the great ancient centers of the world, including Egypt, the Middle East, Greece, and large parts of Asia and Europe. He became a regular visitor to the British Museum reading room in London, and observed:

The great center of learning in England is the British Museum, with its miles of bookcases, which caused De Quincy to sit and weep because he could not read all the volumes. In order to gain access to the two principal departments of the museum—one of rare books, and the other of manuscripts—it was necessary to be appropriately sponsored. I had the good fortune of becoming acquainted with General Sir Francis Younghusband, the man who led the British expedition into Tibet in 1903–1904, and camped his army at the foot of the Potola at Lhasa. While dining one day at the Officer's Club, Sir Francis confided to me that he was known as the conqueror of Tibet, but he regarded this as a dubious honor. The real fact, he said, was that Tibetan religion and philosophy had conquered him. A note from Sir Francis immediately gave me admission to the most valuable parts of the British Museum, and I was able to examine the originals of many of the world's most priceless books and manuscripts.

It is not at all clear how Manly P. Hall financed his travels and research, but legend has it that his secret benefactor was a rich oil baron's wife in California. The story goes that she had heard one of Hall's many lectures in Los Angeles and had been so impressed by the young speaker that she offered to pay for his travels, research, and quest for ancient wisdom, encouraging him to build a library of rare and arcane material from the four corners of the world. A recent biographer of Hall (Louis Sahagun in *Man of Mystery*) claimed that his sponsors were a mother and daughter, Caroline and Estelle Lloyd, from a very wealthy family in Ventura.

During these travels, Hall become convinced that it was through the study of comparative religions that true wisdom would be found, and so he set about not only learning as much as he could about the major religions of the West and East but also delving into the mysteries of many of the lesser-known sects and orders.

The impact of *The Secret Teachings of All Ages* cannot be overstated. This incredible volume was published by Hall himself initially, at a staggering cost of some $100,000, a huge sum of money in 1928.

Pictures of the young Manly P. Hall show a handsome man who seems to radiate charisma and has the look of a movie star. His influence within esoteric circles was certainly growing, and his fan base from his extensive lecturing was growing by the month. Hall was to become the darling of the elite, being seen as a wise, sagelike figure by many.

In 1934 he founded the Philosophical Research Society in Los Angeles. The facility still operates today, hosting lectures and degree courses, publishing and selling books, and housing one of the most complete libraries of ancient wisdom, esoterica, and the occult in the world. Carl Jung was reputed to have used the library extensively when formulating many of his theories on psychology. A plaque in the center's courtyard reads, "Dedicated to Truth Seekers of All Time."

Manly P. Hall counted movie and music stars, politicians, and business moguls among his admirers. It is rumored that Elvis Presley was a fan of his work; supposedly, he once sent his wife, Priscilla, to a

Hall lecture because he was afraid of being mobbed if he went himself. Hall, writing about his newfound fame, reflected, "All followers who offer to adorn and deify their teachers set up a false condition . . . human beings, experience has proved, make better humans than they do gods."

Today Manly P. Hall and his work seem dusty and arcane, out of step with modern ideas about ancient spiritual knowledge. Hall wasn't a media-savvy self-promoter like so many of the New Age fraternity. His was a gentler understanding of the Mysteries but also a much more in-depth and personal one. Hall was a real thinker, and his photographic memory enabled him to recall vast stores of knowledge and data when needed.

During his heyday in the late 1920s and 1930s, Hall befriended the Russian mystic, author, and painter Nicholas Roerich, and the two men soon found common ground in their love of the work of Helena Blavatsky, the Russian founder of the movement known as Theosophy. Hall and Roerich began to move in exalted circles and their influence ranged far and wide. It was even rumored that Hall and Roerich were responsible for adorning the newly designed dollar bill with the Great Seal of the United States, which features the so-called Eye of Providence hovering above an unfinished pyramid. Hall was familiar with such symbolism, of course, and would have recognized in the Great Seal its deeply esoteric and occultic meanings.

Manly P. Hall believed that the United States held a special, predestined place in the world and wrote *The Secret Destiny of America* with this in mind. He writes, "Thousands of years ago, in Egypt, these mystical orders were aware of the existence of the western hemisphere and the great continent which we call America. The bold resolution was made that this western continent should become the site of the philosophic empire. Just when this was done it is impossible now to say, but certainly the decision was reached prior to the time of Plato, for a thinly veiled statement of this resolution is the substance of his treatise on the Atlantic Islands."

Hall was also a firm proponent of the theory that Sir Francis Bacon had been the real writer of William Shakespeare's body of work.

In a 1973 ceremony at the Philosophical Research Society, Manly Palmer Hall was inducted as a thirty-third degree Freemason under the Scottish Rite of Freemasonry. Hall had been a lifelong Freemason, writing extensively on the subject, and this honorific degree was conferred upon him in recognition of his study of the craft and its underlying philosophy.

Manly P. Hall's death in 1990 was as mysterious as his life. At the age of eighty-nine, and in frail health, Hall was found, seemingly dead for many hours, with thousands upon thousands of ants streaming from his nose and mouth and around his body. The cause of his death has never been confirmed, but many speculate that his assistant had plotted against him in order to benefit from Hall's will.

The legacy of Manly Palmer Hall will live on indefinitely. His *The Secret Teachings of All Ages* remains a standard reference work for seekers of ancient truths and mysteries, and his library (which, incidentally, President Franklin D. Roosevelt was very interested in) still stands as a testament to his quest for knowledge and his undying love of the Ancient Mystery traditions.

See also: *Dollar Bill Symbolism*, *Great Seal of the United States*.

Hand of the Mysteries

In *The Lost Symbol*, the Hand of the Mysteries is physically re-created when Mal'akh severs Peter Solomon's right hand and literally transforms it into a Hand of the Mysteries, which he then places in the rotunda of the U.S. Capitol. We learn that its fingers have been tattooed, in effect turning a human hand into the symbolic Hand of the Mysteries: with a crown on the thumb and a star on the index finger, followed by a sun, a lantern, and, on the little finger, a key.

The Hand of the Mysteries is referenced in the 1928 book called *The Secret Teachings of All Ages*, by the mystic and philosopher Manly P. Hall. It could be said that *The Lost Symbol* starts and ends with Manly P. Hall. The book begins with a quote from *The Secret Teach-*

ings of All Ages and in the final chapter, 133, we are treated to a second quote. Certainly much of the content of the novel is in accord with the writings of Manly P. Hall, a philosopher and mystic who wrote his magnum opus aged just twenty-five. It is still hard to comprehend what a masterly work this book is. It would have been a glorious achievement for someone with a lifetime's experience of such esoteric subjects, but for a young man it is simply remarkable. It will probably not come as a surprise to discover that Hall later became a thirty-third degree Freemason.

Hall had illustrator Augustus Knapp reproduce an image of the Hand of the Mysteries, taken from an eighteenth-century watercolor of unknown provenance. In the illustration we see that rather than having the five symbols Robert Langdon highlights tattooed onto the fingers, the symbols are here floating above the extended fingers and thumb of the hand. In addition, there is a fish swimming in an oval background of green, surrounded by a ring of flames placed over the palm of the hand.

In the accompanying text, Hall cites a quote that he found along with the watercolor which reads "The wise take their oath by this hand that they will not teach the Art without parables."

Just as Robert Langdon points out in *The Lost Symbol*, Hall suggests that the Hand of the Mysteries was offered as an invitation from a master to an initiate: "The original drawing from which this plate was taken is designated the hand of the philosopher which is extended to those who enter into the mysteries. When the disciple of the Great Art first beholds this hand, it is closed, and he must discover a method of opening it before the mysteries contained therein may be revealed."

If you remember, in *The Lost Symbol*, the severed hand has to be pried opened to reveal a code, "SBB XIII," which has been inscribed onto the palm. This leads Langdon and others to the room deep below the Capitol where the granite pyramid is located.

The Hand of the Mysteries is an allegorical device that suggests the workings of the great alchemists, who encoded many of their works with symbols. Manly Hall's *The Secret Teachings of All Ages* explains the significance of the image of the fish: "The fish is mercury and the flame-bounded sea in which it swims is sulfur, while each of the fingers bears the emblem of a Divine Agent through the combined operations of which the great work is accomplished."

He goes on to illuminate the symbols associated with the fingers and thumb:

Philosophically, the key represents the Mysteries themselves, without whose aid man cannot unlock the numerous chambers of his own being. The lantern is human knowledge, for it is a spark of the Universal Fire captured in a man-made vessel; it is the light of those who dwell in the inferior universe and with the aid of which they seek to follow in the footsteps of Truth. The sun, which may be termed the "light of the world," represents the luminescence of creation through which man may learn the mystery of all creatures which express through form and number. The star is the Universal Light which reveals cosmic and celestial verities. The crown is Absolute Light— unknown and unrevealed—whose power shines through all the lesser lights that are but sparks of this Eternal Effulgence.

The human hand has been regarded as an important symbol itself for many thousands of years. Magic, alchemy, and even Noetic Science revolve around the application of the human will over the material world. As Hall described it, the human mind is the "product of the will to know," whereas the hand is the "product of the will to grasp."

So it is that the hand is the ultimate instrument of the mind, for while the mind can conceive of the material world, only the hand can manipulate it. For this very reason, the hand has always been a potent symbol. In ancient Egypt, we find inscriptions showing hands placed at the end of rays emanating from the sun, to signify the interaction between God—the sun disk—and mankind. Often those hands of the sun hold ankhs, a symbol which is often described as meaning "life" or "breath."

In another scene of *The Lost Symbol*, Mal'akh reveals that he'd cut off his father's right hand so that Peter Solomon would have to sacrifice him using his left hand. The left hand is said to be reserved for the dark and black arts. This often stems from a belief that early cultures would practice all good and constructive deeds with the right hand and leave all unclean or unsavory tasks for the left hand. Manly P. Hall reveals another intriguing aspect of this as part of a discussion of sacred writing—not so much which hand it was created with but the direction in which it was committed to paper:

> Some philosophers further declared that there were two methods of writing: one from left to right, which was considered the exoteric method; the other from right to left, which was considered esoteric. The exoteric writing was that which was done out or away from the heart, while the esoteric writing was that which—like the ancient Hebrew—was written toward the heart.

One final point about the Hand of the Mysteries: In *The Lost Symbol*, we are told that Peter Solomon's severed hand was manipulated so that the forefinger and thumb pointed up toward the heavens—in this case, literally, for it pointed to the portrayal of George Washington sitting in heaven in *The Apotheosis of Washington*, which is painted on the inside of the Capitol's dome. We are further told that the hand was positioned exactly like that of George Washington in a famous statue depicting him as the god Zeus, bare chest and all. The first president of the United States points heavenward in what Lynn Picknett and Clive Prince, coauthors of *The Templar Revelation: Secret Guardians of the True Identity of Christ*, refer to as the "John gesture"—because it is found so often in the works of Leonardo da Vinci and seems to be used to represent John the Baptist. Readers of Dan Brown's *The Da Vinci Code* will find this familiar territory. The severed hand in the rotunda makes this exact same gesture, with the index finger and thumb extended.

Recalling Manly P. Hall's description of the symbols associated with the thumb and index finger of the Hand of the Mysteries—the crown and the star, respectively—we find that both are associated with the Light: the index finger representing the Universal Light and the thumb the Absolute Light. It seems very fitting that Peter Solomon's hand should point to *The Apotheosis of Washington* with the two digits that correspond with the two symbols for the Light. The central theme of *The Lost Symbol* is illumination and discovering God within, so Brown's use of the Hand of the Mysteries is a very clever device.

See also: *The Apotheosis of Washington, Capitol Building.*

Heredom

In *The Lost Symbol*, the word *Heredom* emerges from a grid of clues solved by Robert Langdon. As its full significance becomes apparent, Robert Langdon and Katherine Solomon need to find a pyramid that is located beneath the House of the Temple in Washington, DC, the headquarters of Scottish Rite Freemasonry—this temple being known as Heredom.

One Masonic website gives the following explanation:

Heredom n. [orig. unknown] 1. a significant word in "high degree" Freemasonry, from French Rose Croix rituals where it refers to a mythical mountain in Scotland, the legendary site of the first such Chapter. Possible explanations include: Hieros-domos, Greek for Holy House, Harodim, Hebrew for overseers; Heredum, Latin for of the heirs. 2. the annual transactions of the Scottish Rite Research Society.

Intriguingly, the word Heredom is also mentioned as a mythical mountain in Scotland as well as the site of a chapter of Freemasons who practice French Rose Croix rituals. So why would a mountain in Scotland have attracted such a legend?

Is it possible that Heredom does indeed point to a mythical Scottish mountain, but if so, which one? Scottish researcher and author Barry Dunford believes that the mythical mountain in question may actually be Mount Schiehallion, located in the center of Scotland, some sixty miles north of the capital city of Edinburgh. Dunford sees in Schiehallion a mythical Mount Zion of the north and speculates that it may be "the Mount of Assembly far away to the north" mentioned in Isaiah 14:13. What is certain is that Schiehallion has been seen as both a mysterious and sacred mountain for many centuries.

Regarding the origins of the concept of Heredom as a Masonic sacred place, Dunford points out on his website that French author Chevalier de Berage wrote in 1747, "Their Metropolitan Lodge is situated on the Mountain of Heredom where the first Lodge was held in Europe and which exists in all its splendour. The General Council is still held there and it is the seal of the Sovereign Grand Master in office. This mountain is situated between the West and North of Scotland at sixty miles from Edinburgh." Mount Schiehallion, with its conical summit and pyramid shape, fits this description very well and was a place of spiritual pilgrimage in the past.

Today the word *Heredom* is also applied to the main publication of the Scottish Rite Research Society, sent annually to members since 1992.

See also: *House of the Temple*.

Hermetica

In *The Lost Symbol,* the phrase "As above, so below" plays a pivotal role in Robert Langdon's search for the location of the Ancient Mysteries; in fact, it is the lost key that unlocks all the other doors.

This principle also forms the basis of Hermeticism, a mystical philosophical tradition and teaching developed in the cosmopolitan Egyptian city of Alexandria around the first century AD. It renounced codified dogma, priestly authority, and the separation of God and man; instead Hermeticism propounded a belief in inner enlightenment, declaring that everyone should aspire to a personal knowledge of the Divine. Hermetic beliefs, a product of Alexandrian syncretism, were heavily influenced by Neoplatonism, Gnosticism, Ptolemaic

Egyptian, Judaic, and Christian thought, and are to be found in the written works referred to collectively as the Hermetica.

The Hermetica covers topics such as philosophical discussions, mysticism, magic, astrology, alchemy, and medicine, and was supposedly written by Hermes Trismegistus (Hermes, the Thrice Great), the central figure of the Hermetica and Hermetic belief. Hermes Trismegistus was the product of fusing Thoth, the Egyptian god of learning, writing, and magic, with Hermes, the Greek god of communication, inventions, language, and travel. Because both gods presided over similar areas of responsibility, the two became combined in Ptolemaic Egypt to become Thoth-Hermes. This much-revered god was believed to know all the secrets of heaven and earth—secrets that might be revealed to the worthy through the power of magic and dreams.

By the time of the early Christian period, Hermes Trismegistus had evolved into an ancient sage on a par with Moses, Pythagoras, and Zoroaster, although having a more ancient existence. It is uncertain why Thoth-Hermes was given the moniker Thrice Great. Some Hermetic texts suggest that it was because of his three incarnations (the previous two being Enoch and Noah) or because he was the greatest philosopher, priest, and king. However, the emerald tablet of alchemy declares that the title paid tribute to his knowledge of the three wisdoms of the universe: alchemy, astrology, and theurgy (the practice of magical rituals). The Egyptian god Thoth had been called Thrice Greatest long before the Hermetica was written, so it would appear that Hermes Trismegistus represented the continuation of a long Egyptian tradition.

The philosophical works and teachings that have survived indicate that the Hermetica once formed a large body of literature. The largest existing collection is known as the *Corpus Hermeticum*, consisting of eighteen tracts originating from Alexandria and written in Greek. The *Corpus Hermeticum* is thought to date from the first three centuries AD. Until the seventeenth century, it was credited to Hermes Trismegistus, although today it is apparent that the *Corpus* was actually the work of a number of individuals.

After a general introduction in the first book, the second book of the *Corpus*, entitled *Poemander* (*Shepherd of Men*), concerns a revelation given to Hermes Trismegistus by a higher being called Poemander, while the other books relate the dialogues between Hermes and his pupils on certain aspects of Hermetic philosophy, hidden wisdom, and secrets of the universe.

Although the *Corpus* is written in Greek, it has been suggested that the authors identified more with their Egyptian ancestry than the Greek world—bearing in mind the claims made in the sixteenth book of the *Corpus* that the Egyptian language was superior to Greek: "This discourse, expressed in our paternal language, keeps clear the meaning of its words. The very quality of the speech and the sound of Egyptian words have in themselves the energy of the objects they speak of. . . ." In contrast, they claim that in translating the writings into Greek, "the greatest distortion" is produced. While it is not generally believed that the main source of these mystical texts is traceable to ancient Egypt, there existed a long Egyptian tradition of wisdom texts written in the style of a man teaching his son, or a sage his pupil.

In 1945, a large number of papyrus texts were discovered in the Egyptian city of Nag Hammadi. The finds included Coptic Hermetic texts, some of which were already known as part of the *Corpus Hermeticum*, but also a previously unknown Hermetic text called *The Ogdoad and the Ennead*, or *The Eight out of the Nine*, which describes the eight stages of Hermetic initiation into gnosis (spiritual knowledge). Also included within the Hermetica is a text on astrology and magic titled *Picatrix*, believed to have been composed in Harran, Turkey, during the eighth century AD; as well as the *Liber Hermetis*, a fifteenth-century work on alchemy and astrological writings that declares Hermes Trismegistus to be its author.

However, in addition to the *Corpus*, numerous fragments, quotes, and references have come down to us through authors such as Iamblichus and Porphyry, and early Christian theologians including Clement of Alexandria (circa AD 150–212), whose writings indicate knowledge of Hermetic works. John of Stobi's *Anthologium*, from around AD 500, also contains some forty passages and fragments of

Hermetic thought, highlighting the written information that has been lost to us.

Perhaps the most famous and concise work on Hermetic philosophy is the emerald tablet. In *The Western Way,* written in 1997, John Matthews and Caitlin Matthews state that the emerald tablet "is one of the most profound and important documents to have come down to us. It has been said more than once that it contains the sum of all knowledge—for those able to understand it."

Alleged to have been written by Hermes Trismegistus, the emerald tablet is where the "As above, so below" principle can be found. The earliest surviving copy of this work appears in the *Book of Balinas the Wise on Causes,* an Arabic book written around AD 650, which relates how, as a youth, Balinas discovered the tablet in a cave in Tyana, Turkey.

The origin of the tablet, if it actually existed, is uncertain, but legend has it that it was written by Seth, the son of Adam, to atone for his father's sins and thus enable man to gain the knowledge required to achieve redemption. Later accounts record that Alexander the Great found the tablet in Hermes' tomb near Egypt's Siwa Oasis, eventually taking it with him when he left the country, and hiding it in an undisclosed location. It was Balinas who then found the tablet many years later, and who then spent his life writing, explaining, and expounding upon its ideology.

The emerald tablet states, "that which is below corresponds to that which is above, and that which is above corresponds to that which is below, to accomplish the miracles of the One Thing." It also notes that the "structure of the microcosm is in accordance with the structure of the macrocosm"—indicating that the universe mirrors the earth, and vice versa; the structure of the smallest atom contains within it the structure of the universe, and vice versa; and the world of matter reflects the Divine so that Man mirrors God and God "creates man in His own image." What happens in one realm affects another, be it in the material world or the spiritual world. Hermetic thinking states, "Know ye not that ye are gods?"

At one point in *The Lost Symbol,* Peter Solomon recites the ancient saying to Robert Langdon, who has been reminded of it twice already that night. It has a tangible depiction in the painting on the ceiling of the Capitol building rotunda, *The Apotheosis of Washington*, which portrays America's first president becoming a god.

Mankind, despite existing in the lowest, material "world," still possesses an internal divine spark; therefore, it was man's duty to try to reunite with the Divine. Since mankind contained the divine spark, it was not necessary to plead with God, for man was not the evil, base creature born with original sin, as purported by Christianity and most other monotheistic religions, but he himself was a god.

Hermetic thought, as highlighted in the macrocosm-microcosm concept, also believed that everything was One. Authors Michael Baigent and Richard Leigh, in their book *The Elixir and the Stone*, describe this as "a single all-persuasive, all-encompassing totality, a single whole in which all dichotomies, all distinctions between body and soul, spirit and matter, were accommodated and harmoniously integrated. Everything, in its own way, was valid. Everything was incorporated in the comprehensive design. . . . For the hermeticist, gnosis entailed direct apprehension of, and integration with, the all-inclusive harmony."

This harmony brought with it the interconnection of everything, so that Man could now play an active role and effectively change his lot in life. No longer would he be the helpless pawn dependent upon the whims and wiles of the gods and fate; he could now be an active participant, manipulating the world around him to his own will in order to bring about significant change. Baigent and Leigh explain that according to the "As above, so below"/macrocosm-and-microcosm principle, "if everything were indeed interconnected, man himself . . . could make things happen to other spheres. If one pulled a particular string or thread in the tapestry of reality, something else, in some other quarter of the tapestry, would ensue."

The emerald tablet explains that "all things have their birth from this One Thing by adaptation," so that Man's actions on earth mirror God's actions in heaven, and so on. Such concepts were conveyed by means of symbols, notably the seal of Solomon: a hexagram with its two interlocking triangles representing "As above, so below," male and female, Man and God. It was thought that these symbols could in turn be used to effect a change, a concept that found favor in activities such as magic, alchemy, and astrology, and which began a new examination of the world of God and Man. In *The Egyptian Hermes,* Garth Fowden states that the "procedures of conventional alchemy are strictly preparatory to the purification and perfection of the soul."

The Hermetic idea of the macrocosm and microcosm thus became a powerful analogy, seen in alchemy as the transmutation of base metals to gold, which likewise created a parallel transformation of the alchemist's soul.

From Harran, in modern Turkey, Hermeticism played a large role in influencing Islamic science and mathematics, eliciting many Arab translations of old Hermetic texts as well as new Arabic ones. Indeed, one Arab writer notes that that twenty-two Hermetic works were available, with thirteen on alchemy alone.

The later Crusades to the Holy Land also brought many people into contact with these ideas for the first time. By the mid-thirteenth century, the Holy Roman Emperor Friedrich III of Germany added his seal of approval to the study and promulgation of Hermetic thought. One of the most famous thirteenth-century alchemists and Hermetic philosophers was the German philosopher and theologian Albertus Magnus, while in the fourteenth century, Nicholas Flamel was a famous proponent of alchemy and magic.

It was the Italian financier and ruler Cosimo de' Medici, however, who had the most crucial role in collecting and promoting the Hermetica, and hence had a direct effect on the enlightenment of Renaissance Europe. In the 1460s, he sent Fra Lionardo del Pistoja to Macedonia to find any philosophical works. Pistoja brought back the *Corpus Hermeticum,* which caused Cosimo such excitement that he immediately ordered his academic translator Marsilio Ficino to translate it into Latin. The newly translated *Corpus* ignited a new interest in Hermeticism and alchemy, which spread to the rest of Europe.

Around this time, some Hermetic occult orders were founded, notably the Rosicrucians, whose emblem was the rose (symbolizing the soul) and the cross (symbolizing the material world). Freemasonry also held Hermetic beliefs in high regard, as noted in the *Morals and Dogma of the Ancient and Accepted Scottish Rite of Freemasonry*, by Albert Pike: "He who desires to attain the understanding of the Grand Word and the possession of the Great Secret, ought carefully to read the Hermetic philosophers, and will undoubtedly attain initiation, as others have done; but he must take, for the key of their allegories, the single dogma of Hermes, contained in his Table of Emerald."

See also: *Alchemy, Freemasonry, Rosicrucians, Seal of Solomon/Star of David*.

House of the Temple

The House of the Temple is home to the headquarters of the Scottish Rite of Freemasonry in the Southern Jurisdiction of the United States. It is located in Washington, DC, at 1733 Sixteenth Street NW, between R and S streets, and is claimed by some to be exactly thirteen blocks north of the White House. It has been the headquarters of the Supreme Council of Scottish Rite Freemasonry since 1915.

This amazing edifice plays a central role within the pages of *The Lost Symbol*, as the setting for the showdown between Mal'akh and his father, Peter Solomon. The confrontation takes place within the central Temple Room of the ornate, stately building, beneath the large oculus in the ceiling. It is upon the central "altar" of this room that Mal'akh demands that his father sacrifice him using the Akedah knife.

Interestingly, the House of the Temple's architect, John Russell Pope, was not a Freemason; therefore, he had an assistant and Masonic advisor named Elliot Woods assigned to help him with incorporating Masonic symbolism into the design. The structure is modeled after the Mausoleum of King Mausolus at Halicarnassus, one of the ancient seven wonders. The building, praised as an architectural wonder, won Pope the 1917 gold medal of the Architectural League of New York. The architect, only thirty-six at the time, would go on to design some of the capital's most famous buildings, such as the Jefferson Memorial, the National Archives, and the National Gallery of Art.

According to David Ovason, the author of *The Secret Architecture of Our Nation's Capital*, the cornerstone of the House of the Temple was laid on the October 18, 1911, with hundreds of Masons in attendance. The ceremony was conducted by J. Claude Keiper, the Grand Master of the District of Columbia, using the same ceremonial gavel that George Washington had wielded at the Capitol building cornerstone ceremony.

Within the temple itself is an alcove that holds the interred remains of Albert Pike, Confederate general and author of what has become the main source book for Scottish Rite Freemasonry, *Morals and Dogmas of the Ancient and Accepted Scottish Rite Freemasonry*, written in 1871. The temple library holds one of the world's largest collections of Masonic-related books, with more than a quarter million titles. There is also a large banquet room, several offices for high-ranking Masonic officials, and exhibition space. Tours are offered on weekdays, and exhibitions of Masonic artifacts are often staged. Above the temple's main door is inscribed the phrase "Freemasonry Builds Its Temples in the Hearts of Men and Among Nations."

Outside the main doorway sit two huge sphinxes. One has its eyes open and signifies "Power"; the other, with its eyes closed, symbolizes "Wisdom." The building itself is known by Scottish Rite Masons as Heredom.

Around the outside of the main structure stand thirty-three columns, each thirty-three feet tall, which can be seen to represent the thirty-three degrees of Scottish Rite Freemasonry. The pyramid-shaped structure that sits atop the temple is some thirteen steps in height, seeming to duplicate the unfinished pyramid on the Great Seal of the United States and, two centuries later, on the dollar bill.

Within the House of the Temple, the fast-paced plot of *The Lost Symbol* is driven forward by a series of dramatic events that take place in the room where the ceremonies and rites of the Ancient and Accepted Scottish Rite are held. The center of the Temple Room features an enormous carved, polished Belgian black-marble altar that dominates the space in a magnificently grand way. Visitors to the House of the Temple notice that around the walls is a black marble frieze inscribed with bronze letters that says: "From the Outer Darkness of Ignorance Through the Shadows of Our Earth Life, Winds the Beautiful Path of Initiation unto the Divine Light of the Holy Altar."

The altar itself is inlaid with Hebrew characters that offer initiates, in particular, the following message: "God Said, 'Let There Be Light' and There Was Light."

Dan Brown notes occasionally throughout his novel that the only light to illuminate the altar at certain times is the "pale shaft of moonlight" that streams in by way of the large oculus at the top of this pyramidal building. An oculus, interestingly, can mean an eye as well as a large domed window. In *The Lost Symbol,* it is both.

Visitors to the House of the Temple are told that the oculus, which is one hundred feet above the altar, is symbolic of the fact that light, as a metaphor for enlightenment and the light of learning, is something that is prized by the Scottish Rite. British Masonic rituals make reference to a similar light-giving window. The dormer window, as it is called, shines on the mosaic pavement, symbolic of opposites: darkness and light. Initiates are told that it gave light to the sanctum sanctorum, or holy of holies, in Solomon's Temple.

The metaphor of the temple representing man provides a link to the Hermetic maxim once again: As above, so below.

In Mal'akh's quest for knowledge, he realizes that the fontanel is the oculus to the brain. He notes that although the portal closes, it is a lost connection between our inner and outer worlds. Langdon too believed that the lost word was right before his eyes when he looked up at to see an oculus to heaven, with the altar below it.

See also: *Heredom, Scottish Rite Freemasonry.*

Institute of Noetic Sciences

The Institute of Noetic Sciences (IONS), a nonprofit organization that encourages and conducts research into human consciousness and its potentials, began life in 1973. It was founded by U.S. astronaut Edgar Mitchell—one of the few to walk on the moon—and Paul N. Temple, an industrialist with a background in the petroleum business. IONS has over twenty thousand members and operates from a two-hundred-acre campus about thirty-five miles north of San Francisco. It produces a quarterly magazine, *Shift: At the Frontiers of Consciousness*, which details the research from the world of consciousness studies.

One of the leading characters in *The Lost Symbol*, Katherine Solomon, is described as a noetic scientist, and there is considerable mention of various research projects showcasing this branch of study.

The word *noetic* comes from an ancient Greek word *noesis*, which roughly translates as "inner knowing." There is no precise English word which corresponds exactly with the original Greek term, but *intuition* comes close. IONS has dedicated itself to exploring the nature of consciousness using rigorous scientific methods in an attempt to establish the connection between the microcosm and the macrocosm as well as the inner and the outer worlds.

Following his return from space aboard Apollo 14 in 1971, Edgar Mitchell related eloquently how walking on the moon and seeing the Earth from such a distance affected him profoundly. Before he went to the moon aboard Apollo 14, he was a man who believed in rational science. But then, on the flight home:

Suddenly from behind the rim of the moon, in long, slow-motion moments of immense majesty, there emerges a sparkling blue and white jewel, a light, delicate sky-blue sphere laced with slow swirling veils of white, rising gradually like a small pearl in a thick sea of black mystery. It takes more than a moment to fully realize this is Earth— home.

On the return trip home, gazing through 240,000 miles of space toward the stars and the planet from which I had come, I suddenly experienced the universe as intelligent, loving, harmonious. We went to the moon as technicians, we returned humanitarians.

When I went to the moon, I was as pragmatic a test pilot, engineer, and scientist as any of my colleagues. But when I saw the planet Earth floating in the vastness of space . . . the presence of divinity became almost palpable, and I knew that life in the universe was not just an accident based on random processes.

Just two years after returning home, Mitchell cofounded IONS. His work at the institute could not have been more different from his career with NASA. You could say that Mitchell used to explore outer space, but his work with IONS is all about exploring inner space—the world that exists only inside our heads, yet which, according to IONS, has the potential to impact the world all around us.

Much of the work done at IONS sounds like science fiction, but it is rooted in real science and study of the human mind. The institute evaluates phenomena that not so long ago would have been classified as magic or firmly in the realm of the occult. The tarot—and divination in general—remote viewing, psychic healing (or what is now known as distant healing), near-death experiences, and meditation are all studied at IONS.

In one scene of *The Lost Symbol*, Peter Solomon and his sister Kate discuss one of the fields of Noetic Science: entanglement theory. As scientists understand more and more about how minute particles operate at the quantum level, this understanding is beginning to have a bearing on consciousness studies. We are starting to learn that particles can seemingly "communicate" with each other even over vast distances. Albert Einstein himself called this phenomenon "spooky action at a distance." The brilliant physicist did not fully understand the process, believing it to be an error in our understanding of quantum mechanics—a flaw that could not possibly exist. We have since learned that it is probable that individual particles can communicate with each other using what is called quantum teleportation: a process whereby a unit of information can be transmitted from one particle to another, irrespective of location or distance. Some scientists predict that these minute particles use equally infinitesimal wormholes to teleport the information from one particle to another, so that the data do not have to travel faster than the speed of light. While this goes way beyond the scope of this book, it is evident that if particles could communicate in this manner, it would open up the possibility that our minds have the potential to communicate with other particles outside our bodies—even other minds.

IONS senior scientist Dr. Dean Radin has written a book about this very subject called *Entangled Minds,* in which he puts forward his belief that this new science of entanglement theory could go a long way toward explaining our psychic abilities. Dr. Radin is probably the institute's best-known face after Edgar Mitchell. He also authored the best-selling *The Conscious Universe,* which serves as a great introduction to the world of consciousness studies.

Along with his work for IONS, Dr. Radin is probably best known for his involvement with the Global Consciousness Project, based at Princeton University. The aim of this experiment is to run a series of random-event generators around the clock in various parts of the world to see if world events can "spike" the REGs—that is, provoke them into recording periods when random numbers suddenly stop being produced and more-ordered patterns are generated. The REGs are analogous to a simple coin flip, where the end result is either tails or heads. The REGs in the Global Consciousness Project produce two hundred flips per second, and instead of heads and tails they produce either a 1 or a 0. Normally there should be no discernible pattern to the strings of 1s and 0s that are recorded. However, Roger D. Nelson who pioneered the work done at the Global Consciousness Project. A scientist working at the Princeton Engineering Anomalies Research, Dr. Nelson first discovered that group consciousness can have an effect on REGs, altering completely random sequences of data and shaping them into recognizable patterns where the numbers stop becoming random.

Since the project's inception in 1998, many major world events have triggered dramatic changes in the patterns created by the REGs, but the most controversial result of the Global Consciousness Project is mentioned in *The Lost Symbol*.

On September 11, 2001, thirty-seven REGs were running at the Global Consciousness Project. On the day of the terrorist attacks on the United States, the REGs indeed seemed to spike, showing that they were affected by the mass outpouring of emotions emitted from the consciousness of humanity. However, while the data show that there was a reaction in the REGs as the whole world came together to watch the terrible events of that day unfold, there was a sting in the tail. The REGs had also recorded anomalies in the hours running *up to* the attacks. The largest spike occurred at five-thirty in the morning New York time—approximately three and a half hours before the first hijacked jet airliner was flown into the World Trade Center—and the anomaly lasted for a half hour.

Debate still rages over the results and the data, but if correct, then the inference is clear: mass global consciousness on our planet has the ability to foretell major events. If true, this has profound consequences for our understanding of the powers of the human mind. The study of the effects the human mind can have on physical outcomes is explored in Lynne McTaggart's book *The Intention Experiment*, which Dan Brown mentions by name in *The Lost Symbol*.

When Edgar Mitchell started IONS, he had two aims: The first was to study the phenomena of human consciousness and prove beyond doubt that the human mind was capable of far greater feats than science had attributed to it. The second was to "apply that knowledge to the enhancement of human well-being and the quality of life on the planet." IONS believes it has accomplished the first of these aims, establishing that human minds really are interconnected with the world around them. While there is still much work to be done in exploring these fields, the institute is now thinking long and hard about how it moves into its next phase, applying what it has learned for the betterment of mankind. For the last few years, IONS has been changing how it operates, gearing up for the challenges that lie ahead.

Noetic Science will always struggle to convince skeptics that these phenomena are really happening, and that the human mind really is as powerful as we are beginning to discover. But the more work that IONS and other agencies complete, the more we will come to understand about this fascinating field. However, it will be a long while before these sciences are accepted into the mainstream. Dr. Radin is only too aware of this and made the following observation in an interview with *Sub Rosa* magazine:

> *Keep in mind that the Wright brothers were actually flying their airplane in plain sight, in front of dozens of witnesses, while skeptics were still denying that flight was even possible. Old ideas die hard, even when pragmatic proof is obvious. Shortsightedness, stubbornness, inability to question fundamental assumptions, ignorance of the philosophy, sociology, and history of science, fear of disrupting the social order, fear of embarrassment, fear of losing one's prestige by tackling a taboo, and so on. Most of the recalcitrance in science is driven by one form of fear or another.*

While the human mind is capable of truly incredible feats, it is equally capable of blindly ignoring what is right in front of it. It will be a long road, but perhaps in a hundred years, humankind will look back at the Institute of Noetic Sciences and appreciate the trail that it has blazed.

See also: *Lynne McTaggart.*

Thomas Jefferson

Thomas Jefferson, one of the mavericks who helped to shape the United States of America, was born in Virginia on April 13, 1743. A remarkable man who became the third U.S. president, he began his education learning Greek and Latin with a local schoolmaster.

Beginning in 1760, he studied law at the College of William and Mary in Williamsburg, Virginia. It was a college where Deist beliefs were prevalent; many teachers and scholars there embraced the idea of a well-ordered world, created by God, but they deviated from traditional Christianity by rejected teachings such as miracles. Jefferson included the writings of Deist thinkers in his copybooks, and as a French speaker, he could access works by Enlightenment writers from France as well as those written in English.

While at college, Jefferson belonged to the Phi Beta Kappa fraternity, which is the oldest academic honor society in America. The fraternity had all the hallmarks of a secret society such as Freemasonry: an elaborate initiation, a special handshake, a secret oath, and a set of rules. Later, in 1779, as governor of Virginia and a member of the Board of Visitors at William and Mary College, he was instrumental in making amendments now referred to as Jefferson's reorganization. They included abolishing the divinity school and creating of new professorships in medicine and modern languages, among others. These changes were consistent with Jefferson's humanist beliefs.

Thomas Jefferson married Martha Skelton, a widow, in 1772, and this increased his wealth and land. It also added to his ownership of slaves—a problematic aspect of his life, from the perspective of today's more enlightened times. Over his lifetime, Jefferson owned around two hundred slaves, and he only freed five; all were relatives of Sally Hemings, an African-American slave with whom Jefferson was reputed to have had a relationship and possibly several children. Recent DNA analysis has proved this fact to many, although some still dispute the findings.

In 1774 his nascent views on American independence were aired when he wrote a tract titled *A Summary View of the Rights of British America*. The following year, Jefferson was appointed as a Virginia delegate to the Second Continental Congress, in Philadelphia. He drafted resolutions and in June 1776 was appointed to a committee—also including Benjamin Franklin—to produce a formal statement justifying a breach with Britain. The document now known as the Declaration of Independence, which included Jefferson's stirring "We hold these truths to be self-evident, that all men are created equal," was debated by Congress and adopted on July 4, 1776.

Returning to Virginia, he applied the principles of fairness under the law to the state legal code; that included the separation of the church and secular functions. When the British launched a surprise attack on Virginia toward the end of the Revolutionary War, Jefferson was forced into an undignified escape, something that political enemies held against him for the rest of his life.

Jefferson was appointed American minister to France and arrived there in 1784, a time when the country was steeped in Enlightenment learning and political turmoil. Among his friends in France was the Marquis de Lafayette, a well-known and confirmed Freemason. Lafayette had fought on the Americans' side at the Battle of Brandywine in 1777 and was well acquainted with George Washington. After returning to France, Lafayette was active as an aristocratic liberal during the turmoil leading up to the French Revolution.

As the French Revolution began the years of violence that were to culminate in the Terror, Jefferson returned to America in 1789 to become the first secretary of state under George Washington. His next high office was the position of vice president under John Adams, from 1797 to 1801. After a bruising and controversial election campaign in 1800, Thomas Jefferson became the third president of the United States and gave his inaugural address in March 1801 in the unfinished Capitol building. Jefferson had worked closely with Washington on the plans and construction of the new capital city.

In the early years of his presidency, Jefferson's policies of dismantling federal government and reducing the national debt were successful. He arranged to buy land from France in 1803 for $15 million in the Louisiana Purchase. Although he had reservations about whether the purchase was constitutional, Jefferson doubled the size of America, gaining 828,000 square miles. Napoléon I, the ruler of France, needed to sell the land to finance his European wars, but the resumption of hostilities in Europe damaged American trade, and the Embargo Act of 1807 banning foreign trade wrecked the economy, backfiring on Jefferson. He was beleaguered when he left office in 1809. Retiring to his estate at Monticello, Jefferson corresponded prodigiously and supervised the construction of the University of Virginia.

In *The Lost Symbol*, the Jefferson Bible is mentioned as a controversial revisionist text. Thomas Jefferson spent sixteen years preparing *The Life and Morals of Jesus of Nazareth*, known as the Jefferson Bible. He'd come to believe that the teachings of Jesus had been corrupted over the centuries by medieval popes and deceitful priests. In his version of the Bible, he omitted from the Gospels the miracles of Jesus and the parts he considered to be unreasonable. This left the parables and teachings of Jesus, but it ended with his crucifixion and burial. Although Jefferson allowed some friends to see his work, it was never published in his lifetime.

Outwardly Jefferson maintained the Anglican tradition, and, when in Philadelphia, he attended a Unitarian church. Writing to a Unitarian minister, Benjamin Waterhouse, he said:

> *I rejoice that in this blessed country of free enquiry and belief, which has surrendered its creed and conscience to neither kings nor priests, the genuine doctrine of only one God is reviving, and I trust there is not a young man now living who will not die a Unitarian.*

It was for Jefferson's religious tolerance that Uriah P. Levy, a Jewish naval officer, gave to the nation a statue of Thomas Jefferson—the first to be erected in the rotunda of the Capitol building. The statue, by French sculptor Pierre-Jean David d'Angers, was presented in 1834 and is mentioned in *The Lost Symbol*. Levy also purchased Jefferson's estate at Monticello the same year and spent heavily to restore the property and open it to visitors.

Thomas Jefferson had an abiding love of collecting books, and he acquired thousands of volumes on such diverse topics as science, the ancient world, and philosophy. During his time in France, he collected extensively and supplemented his library at Monticello. After the British burned the Library of Congress during the War of 1812, Jefferson sold Congress his collection—the largest private collection in the United States, consisting of 6,487 books. In a letter, he wrote: "I do not know that it contains any branch of science which Congress would wish to exclude from this collection . . . there is in fact no subject to which a member of Congress may not have occasion to refer."

When his old friend the Marquis de Lafayette visited America in 1824, he visited Monticello, reuniting the two men after thirty-five years. In his memoirs, Lafayette described Jefferson as "bearing marvelously well under his eighty-one years of age, in full possession of all the vigor of his mind and heart which he has consecrated to the building of a good and fine university." This referred to the University of Virginia, which Jefferson not only founded but established its curriculum. He even designed the school's buildings, including its distinctive rotunda.

Among his many other achievements—and something that Dan Brown's character Robert Langdon would no doubt have known—Jefferson invented the wheel cipher, leading historians to regard him as the father of American cryptography. The wheel cipher consisted of twenty-six wooden cylinders on a spindle, with all the letters of the alphabet carved into the edge of each wheel. According to David Khan, in his book *The Codebreakers: The Comprehensive History of Secret Communication from Ancient Times to the Internet*, "Jefferson's wheel cipher was far and away the most advanced device in its day. It seems to have come out of the blue rather than as a result of mature reflection upon cryptography."

As befitting the author of the Declaration of Independence, Thomas Jefferson died at his estate on July 4, 1826. In his famous last recorded words, he had asked on the previous day, "Is it the fourth?"

In recognition of his immense contributions to his country, Jefferson is one of the four U.S. presidents whose visages make up the famous sculpture at Mount Rushmore, the others being George Washington, Theodore Roosevelt, and Abraham Lincoln. This colossal carving, in South Dakota, has sixty-foot-high heads carved out of the granite mountain, and symbolizes elements of the first 150 years of the history of the United States. Jefferson takes his place among the great leaders of America for his role in enshrining the principles of democracy in the country and for expanding the young nation westward with the Louisiana Purchase.

The Jefferson Memorial was dedicated in Washington, DC, on April 13, 1943, two hundred years after Jefferson's birth. The design was based on the rotunda at the University of Virginia, Jefferson's own project, and the Pantheon in Rome. Three architects—John Russell Pope, Otto Eggers, and Daniel Higgins—took part in the design. The memorial sits across the Potomac Tidal Basin from the White House and the Washington Monument,. On the interior frieze of the dome is a quote from Jefferson: "I have sworn upon the altar of God eternal hostility against every kind of tyranny over the mind of man."

On the dust jacket of the U.S. edition of *The Lost Symbol*, there is a sequence of numbers running around a circular design. Each number corresponds to a chapter number in the book. If you write down the first letter of these chapters, the phrase spelled out is "popes pantheon," an effective description of the Jefferson Memorial. Another prominent Washington, DC, building designed by John Russell Pope is the House of the Temple, the Masonic Temple that serves as the headquarters of Scottish Rite Freemasonry and is the setting of a climactic showdown in *The Lost Symbol*.

There has been speculation that in common with many of the Founding Fathers, Jefferson may have been a Freemason. There seems to be no documentation that he was ever initiated into a lodge, although, of course, if this had happened in France during the revolution there, any records might have been lost. Although Thomas Jefferson may not have been a Freemason, it is undoubtedly true that many of his contemporaries belonged to various lodges and societies. It is beyond a doubt that Jefferson would have been exposed to these societies and that a man of his intellect and standing would have been intimately familiar with the rites, rituals, and symbolism of many or all of them. It is clear that Jefferson followed a path of Deism, and this fact alone demonstrates that he would have had sympathies for and an understanding of Freemasonic principles.

See also: *House of the Temple*.

Kryptos

Kryptos is a sculpture hiding an encrypted message that sits in the courtyard of the New Headquarters Building at CIA headquarters in Langley, Virginia. The sculpture is actually composed of a number of components: a large S-shaped metal scroll containing four blocks of text, granite slabs inscribed with copper Morse code messages, an engraved compass pointing to a lodestone, and a reflective pool, among other features in the landscaped area. A full description of the materials reads: polished red granite, quartz, copperplate, lodestone, miscanthus grasses, water, and petrified wood.

Kryptos means "hidden" in ancient Greek, and the sculpture does indeed contain a hidden message—several, in fact. However, the artist, Jim Sanborn, has indicated that there is one overall solution to the sculpture, probably arrived at by unraveling all the disparate elements.

Sanborn, born in Washington, DC, in 1945, was commissioned to create the artwork in 1988, for which he was paid $250,000. Since the piece was dedicated in 1990, code breakers, including many CIA employees, have attempted to decipher the message in the sculpture.

Sanborn had never created such a complex piece before, and, in fact, he knew hardly anything about cryptography. However, he worked closely with Ed Scheidt, a former head of the CIA's Cryptographic Center. Scheidt taught Sanborn how to devise such a complex code, after first schooling him in the arts of code making and code breaking, teaching him all the techniques from the nineteenth century through World War II. Nevertheless, it was Sanborn who came up with the final solution to the puzzle.

As of this writing, three of the four panels on the main copper scroll, known as K1, K2, and K3, respectively, have been solved and the text revealed. K1 reads as follows, the misspelling said to be intentional: "Between Subtle Shading and the Absence of Light Lies rhe Nuance of Iqlusion."

K2 conveys in a longer message, with X indicating a line break:

It Was Totally Invisible Hows That Possible? They Used the Earths Magnetic Field X The Information Was Gathered and Transmitted Undergruund to an Unknown Location X Does Langley Know About This? They Should Its Buried Out There Somewhere X Who Knows the Exact Location? Only Ww This Was His Last Message X Thirty Eight Degrees Fifty Seven Minutes Six Point Five Seconds North Seventy Seven Degrees Eight Minutes Forty Four Seconds West X Layer Two.

K3 turns out to be a section of text from Howard Carter's account of the moment when he and Lord Carnarvon first broke into the tomb of King Tutankhamen in Egypt's Valley of the Kings in 1923. The full text is:

Slowly Desparatly Slowly the Remains of Passage Debris That Encumbered the Lower Part of the Doorway Was Removed with Trembling Hands I Made a Tiny Breach in the Upper Left Hand Corner and Then Widening the Hole a Little I Inserted the Candle and Peered the Hot Air Escaping from the Chamber Caused the Flame to Flicker but Presently Details of the Room Within Emerged from the Mist X Can You See Anything Q (?)

The final section of the text, K4, a sequence of ninety-seven characters, still has not been solved. A group of determined code breakers has assembled on the internet to try to solve the K4 panel of *Kryptos* and now number 1,300. They've agreed to make a joint announcement should any of the members discover a solution. Needless to say, they are still hard at work.

Some of the Morse code messages on other sections of the sculpture read: "Sos, T Is Your Position, Shadow Forces and Virtually Invisible."

It is thought that the coordinates in the K2 section point to a location just southeast of the sculpture. If we read the message, it seems to suggest that something is buried in this location. To paraphrase the solution of K2: "The information was gathered and transmitted underground to an unknown location . . . Does Langley know about this . . . They should; it's buried out there somewhere . . . Who knows the exact location? Only ww . . ."

This, together with the coordinates, makes for a highly intriguing puzzle, possibly even as dramatic as a Dan Brown thriller. The truth is that the meaning within the sculpture, "hidden in plain sight," clearly does not just relate to the code secreted in the piece of art. When we combine these tantalizing clues from the decoded message, together with the extract detailing Howard Carter's uncovering of a long-lost tomb, it is likely that the sculpture is pointing to a hidden artifact. However, until the fourth section of the copper screen is decoded, we will have to wait to find out the exact answer.

We do know who "ww" is, though. He seems to be William Webster, director of the CIA from 1987 to 1991. At the beginning of *The Lost Symbol*, Dan Brown tells us in one of his facts that a cryptic document was locked in the director of the CIA's safe. We know for certain that Webster was given the answer to the sculpture's riddle. However, Sanborn claimed in a 2009 interview that even Webster doesn't have the full solution.

So, we wait, until someone manages to crack the mystery of *Kryptos* and solve the whole puzzle. It may be a long wait, though: in a 2009 interview with *Wired* magazine, cryptographer Ed Scheidt remarked, "There may be more to the puzzle than what you see. Just because you broke it doesn't mean you have the answer." This suggests that there may be more layers to the puzzle, even once we have all four sections of the text deciphered.

Dan Brown's previous novel featuring Robert Langdon, *The Da Vinci Code*, included actual snippets of the deciphered *Kryptos* code on its U.S. cover, leading commentators to suggest that the follow-up (what, in effect, became *The Lost Symbol*) would feature the *Kryptos* prominently. However, it plays only a minor role in the book. Whether this was due to artist Jim Sanborn's resistance to Dan Brown's using the sculpture in the book is not known. Between the publicity stirred up by both *The Da Vinci Code* clues and now *The Lost Symbol*, one thing is certain: there are now likely to be many more people wanting to get involved in solving the puzzle of *Kryptos*.

And in answer to the question posed in the section of *Kryptos* known as K3 . . .

Yes, it is wonderful.

See also: *CIA—Office of Security*.

Library of Congress

Having been rescued by Warren Bellamy from the clutches of the CIA, Robert Langdon and his rescuer arrive at the Library of Congress by way of a tunnel from the Capitol building. Once inside, they pass through the Great Hall and into the Main Reading Room, which Bellamy, Architect of the Capitol, had promised would be a "safe place." Despite his desperation at the turn of events, Langdon pauses to consider the room's splendor, reflecting that this was possibly the most amazing room in the world.

The conception of the Library of Congress dates to 1800 when an act of Congress made $5,000 available for the provision of "such books as may be necessary for the use of Congress." These were to be housed within the original Capitol building, in "a suitable apartment for containing them therein." However, following the American defeat at the Battle of Bladensburg on August 24, 1814, British troops entered Washington, burning and looting many public buildings, including the Capitol. In the process, three thousand volumes from the library's collection were destroyed. To compensate for the loss, former president Thomas Jefferson offered to sell his personal collection of more than six thousand books to Congress for whatever it wished to pay, which turned out to be $23,950, thus forming the basis of the new collection. Unfortunately, another fire on Christmas Eve 1851 destroyed thirty-five thousand titles, including two-thirds of the books that had been purchased from Jefferson. Although more funds were forthcoming from Congress to again expand the Library's collection, it was not until the library came under the auspices of Ainsworth Rand Spofford, Librarian of Congress from 1864 to 1897, that the collection expanded considerably, aided by the 1870 copyright law, which stated that two copies of every copyrighted book and print material had to be sent to the Library of Congress. The resulting influx soon necessitated moving the collection to a larger, purpose-built building, with work on its construction begun in 1892. Built in the Renaissance style, the Thomas Jefferson Building has been called "the largest, the costliest, and the safest" library building in the world.

The library is the research facility for Congress, its official mission statement being "to make its resources available and useful to the Congress and the American people and to sustain and preserve a universal collection of knowledge and creativity for future generations."

The Library of Congress has the largest collection in the world, with nearly 142 million items in all, including more than 32 million books and 62 million manuscripts housed in over 650 *miles* of bookshelves. Each day a staggering 10,000 items are added to the collection, due mainly to the copyright requirement. As the collection has expanded, so has the library itself, to two buildings on Capitol Hill: the John Adams Building, built in 1938, and the James Madison Memorial Building, which opened in 1981. In addition to the library, other resources include the Office of the Librarian, the Congressional Research Service, the U.S. Copyright Office, and the Law Library of Congress, which alone holds over 3 million volumes.

The building that Langdon found himself in is the magnificent Thomas Jefferson Building. Its rectangular exterior is inset with a T-shaped structure that forms the Great Hall and the Main Reading Room. The Great Hall's interior is opulently finished in Italian marble, with a marble floor inlaid with brass to form a sun surrounded by the twelve signs of the zodiac. The stucco ceiling is decorated with gold leaf, while the roof's paneled beams are decorated with aluminum leaf and set between stained glass windows.

Looking down on this are eight statues of Minerva, the Roman goddess of learning and wisdom, in her guises as Minerva of war and Minerva of peace. Minerva was the Roman equivalent of the Greek goddess Athena, whose many images are to be found throughout Washington, DC. A large mosaic depicting Minerva stands in the Great Hall. This mosaic was executed by artist Elihu Vedder, who had strong Masonic and Rosicrucian ties. The Great Hall is decorated with many examples of the trades and hobbies of Americans circa 1897, when the building was completed. The two grand staircases are decorated with small children, known as *putti*, in various guises, as well as a gardener complete with gardening tools, and a physician with a vessel, mortar, and the snake-entwined rod of Asclepius, still a symbol of medicine today. A mechanic, entomologist, farmer, and cook, to name but a few, are also in attendance.

The East Corridor pays particular homage to America's important role in scientific discoveries and advancements in the arts, humanities, law, and medicine. It is here also that Langdon passes the bulletproof display cabinets holding the Gutenberg Bible, the first printed book, and the handwritten Giant Bible of Mainz, both of which were produced in Germany in the 1450s. Just below the ceiling are six paintings by John White Alexander, *The Evolution of the Book*, highlighting the stages of human development up to the printed word.

Leading off from the Great Hall, the Main Reading Room provides access to the library's general collections of 70,000 volumes and is a free resource open to anyone over the age of sixteen. This most striking room is octagonal in shape, reaching up 160 feet to its domed roof. Around the octagon, each of eight marble columns supports a plaster female statue symbolizing art, commerce, history, law, philosophy, poetry, religion, and science.

The eight stained glass windows in the archways beneath the dome represent the forty-eight state seals of the United States; Hawaii and Alaska were not part of the nation when the building was constructed. Around the galleries above are sixteen bronze statues of men who exemplify the human endeavors represented in the eight female statues: art is embodied by Michelangelo and Ludwig van Beethoven;

commerce by Christopher Columbus and Robert Fulton; history by Herodotus and Edward Gibbon; law by Solon and James Kent; philosophy by Plato and Sir Francis Bacon; poetry by Homer and William Shakespeare; religion by Moses and Saint Paul; and science by Isaac Newton and Joseph Henry.

It is the statue of Moses, complete with horns, that prompts Langdon to explain to an impressed Warren Bellamy that this stems from Saint Jerome's mistranslation of a biblical passage from the book of Exodus. Apparently the saint mistook the phrase "his face was radiant"—meaning that Moses was glorified/enlightened by being in the presence of God—for "his face was horned." This occurred around AD 400. From then on, artists and sculptors faithfully depicted Moses with a pair of horns.

The architectural and decorative grandeur continues through the library's other rooms and galleries set on the building's two floors. They include the Members of Congress Room, Jefferson Congressional Reading Room, Asian Reading Room, European Reading Room, and American Folklife Center, among many others.

The Rare Book and Special Collections Reading Room contains some 650,000 books and other printed materials, including medieval manuscripts and the Jefferson Collection Exhibition. Since 1998, the library has been able to replace most of the Jefferson titles lost in the destruction of 1814, achieving this by scouring its records, Jefferson's personal papers and correspondence, and other historical sources in order to collate a list of Jefferson's original books so that the library could obtain the exact same editions as the ones Jefferson had collected.

See also: *Thomas Jefferson*.

Pierre L'Enfant

An architect named Pierre Charles L'Enfant was originally responsible for the geometrical layout of the city of Washington, which was later modified by George Washington and Thomas Jefferson, along with Andrew Ellicott. Early in *The Lost Symbol,* Dan Brown credits L'Enfant with adorning the capital city with Masonic symbolism.

Shortly afterward, Brown avers that poor Pierre's ghost has been seen manifesting itself in the Capitol building, trying to collect payment of his bill, now rather overdue, having awaited settlement for over two hundred years. On the same page Brown speaks of L'Enfant, along with George Washington and Benjamin Franklin, as master Freemasons. The books mentions elsewhere that many of the capital's monumental buildings were dedicated by Freemasons in accordance with their ceremonies.

So who was this man with the French name who is mentioned in such august company? Pierre Charles L'Enfant was born in Paris, France, in 1754. His father taught at the French Royal Academy of Painting and Sculpture, and young Pierre Charles studied there under him. In 1776 he enrolled as a volunteer in the American Continental army and traveled to America with the Marquis de Lafayette.

Lafayette, despite his own aristocratic French background, was committed to the cause of American independence, and was commissioned by Congress as a major general. The marquis was a well-attested Freemason, and at the Masonic Temple in Philadelphia there is a Masonic apron given by Lafayette to his friend George Washington, with whom he had served at Valley Forge. The apron is replete with symbolism, including the pillars of Boaz and Jachin and the All Seeing Eye.

L'Enfant was wounded at the siege of Savannah and subsequently served on General Washington's staff as an engineer. The fledgling Congress appointed him a major of engineers in 1783 as a tribute to his service.

He was responsible for designing a medal and diploma for a company of onetime officers from the Continental army who called themselves the Society of the Cincinnati after the legendary Roman patriot of early republican times. Returning to France, he assisted in forming a French branch of this society, the purpose of which was, and still is, to keep alive the ideals of the officers who took part in the Revolutionary War. L'Enfant suggested that the medal and diploma should prominently feature a bald eagle, on the grounds that it "is peculiar to this continent, and is distinguished from those of other climates by its white head and tail [so it] appears to me to deserve attention."

L'Enfant returned to America in 1784, making a living as an architect and doing work for Congress. An odd project he undertook around this time was Morris House in Philadelphia, which was in practice a flamboyant folly and was never completed. Financier Robert Morris had commissioned a substantial dwelling, but his architect, L'Enfant, was overly ambitious, and it quickly became obvious that the whole concept was far too extravagant.

In 1788 L'Enfant was employed to transform the city hall in New York into a building fit to house the infant federal government. Being anxious to symbolize the newly independent thirteen states, he used an eagle holding thirteen arrows as well as thirteen stars and rays. When Congress soon decided to construct a new capital city for the federal government, President Washington engaged L'Enfant to draw up plans for official approval.

Pierre L'Enfant knew, of course, that the ideal city of the classical world had been based on a grid system, and decided that these young United States, with political principles drawn from the past, should have such a city. Accordingly, his streets were planned as gridirons, forming irregular rectangular blocks. The centers of attraction were to be the president's dwelling and the Capitol building, and the squares in their vicinity would afford spaces in which to place monuments and water features. Thomas Jefferson, then secretary of state, obtained maps of chosen European cities to provide inspiration to Pierre Charles. The works of outstanding designers such as Christopher Wren in England and André Lenôtre in France were drawn upon.

Unfortunately, L'Enfant allowed the importance of his brief to develop into an overweening sense of his own importance. He would not accept as mandatory his instructions from the city commissioners, even when he was ordered to do so by the president. His schemes were recognized as impossibly grandiose, and he was deeply resented for his ruthless action of having the house of an influential citizen demolished because he wanted to put an avenue in its place. It must have been difficult for George Washington, then living in Philadelphia, to keep a restraining hand on his friend L'Enfant, who was displaying his volatile temperament in the future Washington, DC; the president, it must be recalled, had been a brother in arms with him. In the end, Pierre L'Enfant threatened to resign, and Washington had little alternative but to dismiss him. Andrew Ellicott was called in to take over the project, and it is largely his work that can be seen today.

In 1812 the United States Military Academy offered L'Enfant the chair of professor of engineering, but for some reason he turned the job down. Two years later, he did a little work on the building of Fort Washington, situated on the Potomac, but within a short time he was replaced.

After a while, L'Enfant claimed over $95,000 for work produced until his dismissal from the Washington job. Congress paid him just less than $4,000, telling him it was all his efforts had been worth. He lived on in Maryland with friends, allegedly without a penny to his name. Presumably it must be his missing $91,000 that his ghost, as recalled by Dan Brown, still awaits inside the Capitol building. In 1909 his remains were reinterred at Arlington National Cemetery in a monument granted rather belatedly to him by Congress. Perhaps he should now be at peace.

The assertion that the layout of Washington, DC, was inspired by Freemasonic principles relies, in large part, on Pierre L'Enfant's having been a Freemason. There seems to be no documentation that he was, and no lodge claims him as a former member. On the other hand, two of his mentors, the Marquis de Lafayette and George Washington, *were* Freemasons, and growing up in 1760s and 1770s France, he would certainly have been very familiar with Freemasonic principles.

Pierre L'Enfant's plans for the layout of Washington, DC, are displayed on a grand scale on the pavement of Freedom Plaza, as described elsewhere in this book. Even as late as 1990, at the completion of the Washington National Cathedral, his original vision of the city was being realized, since it was he who had first proposed a "great church for national purposes."

See also: *Freedom Plaza, Washington, DC*.

Magic Squares

4	9	2
3	5	7
8	1	6

For a symbologist like the character Robert Langdon, solving puzzles and cracking codes are second nature; interestingly, Dan Brown's father was a mathematician. Brown has described how he was often given codes to solve as a child. In much the same way that we relax now with crosswords or number puzzles, it appears that for centuries, people have taken pleasure in manipulating numbers for fun. The creation of so-called magic squares has been associated with many civilizations, and their ingenuity is appealing on many levels. It is said that mathematics is the universal language; as such, the ability to understand, or "read," a magic square is universal.

In a magic square, the rows, columns, and diagonal lines of numbers all add up to the same figure. The complexity can be extended by including a wraparound level or imagining the grid as a cube. The numbers used to create the square are usually sequential; for example in a three-by-three grid, they will be the numbers 1 to 9.

The Lo Shu square, thought to date from around 650 BC in China, is a three-by-three (or "order 3") grid where all the axes add up to the number 15. The legend associated with the Lo Shu square is that a series of grids containing dots were seen on the back of a tortoise that was observed by the river Lo. The Kubera Kolam is a variation on the

Lo Shu square, in that 19 has been added to each number, so the digits are 20 to 29, and the magic total is 72. The Kubera Kolam, mentioned by Dan Brown in the novel, and common in India, is a magic square pattern; it's generally created out of rice flour that is laid out freshly each day on the floor of a house, and thought to bring prosperity to the home.

Magic squares are also found in Arab works from the tenth century AD, such as an encyclopedia published in Baghdad that has the first examples of grids of the orders 5 and 6. The *Rasa'il Ikhwan as-Safa*, as this encyclopedia is called, was linked to a group known as the Brethren of Purity. The Masonic researcher Chris McClintock, in his *Sun of God* thesis, has recently suggested that the Brethren was a conduit between ancient teachings and modern-day Freemasonry.

The first magic square that Langdon encounters in *The Lost Symbol* is the four-by-four grid depicted by the German painter and engraver Albrecht Dürer in his engraving *Melencolia I*. In this square, there is the additional element that the date of the picture's creation, 1514, is depicted in two adjacent squares on the bottom row.

Heinrich Cornelius Agrippa, a writer of Renaissance esoteric material, produced his *De occulta philosophia*, which was written between 1509 and 1510. In the three books that make up the work, he includes a series of magic squares. Agrippa claimed that the best way for man to know God and nature was through the study of magic. Despite modern opinions that the study of the occult or magic would be nonreligious, in the third book of *De occulta philosophia*, Agrippa reveals the name of Jesus to contain the power of the Tetragrammaton, the sacred name of God.

Agrippa constructed a series of magic squares, each one relating to one of the planets and known as kameas. Another layer of mystery is added when a name or word is translated from letters to numbers and its shape is then traced around the position of the numbers in the kamea. The resulting pattern when produced for magical purposes is one example of a sigil, and we are told in *The Lost Symbol* that the character Mal'akh has a number of sigils tattooed on his body.

Benjamin Franklin produced an eight-by-eight grid. It forms a central puzzle in *The Lost Symbol*, enabling Langdon to solve the arrangement of 64 symbols that forms the map pointing to the location of the "lost" symbol. In Franklin's grid, the rows and columns add up to 260, but, unlike many other magic squares, the diagonal rows do not.

Langdon, after first mistaking the clue "Eight Franklin Square" for an address, finally realizes that it refers to Franklin's mathematical square. This confusion points to the building of a Masonic group commonly called the Shriners: the Almas Shrine Temple located on K Street NW and directly facing Franklin Square in Washington, DC.

Franklin once wrote that he had been "induc'd to amuse myself with making magic squares, or circles" when bored. Given his many other accomplishments, we may wonder where this spare time came from, but Franklin is also famous for producing a sixteen-by-sixteen magic square, a phenomenal undertaking.

Franklin also wrote in a letter, "Being one day in the country at the house of our common friend the late learned Mr. Logan, he showed me a folio French book, filled with magic squares, wrote, if I forget not, by one M. Frenicle . . . he did not recollect that any one Englishman had distinguished themselves in the same way."

Does this account for the fact that the UK cover of *The Lost Symbol* does not contain the magic square puzzle present on the back of the U.S. edition?

In a replica of the Dürer square that Brown has trained his readers to solve within the novel is the message "Your Mind is the Key." Considering the discussion toward the end of the novel between Langdon and Katherine Solomon on the power of human thought and the mind of man receiving enlightenment, this would seem to be a message close to Dan Brown's heart.

See also: *Albrecht Dürer, Benjamin Franklin, Melencolia I, Shriners.*

SIMON COX

Lynne McTaggart

Lynne McTaggart is mentioned in *The Lost Symbol* because her book *The Intention Experiment* is cited as a work that inspired Katherine Solomon to continue her research within the field of Noetic Science.

McTaggart, born in 1951, is a journalist and author. She has written five books to date, two of which have been best sellers, *The Field* and *The Intention Experiment*.

McTaggart also runs the much lauded *What Doctors Don't Tell You* health newsletter, which was launched in 1989. The premise was to create a truly independent journal, free from the influence of major pharmaceutical companies and government bodies.

However, McTaggart is best known for her body of work known as *The Intention Experiment*. It is not just a book but also an active internet community of volunteers that McTaggart has put together with her husband, Bryan Hubbard, and a team of scientists. They work with groups of volunteers who conduct web-based experiments and pool the collective power of their minds to achieve specific aims.

We discover in *The Lost Symbol* that Katherine Solomon's research has already proven that focused thought can affect any living organism, including the growth rate of plants. This chapter seems to have been based precisely on the work of McTaggart and her team, and mirrors an experiment of theirs known as the "water germination experiments." In 2008 McTaggart asked an audience at one of her lectures in Hamburg, Germany, to choose a bottle of water from four samples, for the purpose of watering a selection of seeds. But before doing so, the volunteers were asked to send out the following thought, or intention, to the water: "My intention is that all the seeds given water from our target bottle will sprout at least three inches by the fourth day of growing."

Five days later, the researchers tabulated their results. The seeds that had been watered with the "special" water grew higher than seeds that received ordinary tap water. Furthermore, in the test sample, 100 percent of the seeds germinated, compared to 90 percent, as could normally be expected. The experiment was deemed a success.

Since then, more experiments have been conducted with much larger groups of people sending out their intentions. The largest to date was the "peace intention experiment," in which a sizable "group mind" of participants connected via the internet and tried to focus their peaceful intentions on war-torn regions of the world.

The description of McTaggart's work in *The Lost Symbol* seems to be accurate, and she herself has welcomed her surprise inclusion in the book, saying on her website, "using the world's best-selling book as a platform to introduce the idea of the power of thought to an entirely new audience will help to promote the work of consciousness research."

She also added a few illuminating passages that highlight some of the remarkable aspects of her ongoing work, including:

> *Intention improves through practice of learned techniques. When writing* The Intention Experiment, *I interviewed dozens of "masters of intentions"—Qigong masters, Buddhist monks, master healers—and all of them discussed particular techniques they learned and practiced to carry out intention. . . . To manifest an intention requires laserlike focus, a full sensory visualization, and a profound belief. . . . Particles are affected by the observer. This is a fundamental principle of quantum physics: observing a subatomic particle turns that potential something into something real.*

This is probably the most fascinating aspect of McTaggart's work: that it is our interaction with the material realm, our consciousness itself, which affects the physical world around us. One of the challenges presented by quantum physics is the behavior of matter at the quantum level. If minute particles of matter can be in all places at once, what is it that forces them to appear in one location and act as solid matter? McTaggart's science provides a tentative answer: it is our living consciousness, our role as observer, that influences those tiny pieces of matter, somehow coalescing them into being. This poses way more questions than it answers. For example, perhaps this proves the idea that we all create our own universe. If each of us influences the behavior of quantum particles and literally brings them into being, then can we be sure that we share the same universe with other observers? Perhaps we really do all create our own private universes that are unique to us. As Katherine hints in *The Lost Symbol*, maybe we really are all masters of our own universe.

Melencolia I

Midway through *The Lost Symbol*, Robert Langdon and Katherine Solomon are trying to decipher the meaning of some numbers and letters that had been carved into a stone box bearing a capstone. "Fifteen-fourteen AD," she points out, assuming it stands for the year 1514. This is in fact a symbature: a symbol used in place of a signature. Robert Langdon realizes immediately that the A and D following the number don't stand for *anno Domini*, used to indicate the Christian era; they're someone's initials. From the stylized presentation—the small D huddling inside the larger A, as if it were seeking shelter—he recognizes it as the mark of the artist Albrecht Dürer. Further intuition leads him and Katherine Solomon to Dürer's famous 1514 engraving, *Melencolia I*.

Despite the fact that the engraving hangs in Washington, DC's National Gallery of Art, Langdon views its image on a computer screen. The design's essential element for their code-breaking purposes is revealed to be a magic square containing sixteen numbers. To admire the work in all its complexity, turn to the plate section in this book.

Entire books and theses have been devoted to trying to explain the elements within the engraving and the concepts that Dürer was trying to express. One of his most enigmatic and studied works, *Melencolia I* was unusual in having the title on the plate. The archaic spelling of *Melencolia* is on a banner being held by a creature that resembles a rodent-bat-snake hybrid.

Dürer has included elements of the science of alchemy, and this engraving is full of symbolic references to that practice. The rainbow in the background represents the colors that allegedly appeared during, for instance, preparation of the philosopher's stone, the instrument needed to transmute base metals such as lead into gold. It was also reputed to have the power to change mortals into an immortal state. Other alchemy-related items and other paraphernalia can be seen in the picture, including a crucible, a sphere, woodworking tools, scales, and compasses. Dürer's *Melencolia I* is in many ways a compendium of symbolism, and the faint image of a skull on the face of the polyhedron further compounds the mystery.

From the Roman numeral I in the title, it seems likely that it was intended to be the first in a series. Perhaps a series of four, since melancholy is one of the four temperaments possessed by different types of people, the other three being choleric, phlegmatic, and sanguine. The temperaments link to the four humors (black bile, phlegm, yellow bile, and blood), to the four elements (earth, air, fire, and water), and to the planets. Physicians, scientists, philosophers, and all those at that time interested in the human condition would have been familiar with, and influenced by, this accepted knowledge. The word *melancholia* actually means "black bile," and it was believed that an imbalance of this in the body would bring about a melancholic disposition. Melancholy was linked to the earth and to the planet Saturn.

Another suggestion has been made that Dürer planned a series of three *Melencolia* engravings, each depicting one of the three elements of the soul described by Aristotle: the imagination, the rational, and the mental.

Frances Yates, analyzing *Melencolia I* in her book *The Occult Philosophy of the Elizabethan Age*, observes:

> Dürer's Melancholy *has a livid hue, the swarthy complexion, the "black face" of the type, and she supports her pensive head on her*

hand in the characteristic pose. She holds compasses for measuring and numbering. Beside her is the purse, for counting money. Around her are tools, such as an artisan might use. Obviously she is melancholic, characterised by the physical type, pose, and occupations of the old, bad melancholy, but she seems also to express some more lofty and intellectual type of endeavour. She is not actually doing anything, just sitting and thinking. What do those geometrical forms mean, and why does a ladder rise heavenward behind the polyhedron?

So is the image a metaphor for wasted genius?

It seems that in every age, great talent and ability are sometimes linked to mental instability or torment. From the fragile genius of Mozart, to the extravagant lifestyle of the poet Lord Byron, to the self-destructive behavior of many rock stars, the idea of the tormented genius is one familiar to us all. This seems to be the suggestion of Raymond Klibansky, Erwin Panofsky, and Fritz Saxl in their book *Saturn and Melancholy*:

> *The humour melancholicus, when it takes fire and glows, generates the frenzy (furore) which leads us to wisdom and revelation, especially when it is combined with a heavenly influence, above all with that of Saturn. . . . Therefore Aristotle says in the* Problemata *that through melancholy some men have become divine beings, foretelling the future like Sybils . . . while others have become poets . . . and he says further that all men who have been distinguished in any branch of knowledge have generally been melancholics.*

Dürer could be showing us the inside of his mind. Mary Margaret Heaton certainly speculated as much in her 1870 book, *The History of the Life of Albrecht Dürer of Nürnberg*: "Perhaps his own soul's wings had beaten in vain against the impassable wall that bounds our mental horizon, before he drew those wings that spring from her powerful shoulders, and seem a mere mockery in the cramped position in which she is placed."

What are we to make of Dan Brown's choice of the artist Dürer and this engraving in *The Lost Symbol*? The character of Robert Langdon is certainly very learned and intelligent, and shows great resourcefulness in tackling the predicaments that Dan Brown conjures up for him. Despite these qualities, Langdon remains a man who finds it difficult to believe. As he admits to Katherine, "faith has never come easily to me." This is the man who found the Holy Grail and saved Rome from certain destruction.

Here is a depiction of someone waiting for the spark of inspiration to lighten the gloom, an echo of the tortured genius that resides in a melancholic inner world but who possesses incredible creativity and that ignition of brilliance when needed. Is it possible that Brown himself identifies not only with his own creation, Robert Langdon, but also with these melancholic, tortured geniuses from history whom he features in his novels?

See also: *Alchemy, Albrecht Dürer, Philosopher's Stone*.

Sir Isaac Newton

Isaac Newton was born in Lincolnshire, England, on January 4, 1643, and received a knighthood from Queen Anne in 1705, becoming Sir Isaac. He was an outstanding example of a polymath: a man possessing a deep understanding and skill across many fields of learning, any one of which would have been sufficient to satisfy an ordinary person. Newton, as we will see, was in no way ordinary. He studied physics, mathematics, astronomy, theology, philosophy, and the arcane subject of alchemy.

Readers of Dan Brown's *The Da Vinci Code* will already be well acquainted with Newton, whose tomb in Westminster Abbey provided a clue to the quest for the Holy Grail. Now, in *The Lost Symbol*, we again have several references to Sir Isaac, in connection with a scale of temperature measurement and his studies as an alchemist.

In 1661 Newton was admitted to Trinity College, Cambridge, on a work-study basis. He much preferred to absorb the ideas of the more modern philosophers and astronomers than devote himself to Aristotelian teachings, as was then the norm. He graduated in 1665, the year of the Great Plague of London, and returned as a fellow of the college two years later.

There is a popular story about Newton's discovery of gravity: while sitting under a tree, he was bonked on the head by a falling apple. According to Newton, he'd merely observed an apple fall to the ground, but however it actually happened, he proceeded to ponder the fact that objects fall toward the earth. Over the course of many years, he formulated his law of universal gravitation. In the twentieth century, this was superseded by Einstein's theory of general relativity, but Newton's law is still accepted as an approximation. This is true except in the case of massive objects or where ultimate accuracy is required. Newton's law appears in his *Philosophiae naturalis principia mathematica*, published in 1687. This book triggered a tremendous argument with Robert Hooke, another brilliant scientist, who claimed that his own research had been hijacked. Newton gave credit to earlier scientists such as Copernicus, Brahe, Galileo, and Kepler, saying, "If I have seen further, it is by standing on the shoulders of giants."

Following Aristotle, it had always been taught that light was white. Newton was the first to dare to contradict this received wisdom; he boldly pointed out that sunlight shining through a prism breaks up into a whole spectrum of colors. Since he wrongly assumed from this discovery that telescopes with refracting lenses would cause problems, he proceeded to invent the reflecting telescope.

Toward the end of the seventeenth century, Newton turned his thoughts toward measuring temperature and devised a thermometer using the Newton scale, which had thirty-three degrees as its boiling point. He began by theorizing about degrees of heat from cold winter air or glowing coals, which was clearly not going very far in determining a scale. So then he decided to heat linseed oil and compare its volume between that at the temperature of melting snow and that at water's boiling point.

The Swedish scientist Anders Celsius had probably heard about

Newton's invention and produced his own temperature scale, almost exactly three times larger. Both have 0 degrees for freezing, and Newton's 33-degree boiling point corresponds to 100 degrees Celsius. Celsius's scale is still used today (sometimes called centigrade), since it is more practical, while Newton's scale will be unfamiliar to most readers of The Lost Symbol. The immersion of a pyramid into boiling water to reveal a luminescent message moves the plot along and provides another link with the symbolism associated with the number 33.

Newton had a great interest in religion but was an unorthodox Christian. His biological father had died before he was born, and his mother had subsequently married a clergyman with whom he clashed. He admitted to threatening to burn their house down at some time during his youth, and it is possible that his Christian faith was colored by his attitude toward his stepfather. It is said that Newton accepted the Arian heresy, which included a belief that Jesus was not of the same substance as God the Father, and that there had been a time when Jesus did not exist. He studied closely the texts in the Bible—scouring them for scientific information in particular—and wrote religious tracts, believing that he'd been chosen by God to shine light on the meaning of the Scriptures. He wrote, "I have a fundamental belief in the Bible as the word of God, written by those who were inspired."

Some of Newton's unpublished documents prophesy that the end of the world will come in 2060, while others predict the creation of a new world that will be blessed with divine peace. Six years after Newton's death, his important work on the Bible was published. This was Observations upon the Prophesies of Daniel, and the Apocalypse of St. John.

In The Lost Symbol, the motto Jeova sanctus unus ("one true God") is revealed, and Robert Langdon explains that this provided a pseudonym for Newton. In Latin, which has no letter i, so a j is substituted, Jeova sanctus unus can be anagrammed Isaacus Neutonuus. Newton used this when writing to friends about alchemical topics and exchanging documents, so that he did not risk his identity being known.

Dan Brown also alludes to a legend regarding Isaac Newton's

dog Diamond, who reputedly tipped over a candle and started a fire that destroyed important documents. In the novel, Peter Solomon's 150-pound mastiff, Hercules, has eaten Langdon's precious seventeenth-century illuminated-vellum copy of the Bible.

While no direct evidence exists that Sir Isaac Newton was a Freemason, there are suggestions that he may well have been a member of the craft. According to some researchers, he was the master of the mysterious Priory of Sion between 1691 and 1727. He was a member of a learned society called the Gentlemen's Society of Spalding, which over the centuries counted among its member the poets Lord Tennyson and Alexander Pope, the physician-scientist Sir Hans Sloane, and the naturalist Sir Joseph Banks. Also, Newton was clearly interested in subjects such as the importance of Noah, which Masons find significant.

It is known that Newton was interested in alchemy, which could have been highly dangerous during his lifetime. Penalties could be severe for someone dabbling in the black art—including public execution. His papers suggest that he might have sought two Holy Grails: the philosopher's stone (a necessary tool) and the Elixir of Life (a supposed universal solvent). James Frazier, in a paper entitled "Contested Iconography: Was Isaac Newton an Astrologer, a Rational Mechanistic Scientist, or Neither?" explains the delay in publishing Newton's alchemical work:

> In an effort designed to protect Newton's image and standing, the deliberate suppression of his alchemical endeavors began almost immediately following his death. . . . The alchemical and theological manuscripts were bundled together and marked by Dr. Pellet as being unsuitable for publication. This included texts and manuscripts on alchemy and theology totaling in excess of two million four hundred thousand words.

Separately, from the German Gottfried Leibniz, another polymath, Sir Isaac discovered differential calculus. A quarrelsome fellow, Newton claimed that the German had not actually done any such thing but had stolen his ideas. This dispute and the ongoing arguments with Robert Hooke and others show a not particularly attractive side to his character. He was also a poor teacher, apparently, since his students avoided his lectures. One commentator was heard to remark, "So few went to hear him, and fewer that understood him, that oft times he did in a manner, for want of hearers, read to the walls." Clearly, students could not keep up with the capacity of his mind, and he would have preferred to be away from them, doing his own research.

Among Newton's other activities, he held the posts of warden and master of the Royal Mint, from 1696 until the end of his life. With his typical vigor, he embarked upon a campaign against forgery, which was rife at the time despite being a capital offense. He belonged to the Royal Society and served as its president from 1703 until his death, and was a member of the British parliament from 1689 to 1690, and again in 1701. On March 20, 1727, Sir Isaac Newton died and was buried in London's Westminster Abbey. This was a singular honor, since he was the first scientist to be interred there.

Newton had a great interest in the learning of ancient peoples, particularly the Egyptians. In his *Chronology of Ancient Kingdoms, Amended,* he reported that the study of astrology had begun in Egypt under the guidance of the priests. The measurements of the Egyptians, especially the cubit, were subject to his analysis.

The economist John Maynard Keynes, who purchased a large part of Newton's manuscript collection, said in a speech to the Royal Society in 1942, "Newton was not the first of the age of reason. He was the last of the magicians."

See also: *Alchemy, Philosopher's Stone.*

SIMON COX

Number Symbolism

Numbers feature prominently in *The Lost Symbol*, whether in the form of magic squares, the encoded location of rooms beneath the Capitol building, or historical dates that act as keys to secret codes.

However, the number that plays the most significant role in Dan Brown's novel is 33. The most obvious case is all the references to thirty-third degree Masons. This is the highest degree within Scottish Rite Freemasonry. Its emblem contains a double-headed eagle, sometimes referred to as a phoenix; the maxim *Ordo ab chao* ("Order from chaos"), which turns up often in *The Lost Symbol*; and the number 33 within a pyramid. This is the emblem that is on Peter Solomon's ring.

Within Freemasonry, the number 33 is very special indeed, and its significance within the Brotherhood has long been debated. Manly P. Hall shed some light on the meaning of the thirty-three degrees, or stages, of Freemasonry in his book *The Secret Teachings of All Ages*. His conflation of the central Freemasonic figure of Hiram Abiff with the concepts of Hindu mysticism is simply staggering:

> *Sufficient similarity exists between the Masonic Hiram and the Kundalini of Hindu mysticism to warrant the assumption that Hiram may be considered a symbol also of the Spirit Fire moving through the sixth ventricle of the spinal column. The exact science of human regeneration is the Lost Key of Masonry, for when the Spirit Fire is lifted up through the thirty-three degrees, or segments of the spinal column, and enters into the domed chamber of the human skull, it finally passes into the pituitary body (Isis), where it invokes Ra (the pineal gland) and demands the Sacred Name. Operative Masonry, in the fullest meaning of that term, signifies the process by which the Eye of Horus is opened.*

The human spine does indeed contain thirty-three segments, and Dan Brown seems to have been at least aware of this potential connection between the thirty-three degrees of Masonry and the spinal column, because Mal'akh has a tattoo of a staircase on his back, with each stair resting on a vertebra as it ascends to the base of his skull. Katherine Solomon also tells Langdon at the end of *The Lost Symbol* that the spine is "Jacob's ladder" and the skull is the true *temple*.

Another interesting point about the thirty-three degrees of Scottish Rite Freemasonry is that there are actually only thirty-*two* degrees to work through; the thirty-third is an honorary degree. Fascinatingly, there are thirty-two paths of wisdom in the Tree of Life of the Kabbalah, the mystical branch of Judaism. This also equates with the thirty-two times that God is mentioned in chapter 1 of the book of Genesis in the Torah. So, when someone successfully contemplates all thirty-two paths, he or she attains enlightenment, which could be thought of as the final, thirty-third path.

In *The Lost Symbol*, Robert Langdon tells us that the origins of the worship of the number 33 began long ago in ancient Greece. Pythagoras, the great mathematician, described the number 33 as the most important of what he called the master numbers: 11, 22, 33, and 44. We will examine Pythagoras and his obsession with the symbolism of numbers in a moment. Meanwhile, Jesus was said to have been crucified at the age of thirty-three, beginning his ministry at the age of thirty and dying three years later, in AD 33 (if we believe that our calendar started precisely with the birth of Jesus).

Furthermore, and more important to Freemasonry, Solomon's Temple in Jerusalem, the First Temple of the Jews, stood for thirty-three years. King David was said to have ruled for thirty-three years in Jerusalem. Sir Francis Bacon, the author of *The New Atlantis*, used a secret cipher number that just happened to be 33, which was the numerical value of his name based upon sacred numerology. That number, 33, occurs again and again in religious, occult, and esoteric teachings throughout history.

The House of the Temple in Washington, the location of the climatic scene between Mal'akh and his father, Peter Solomon, is the home of the Supreme Council, or, as it says on a plaque at its entrance: "The Temple of the Supreme Council of the Thirty-third and last degree of the Ancient and Accepted Scottish Rite of Freemasonry for the Southern Jurisdiction of the United States, Erected to God and Dedicated to the Service of humanity, Salve Frater!" (translates as "welcome, brother").

The building has 33 outer columns, each of which is 33 feet tall; and inside, in the Executive Chamber, there are 33 ceremonial chairs, one for each of the because the Supreme Council has 33 members.

The Capitol building in Washington also has its connections to number 33. William Henry and Dr. Mark Gray describe this in their book *Freedom's Gate: The Lost Symbols in the U.S. Capitol:* "The Capitol Rotunda is a large, circular room located in the center of the Capitol Dome on the second floor. Ninety-six feet in diameter, it is the symbolic and physical heart of the U.S. Capitol. It is the ceremonial center of the United States of America. After Barack Obama was sworn in on January 20, 2009, on the West Porch of the Capitol, he ascended 33 steps into the Rotunda."

When we look at an early sketch of *The Apotheosis of Washington*, the fresco painted by Constantino Brumidi, high above the rotunda floor, we see that initially he placed thirty-three maidens around George Washington. In the second draft he replaced the thirty-three maidens with the thirteen that we see in the final painting, except that in this sketch, he painted thirty-three stars over the maidens' heads.

Taking the symbolism a stage further, *The Lost Symbol* was published on September 15, 2009, or 09.15.09. If we add those numbers, we arrive at 33.

Dan Brown is not the first to become obsessed with numbers and their meaning, Numerology is an ancient discipline with a history that goes back through the ages and is closely linked to divination. Pythagoras himself said, "the world is built upon the power of numbers," and much of what we know of numerology comes from the teachings of the great ancient Greek mathematician. Pythagoras assigned meaning to certain numbers and then applied this "code" to the names of people and the gods in an attempt to divine something about their true nature. In trying to explain this complex combination of science and magic, he said, "All things of the universe have a numerical attribute that uniquely describes them." This is essentially the core of numerology.

The ancient Greeks weren't the only people to devote their attention to numerology. The Hebrews devised an incredibly complex system of numerology known as gematria, which built upon the numerology of Pythagoras and took it a step further, applying values to whole phrases, prayers, and sections of the Judaic Talmud.

We could discuss gematria for years and not learn all its secrets, but this passage from Manly P. Hall's *The Secret Teachings of All Ages* provides a quick example of how it worked and how layers of meaning could be secreted within sacred texts:

> All higher numbers can be reduced to one of the original ten numerals, and the 10 itself to 1. Therefore, all groups of numbers resulting from the translation of names of deities into their numerical equivalents have a basis in one of the first ten numbers. By this system, in which the digits are added together, 666 becomes 6 + 6 + 6 or 18, and this, in turn, becomes 1 + 8 or 9. According to Revelation, 144,000 are to be saved. This number becomes 1+ 4 + 4 + 0 + 0 + 0, which equals 9, thus proving that both the Beast of Babylon and the number of the saved refer to man himself, whose symbol is the number 9. This system can be used successfully with both Greek and Hebrew letter values.

While the exact meaning of numbers such as 33 has been lost to most of us, the ripples of this sacred, encoded knowledge make themselves felt even in the modern world. In the example of Jesus Christ being thirty-three at the time of his death, it is very unlikely that this was his actual age; yet this is now a number encoded into the story of

Jesus. Whoever devised such an idea wanted this number to be passed down through the ages and wanted us to remember.

So it is with the rituals of the Freemasons. Not all participants understand the full meaning behind the symbolism of the numbers and themes involved, but the process ensures that the knowledge is kept alive and is transmitted throughout the ages.

See also: *Manly P. Hall, House of the Temple*.

One True God

This phrase is found on the granite pyramid that Robert Langdon locates in room SBB XIII deep beneath the Capitol building. After he and Katherine Solomon decode the symbols found on the side of the pyramid, they end up with the phrase *Jeova sanctus unus*.

Langdon explains that the phrase is Latin, and Katherine Solomon tells us that it is synonymous with the name of God found in the Jewish Torah: Jeova, Jehova, Yahweh. *Jeova sanctus unus* means literally "one true God."

According to the holy books of the Jews, Yahweh is indeed the One True God, the same God who guided Moses from Egypt and who then passed to mankind the Ten Commandments. We see this precise moment when God reveals himself in the book of Exodus 20:1–3: "You shall have no other gods to rival me.' "

However, the modern name Yahweh is only the English form of the original Hebrew, which was made up of four letters: Yhwh. The term is also known as the Tetragrammaton—literally, "having four letters" in Greek. This hints at just how sacred the name was. In fact, this name was known as the Ineffable Name, or the Unutterable Name.

Because it is considered the true and personal name of God, Orthodox Jews regard the pronunciation of this name as too sacred for everyday usage. If we remember the Ten Commandments, we find (in Exodus 20:7): " 'You shall not misuse the name of Yahweh your

God, for Yahweh will not leave unpunished anyone who misuses his name.' "

So, Orthodox Jews never speak the word aloud. When Solomon's Temple stood in Jerusalem, the name was spoken by the high priest on the Jewish holiday known as Yom Kippur, but since the destruction of the Temple in Roman times, the term has not been vocalized. In fact, it is said that the true and correct pronunciation of the name has been lost through the ages. In common usage, the word *Lord* is used instead.

The concept of One True God is known as monotheism. While the Abrahamic religions are monotheistic, the roots of monotheism are found further back in time. Zoroastrianism, founded in Persia sometime during the first millennium BC, has at its core the belief in one god known as Ahura Mazda. Zoroastrianism was influential in the creation of Judaism, a religion that in turn helped shape Christianity. The true age of Zoroastrianism is not known for certain, and it could have been predated by another monotheistic faith: Atenism in ancient Egypt. The Pharoah Akhenaten worshipped the Aten, in its form as the sun disk. Atenism was short-lived, however, flourishing only during the lifetime of the heretic Pharaoh Akhenaten. When he died, sometime around 1355 BC, the religion died with him. However, we still have records of the beliefs of Akhenaten's religion, and a text now known as "The Great Hymn to the Aten" was found at Amarna, the city that Akhenaten built in honor of the god Aten:

> *How manifold it is, what thou hast made!*
> *They are hidden from the face (of man).*
> *O sole god, like whom there is no other!*
> *Thou didst create the world according to thy desire . . .*

This hymn bears an uncanny resemblance to a passage found in the book of Psalms in the Bible, known as Psalm 104 though it is not clear if "The Great Hymn to the Aten" influenced its writing. However, an intriguing aspect of Psalm 104 is that it starts by ascribing characteristics that could be considered those of the sun to God, again reinforcing the idea that the psalm could be based in part on the hymn. Psalm 104 begins:

Bless Yahweh, my soul, Yahweh, my God, how great you are! Clothed in majesty and splendour, wearing the light as a robe! You stretch out the heavens like a tent, build your palace on the waters above, making the clouds your chariot, gliding on the wings of the wind, appointing the winds your messengers, flames of fire your servants.

Scholars still debate whether or not "The Great Hymn to the Aten" really is the earliest reference to the worship of One True God, but one thing is clear: monotheism and the belief in one God is an ancient concept.

In Masonic symbolic lore, the One True God concept is represented by the title Great Architect of the Universe.

In *The Lost Symbol*, it turns out that the phrase "One True God" has more significance than just revealing the name of God. Langdon reveals that *Jeova sanctus unus* was also the pseudonym of the famous scientist Isaac Newton. Langdon explains that the name of Isaac Newton in Latin was *Isaacus Neutonuus*—an anagram of *Jeova sanctus unus*, with the *I* in Isaac substituted for the *J*.

It is true that Newton signed all of his alchemical works in this way. In his lifetime, Sir Isaac Newton committed millions of words to paper, and he seems to have spent much of his later life examining the Bible, believing that sacred knowledge was encoded within.

John Maynard Keynes, who collected much of Newton's prolific output, claimed—after reading his full works—that Sir Isaac believed "the universe is a cryptogram set by the Almighty."

See also: *Great Architect of the Universe, Sir Isaac Newton.*

Ouroboros

Dan Brown writes in *The Lost Symbol* that the character Mal'akh's scalp bears a tattoo of a snake devouring its own tail, which he calls the ouroboros. Is this something invented by the author or is it something real? At the start of chapter 128, we are supplied with important information: no less than an illustration of the ouroboros. It is the seventh symbol in a sequence of images that Robert Langdon is trying to decipher, and is introduced as a symbol for wholeness. There it is again: the snake swallowing its own tail, forming an O.

The symbol of the serpent biting its own tail seems to have first been designed by ancient Egyptians sometime around 1500 BC. Several hundred years later, during the Zhou dynasty (700–256 BC) in China, the dragon or snake swallowing its own tail was being illustrated. Is it coincidental that two great civilizations—divided by a massive continent—each developed the concept of this symbol entirely independently?

The Phoenicians took to the symbol of the ouroboros, and it became part of their culture. These people originally inhabited the present-day Syrian coastal area of the Mediterranean Sea. They prospered as sailors and merchants, and through their trading links, disseminated their ideas widely.

The ancient Greeks were next to adopt the tail eater and gave it the name by which we know it today. Alternative spellings include *uroboros* and *oureboros*. The ouroboros has come to symbolize the cycle of nature: life out of death, creation out of destruction, and so on. Some historians have proposed that the Egyptians based the ouroboros on the Chinese symbol for yin and yang, which predated it.

After all, yin and yang represents creation, and the ouroboros constantly re-creates itself. Yin is symbolic of earth, female, dark, and negative, while yang corresponds to heaven, male, light, active, and positive. To create a balance, each half needs to feed off the other. Of course, there's also a school of thought that insists the ouroboros appeared first and inspired the yin-and-yang symbol.

In alchemy, the ouroboros is a snake, or sometimes a dragon, which in earlier times was often referred to as a worm. Alchemists also regard the ouroboros as symbolizing the clash of opposites.

Gnosticism, a form of spiritual teaching holding that its followers possessed special enlightenment, taught that the sun disk could be thought of as a huge dragon holding its own tail in its mouth. Most Gnostics referred to God as Monad (One.) An imperfect God had created an equally imperfect world, they believed, and this was inhabited by divine souls, namely people.

Another form of mysticism, Hermeticism, is a compendium of beliefs based on the supposed writings of Hermes Trismegistus (Hermes the Thrice Great), alleged to have been a brilliant Egyptian priest. He was believed to have been associated with the god of wisdom, Thoth. During the Renaissance, these beliefs greatly influenced dabblers in magic and the occult. One of their symbols? The ouroboros, symbolizing the continuous cycle of life.

In several higher degrees of Scottish Rite Freemasonry, the regalia, especially aprons of those who have attained these degrees, is adorned with the image of the ouroboros.

Norse mythology contains its own version of the ouroboros: the snake Jormundgand. It was one of the three children of the great god Loki, the shape changer, the sly one. Long ago, Odin, the greatest of the gods, realized that one day Jormundgand would bring great trouble, so he threw the snake into the deep ocean surrounding the world. However, the creature was so huge that it could circle the world, biting its own tail. Gods and men were caught in its grip.

It is said that Friedrich August Kekulé, a German chemist of the nineteenth century, dreamed of the tail-consuming snake. At the time, he was researching the chemical benzene, and was finding progress impossible. He awoke, pondered the circle that the snake had formed, and realized that his dream provided the solution: his snake was a closed carbon ring. He had solved his problem by falling asleep on the job!

The ouroboros has held significance for diverse peoples over a very long span of history. While at first glance it might be thought that they had little in common, they were all united by the symbol of the snake that eats itself.

See also: *Alchemy, Hermetica.*

Philosopher's Stone

The philosopher's stone was one of the greatest secrets of alchemy— so secret, in fact, that we don't know precisely what it was. Its true nature has been veiled in so many secrets over the centuries that the true meaning is hard to divine.

In *The Lost Symbol*, Robert Langdon discovers the acronym *VITRIOL* written on the wall of a room deep below the Capitol building. He tells Inoue Sato that it stands for *visita interiora terrae rectificando invenies occultum lapidem*, which translates as "visit the interior of the earth, and by rectifying, you will find the hidden stone."

The most interesting part of that phrase is *occultum lapidem*: the "hidden stone." We learn that this could relate to the philosopher's stone of the alchemists, truly their Holy Grail.

So, before we go any further, what exactly do we know about the philosopher's stone? Well, this fabled object or substance was described as an elixir of immortality; the fountain of youth that appears in countless cultures in one form or another. In the Middle Ages, the concept of an elixir that could confer eternal life was known as the philosopher's stone, and alchemists were obsessed with attempting to create it.

Some of the greatest alchemists of Europe and the Middle East turned their hands and minds to discovering this elusive substance, among them Ostanes, Nicolas Flamel, Count St. Germain, Fulcanelli, and even Sir Isaac Newton.

In addition to granting immortality, the elixir supposedly could transmute lead to gold. Despite being the subject of many experiments and much debate over the centuries, many doubt that it truly existed; rather, it was an *ideal*—perfection itself. As Zosimus, the Byzantine historian who lived toward the end of the fifth century, wrote of the philosopher's stone: "Receive this stone which is not a stone, a precious thing that has no value, a thing of many shapes which has no shapes, this unknown which is known to all."

We know that alchemy had two paths. One we could term exoteric: concerned with the pursuit of turning base metals into higher states, such as gold. The other, esoteric path was more interested in the transformation of a mortal man's soul into the divine. It is interesting that many have equated the philosopher's stone with the Holy Grail itself, because one of the earliest accounts of the Grail, the epic poem *Parzival* (written by Wolfram von Eschenbach sometime in the first part of the thirteenth century), says quite clearly that the Grail is in fact a stone:

If you do not know it, it shall here be named to you. It is called lapsit excillis. *By the power of that stone the phoenix burns to ashes, but the ashes give him life again. Thus does the phoenix moult and change its plumage, which afterwards is bright and shining and as lovely as before. There never was a human so ill but that, if he one day sees that stone, he cannot die within the week that follows. And in looks he will not fade. His appearance will stay the same, be it maid or man, as on the day he saw the stone, the same as when the best years of his life began, and though he should see the stone for two hundred years, it will never change, save that his hair might perhaps turn grey. Such power does the stone give a man that flesh and bones are at once made young again. The stone is also called the Grail.*

This is fascinating because here we find the same properties as the elixir known as the philosopher's stone. Could it be that the alchemists were looking not for an "elixir" after all but this legendary stone? In *The Elixir and the Stone*, Michael Baigent and Richard Leigh discuss the possible meaning of *lapsit excillis*:

> Scholars have suggested numerous interpretations of the phrase "lapsit excillis," all of them more or less plausible. It might be a corruption of lapis ex caelis—"stone from the heavens." It might be a truncation of lapis lapsus ex caelus—"a stone fallen from heaven." Most obviously, of course, it might be lapis elixir, the philosopher's stone and elixir of alchemy. [Wolfram's Parzival] is laden with alchemical symbolism. The phoenix, for example, is a familiar image in alchemical works, and Wolfram invokes it in a familiar alchemical context.

Yet another curious candidate is *lapis lapsus exiliens*, which seems to be a translation of the name of a legendary stone mentioned by the twelfth-century Arabic geographer al-Idrisi, which he termed "the stone that rose and fell." *Lapis lapsus exiliens* was associated with the rock found within the Dome of the Rock in Jerusalem, the stone from which the prophet Muhammad ascended to heaven. This stone is known by Jewish scholars as the *eben shetiyah*, or "stone of foundation."

Another clue that leads us to consider whether the Holy Grail and the philosopher's stone might be one and the same is the story of the legendary Hermes Trismegistus ("Hermes, the Thrice Great"), whose writings are the foundation of Hermeticism and alchemy. Hermes Trismegistus is ascribed with writing the emerald tablet, a treatise full of alchemical knowledge. Isaac Newton himself translated the text, which included the following lines: "It ascends from the Earth to Heaven and again it descends to the Earth and receives the force of things superior and inferior."

Notice the curious similarity here between what Newton describes as an object that "ascends from the Earth to Heaven and again it descends to the Earth" and "the stone that rose and fell," as described by al-Idrisi.

The question is, did the emerald tablet really exist in a physical form? Looking again at *lapis ex caelis*, "stone from the heavens," leads us toward meteorite, which we know were highly prized in antiquity. (See this book's discussion on the Akedah.) When a meteorite strikes the earth, it produces the formation of moldavite. This semiprecious stone, which resembles green glass, has gemlike qualities and is often used in jewelry. Looking again at Isaac Newton's translation of the emerald tablet provides a tantalizing clue: "Its force or power is entire if it be converted into earth." This describes moldavite *exactly*. It is created through fire when the "power" or "energy" of a meteorite impacts the earth, creating this new substance through sheer force. Sacred chemistry of the gods, if you happen to be an alchemist.

In a recent translation of the emerald tablet from the original Arabic, by Nineveh Shadrach, the line in question appears as "It is a fire that became our earth," which again precisely describes the creation of moldavite. This new translation also contains an intriguing variation of the line from Newton's version: "It extracts the lights from the heights and descends to the earth containing the power of the above and the below for it is with the light of the lights. Therefore the darkness flees from it."

Is it possible that the emerald tablet was a large piece of moldavite engraved with the words of Hermes Trismegistus? This would be fascinating because the word *Grail* is very likely descended from the Persian word *ghr*, meaning "pearl" or "stone." Furthermore, the Persian word *ghr'al*—which looks very much like the word *grail*—means "engraved stone." The implications of this are literally astounding, for it means that we don't have to decide between *lapis ex caelis*, "stone from the heavens," and *lapis elixir*, "the philosopher's stone," as a meaning for the Holy Grail. If the emerald tablet was a graven piece of moldavite, then the philosopher's stone is both of these concepts at the same time, a sacred meteoritic stone from heaven with magical properties that was in turn engraved with the alchemical teachings of Hermes Trismegistus. Considering that meteorites have been worshipped in many cultures worldwide, it is not surprising to discover that one of the most sacred objects of myth and legend, the philosopher's stone, could have its origins in the very heavens themselves.

See also: *Alchemy, Hermetica, Sir Isaac Newton.*

Pineal Gland

This tiny part of the brain is responsible for the efficient functioning of several metabolic systems within the body. It is also imbued by some with a symbolic link to the so-called third eye.

The Lost Symbol contains a conversation between Robert Langdon and Katherine Solomon in which they discuss the human brain, particularly the pineal gland. It is described as being active in meditative states and producing a rare waxlike substance that can heal the body, likened to the biblical manna that sustained the followers of Moses in the wilderness.

They discuss the notion that perhaps biblical references to "the Temple" actually mean the human mind, and Katherine quotes from 1 Corinthians 3:16 to support her argument. The skeptical Langdon raises the fact that the Temple is described as having an inner section and an outer section, separated by a veil. He may have been thinking of the passage describing the construction of the Temple, in some translations of Exodus 26:33: "and the veil shall divide unto you between the holy place and the most holy."

Once again Katherine has an answer for him: the two parts of the brain are separated by the arachnoid, "a veil of weblike tissue." Whether or not the Bible is describing a metaphor for the human brain, the pineal gland attracts interest from scientists and philosophers.

The gland is approximately seven millimeters long in humans and is located near the center of the brain, between the left and right hemispheres. It is responsible for producing a hormone called melatonin, which regulates the body's daily rhythms. When light stimulates the retina of the eye, impulses are sent down the optic nerve to a part of the brain called the hypothalamus. From here, sympathetic nerves link to the pineal gland and inhibit melatonin production. But during times when no light reaches the eye, like at night, the pineal gland is free to make more of the sleep-inducing hormone.

As with so many other aspects of anatomy, the pineal gland was first described by Galen (c. AD 130–210), the Greek doctor and philosopher whose opinions were followed until the seventeenth century. It was Galen who explained that the gland takes its name from the pinecone—*pinea*, in Latin—which it resembles in shape. In Galen's opinion, the gland's function was to support blood vessels, and he was dismissive of other suggestions that it regulated the flow of so-called psychic pneuma in the brain.

René Descartes, the seventeenth-century French philosopher, believed that the pineal gland was the "seat of the soul." In 1640 he wrote: "Since it is the only solid part of the brain which is single, it must necessarily be the seat of the common sense, i.e., of thought, and consequently of the soul; for one cannot be separated from the other. . . . My view is that this gland is the principal seat of the soul, and the place in which all our thoughts are formed."

The pineal gland attracted the attention of Helena Blavatsky, an esoteric writer who cofounded the Theosophical Society in 1875. She linked it to the "eye of Shiva," or the third eye, and said that the pineal gland in modern man was a vestigial version of an "organ of spiritual vision." In some animals, the cells that make up the pineal gland closely resemble the eye's photoreceptor cells; the discovery of early vertebrate fossils with a pineal opening have further fueled the view of this gland as a third eye.

The pineal gland is associated with the sixth chakra (*ajna* chakra), which is referred to as the third eye. In Hinduism it is known as the *gyananakashu,* or eye of knowledge, and many Hindus wear a mark known as a *tilak* between their eyebrows to symbolize this. Similarly, the way that ancient Egyptians used to position the cobra headdress, or *ureus*, in the center of the forehead may have indicated an appreciation of this function.

The hormone melatonin was first isolated in 1958. It has become very popular as a supplement and has been suggested as a cure for jet lag and other sleep disorders, while psychiatric conditions such as seasonal affective disorder (recurrent depression that tends to come on as the days grow shorter during the autumn and winter seasons) may be related to its production.

Rosicrucians

An A to Z of the Occult, by Simon Cox and Mark Foster, explains that the Society of Rosicrucians "was an esoteric society formed with the intention of bringing about a change in European civilization, of creating a more perfect society based on hermetic values and alchemical teachings."

As with the vast majority of esoteric societies, including the Freemasons, trying to ascertain actual origins are difficult if not impossible to prove. Many writers long before Dan Brown have suggested that the Rosicrucians originated Freemasonry. The character of Robert Langdon, in *The Lost Symbol*, explains that the rose cross is a symbol of Freemasonry in honor of the early Rosicrucians and their contribution to Masonic philosophy.

Freemasonry does indeed contain various rituals referring to the Brotherhood of the Rose and Cross. The eighteenth degree of the Ancient and Accepted Scottish Rite is called the rose croix degree, and a rosy-cross degree forms part of the ceremonies of the Royal Order of Scotland. There are also Rosicrucian Societies, with membership restricted to Freemasons alone. One such society, the Societas Rosicruciana in Anglia (SRIA), was founded in London, England, in 1867. This should not be confused with the non-Masonic Societas Rosicruciana in America (also SRIA), founded in 1912. Adding to the confusion, there is also an American Freemasonic equivalent known as the Societas Rosicruciana in Civitatibus Foederatis (SRICF).

The grade structure of these societies is:

First Order
Grade I	Zelator
Grade II	Theoricus
Grade III	Practicus
Grade IV	Philosophus

Second Order
Grade V	Adeptus Minor
Grade VI	Adeptus Major
Grade VII	Adeptus Exemptus

Third Order
Grade VIII	Magister
Grade IX	Magus

Each grade invites the member to study further into the Rosicrucian mysteries. Many members of the English SRIA were particularly mystical-minded Masons who founded the famous occult school known as the Hermetic Order of the Golden Dawn, in 1888.

A later member of the Golden Dawn was accused of black magic and of creating his own religion. He was none other than the infamous magician Aleister Crowley. He is also alleged to have been a thirty-third degree Mason, although this has been contested. Mal'akh, the villain of *The Lost Symbol,* is said to have studied Crowley in his quest for power and knowledge.

The Christian mystic Arthur Edward Waite, a contemporary of Crowley's, was both a Freemason and a member of the Golden Dawn. He is most famous for the Rider-Waite tarot deck, perhaps the most popular tarot cards of all time. A prolific writer on all things esoteric, he authored *A New Encyclopaedia of Freemasonry,* in which he said that "we have further to remember that the Rosicrucian Mystery was one of Divine Rebirth, such indeed as we meet with—though under many veils—in the ceremony of Freemasonry."

This divine rebirth needs to take place within the individual and relates to the message in the climactic chapter of *The Lost Symbol*. At the Washington Monument, Peter Solomon reveals to Robert Langdon that the truth of the Ancient Mysteries is the realization that people are not God's subjects but in fact possess the capability to be gods themselves through the realization of this truth.

Langdon mentions the American-based Rosicrucian Order known as the Ancient and Mystical Order Rosae Crucis (AMORC), which states its purpose as "the study of the elusive mysteries of life and the universe." This "ancient" organization was actually founded in New York in 1915. In its defense, however, AMORC does claim to have inherited an "oral tradition" dating back some 3,500 years to the reign of the Egyptian Pharaoh Tuthmosis III. AMORC further claims that its influences include the "heretic" Pharaoh Amenhotep IV, who became known as Akhenaten. He is regarded as the revolutionary pharaoh who threw out the old gods of Egypt and replaced them with one God, the Aten. This was the first record of the One True God concept in history—in other words, monotheism, which forms the basis of all the great religions of the book.

What did the Swiss-born alchemist Paracelsus and Sir Francis Bacon have in common? Both were Rosicrucians, as were the alchemists Michael Maier, Robert Fludd, and John Dee, Sir Isaac Newton, the Freemason and antiquarian Elias Ashmole, the mystic Jacob Boehme, and Benjamin Franklin. This is suggested by Robert Langdon and therefore may be a hint at where this plot element was gleaned.

In terms of documentary proof, the first mention of the society appears within a series of early-seventeenth-century pamphlets known as the *Rosicrucian Manifestos*. *The Lost Symbol*'s Katherine Solomon, the noetic scientist and sister of Peter Solomon, studied these documents as part of her research.

The manifestos circulated in Germany before word of the mysterious and mystical Brotherhood spread across Europe, eventually finding its way to the United States and the rest of the world. The first manifesto, entitled *The Fama Fraternitatis, or, A Discovery of the Fraternity of the Most Laudable Order of the Rosy Cross,* was printed in Kassel, Germany, in 1614. (Earlier handwritten copies dating from 1610–11 have since come to light.) The second manifesto, *The Confessio Fraternitatis, or The Confession of the Laudable Fraternity of the Most Honorable Order of the Rosy Cross, Written to All the Learned of Europe,* followed in 1615. It is not known who wrote these manifestos. Some academics have questioned whether or not an original group actually really existed, or if this was all just an elaborate hoax. What followed, however, was real, in that self-styled Rosicrucian groups began to appear and have done so ever since.

A year later, there appeared another Rosicrucian document, *The Chemical Wedding.* This was in a slightly different style and has been attributed to the Lutheran pastor Johannes Valentinus Andreae. The phrase "chemical wedding" is an alchemical reference to the process of spiritual transmutation, whereby a marriage of opposites is sought in order to discover the elixir of life or the philosopher's stone to achieve knowledge of God.

Explanations as to why the society was called the Rosy Cross or Rose Cross vary, but it is certainly connected to symbolism. As Robert Langdon explains to Katherine Solomon, it is a binary symbol, or "two symbols fused to create one." The idea is that the Egyptians used a cross to express the intersection of the celestial and human realms, or the famous concept "as above, so below."

This is also the meaning behind the Freemasons' use of the square-and-compass configuration, representing transformation. The rose represents love, or spirit, and the equal-armed cross equates to matter. Thus, spirit is crucified in matter, and the work of the Rosicrucian mystic is to set this free by exploring, understanding, and balancing, or marrying, rational thinking with spirituality. The allusion to Christ and the promise of resurrection within the Christian tradition is also obvious.

The early documents state that what is being made public for the first time is an order founded by a mystic named Brother Christian Rosenkreuz, said to have been born in 1378. A wise and learned man, he is said to have traveled abroad to study with Arab mystics, from whom he learned esoteric wisdom such as the Kabbalah, Hermeticism, and alchemy. On his return to Europe, he was shunned by the academic community, so he instituted a society to do good works in secret. In Rosicrucianism, each brother is asked to blend into the surrounding culture and keep unknown, then report on his progress once a year. It is further stipulated that each will choose a successor, with whom he will share his mysteries and secrets. When Christian Rosenkreuz died, he was placed in a secret seven-sided, three-level vault full of books and occult equipment. Apparently, the tomb was rediscovered around 1604, though its location was kept secret. It was described as having eternally burning lamps—which were still glowing—and the founder's body lay perfectly preserved.

The earliest known printed version of the *Fama Fraternitatis* in English is the translation by the philosopher Thomas Vaughan in 1652. However, according to Frances Yates's book *The Rosicrucian Enlightenment*, a handwritten copy dated 1633 was found preserved in the library of Sir David Lindsay, first Lord Lindsay of Balcarres, who is known to have had an interest in alchemy. Perhaps it is just a wonderful coincidence, but his granddaughter married Sir Robert Moray, the founder of the Royal Society, or the "Invisible College," and who was arguably the first true "gentleman mason" or Freemason.

It cannot be coincidence, however, that in 1638, a Scotsman named Henry Adamson wrote a strange poem that includes these much-quoted lines:

> *For we be brethren of the Rosie Cross;*
> *We have the mason-word and second sight,*
> *Things for to come we can foretell aright.*

See also: *Alchemy, Aleister Crowley, Freemasonry, Hermetica, One True God.*

SIMON COX

The Royal Society and the "Invisible College"

The Royal Society, or to give its full title, the Royal Society of London for the Improvement of Natural Knowledge, is an august body of the most respected scientists of our age. Current fellows include Stephen Hawking, Richard Dawkins, and Sir Timothy Berners-Lee. Given this highly respectable pedigree, one wonders how such an institution could be mentioned within *The Lost Symbol* as linked to the arcane study of alchemy.

The "Invisible College" is the title given to a society of learned and brilliant minds who joined together to share their knowledge and advance their studies. Dan Brown credits them with being a group of elites within the Royal Society who benefited from their understanding of ancient knowledge, passed down through the centuries from the mystery schools of Egypt. The character Peter Solomon in *The Lost Symbol* has ancestors who belonged to the Royal Society.

The Royal Society, successor body to the Invisible College, emerged from the collaboration of a group of philosophers who respected and discussed the work of Sir Francis Bacon. In his book *The New Atlantis*, Bacon described an establishment called "Salomon's House," where investigations into the natural world were made. It is this concept of a group of sages seeking to widen the extent of human knowledge, and the principles of experimental science outlined by Bacon in his *Advancement of Learning*, that inspired the founding of the Invisible College.

Robert Boyle, one of those who followed Bacon's investigative principles, referred to the Invisible College by name in 1646. Boyle was an alchemist as well as the author of *The Sceptical Chymist*, and in a letter to his former tutor, he wrote:

The best of it is that the cornerstones of the Invisible (or as they term themselves the Philosophical) College, do now and then honor me with their company, which makes me sorry for those pressing occasions that urge my departure.

The Royal Society was founded November 28, 1660, at Gresham College after a lecture by Christopher Wren. The twelve founding members aimed to form a "College for the Promoting of Physico-Mathematical Experimental Learning." Wren was the renowned architect who designed St. Paul's Cathedral in London, among many other masterpieces. Like so many enlightened men of his time, he did not confine himself to one field of study, and his scientific inquiries included medicine, astronomy, and microscopy.

A key founding member was Robert Moray, a leading Freemason and almost certainly the same Robert Moray whose Masonic initiation in 1641 was the first recorded example of a "speculative" (that is, a nonworking mason) becoming a member. Moray was a soldier who had fought for the French army and had been in contact with King Charles II of England during his exile. King Charles II was interested in science, as attested by his involvement with the Royal Observatory at Greenwich, and when Moray informed him of the Royal Society's formation, he gave his approval. In 1663 a second royal charter was granted to what was by then known as the Royal Society of London for Improving Natural Knowledge.

Another founding member of the Royal Society, Elias Ashmole, was initiated as a Freemason in 1646. Ashmole was a true Renaissance man, interested in such diverse subjects as politics, history, the military, and astrology, but most of all alchemy. During the English Civil War, Ashmole was a fervent supporter of the Royalist side, and when Charles II gained the throne, Ashmole was rewarded with lucrative posts. His legacy can be seen today in the city of Oxford, home to the Ashmolean Museum, which displays his vast collection of antiquities, books, and research.

Robert Hooke, who is known as the father of microscopy, was the society's first curator of experiments and also a surveyor after the Great Fire of London in 1666. His multiple talents and interests typify the early members of the society.

The scientific advances made by members of the Royal Society are tangible, which is not true of the Invisible College concept. So did an elite group within the society's ranks continue to base its philosophy on ancient mystical teachings?

Certainly many members of the Royal Society through the years have been Freemasons—in some cases, with high positions within the craft. For example, Masonic author Robert Lomas, in his book *The Invisible College*, comments on the career of the French philosopher John Theophilus Desaguliers:

> *Desaguliers had been introduced to Freemasonry while employed by the then President of the Royal Society Isaac Newton, as an experiment demonstrator for the Society's meetings. Desaguliers started out as an employee of the Royal Society. Under the patronage of Newton he became a Fellow of the Royal Society, and he also rose to the highest rank in English Freemasonry.*

In fact, Desaguliers was the Grand Master of the Premier Grand Lodge of England in 1719. The name of Sir Isaac Newton appears whenever hidden knowledge or esoteric involvement in science is discussed. Newton was the president of the Royal Society from 1703 until his death in 1727.

The men who formed the Royal Society, learned across many disciplines and able to read Latin and Greek texts in their original languages, were undoubtedly familiar with ancient teachings and philosophies, including those described as alchemical or Hermetic.

In *The Advancement of Learning*, Sir Francis Bacon wrote that "there should be a fraternity or brotherhood in learning, through which learned men might exchange knowledge and help one another. . . . The brotherhood of learning should transcend national boundaries." The Royal Society most certainly fulfilled that ideal.

For the brightest and most innovative scientific minds of any age, to have a forum in which to share and develop their ideas, is indeed the dream that Sir Francis Bacon seems to have had, and is a true stage for enlightenment.

See also: *Sir Francis Bacon, Sir Isaac Newton.*

Scottish Rite Freemasonry

A major element in the story line of *The Lost Symbol* is Scottish Rite Freemasonry, especially its thirty-third degree. Dan Brown shows this to be the highest degree in all of Freemasonry; the ultra-elite members who achieve this level supposedly receive some special information or profound wisdom. The symbol of Scottish Free Masonry is a double-headed eagle, or phoenix. The home of the Scottish Rite is the House of the Temple in Washington, DC; members know it as Heredom, named after a mythical mountain in Scotland.

With all the references to Scotland, Scottish, and *Ecosse* Rites and degrees, many have wondered why the home of Scottish Rite Freemasonry is in the United States. According to *Coil's Masonic Encyclopedia*, written by Henry Wilson Coil, himself a thirty-third degree Mason, and edited by three other thirty-third degree Masons, "Scotch, Scots, and Scottish are among the most troublesome words in Masonic writing. So long as they referred only to Scotland, all was well. But, about 1740, they began to be used to describe numerous degrees which were produced in Europe by authors who never saw Scotland."

As was discussed in the entry on the development of Freemasonry, when the first Grand Lodge of Freemasons was formed in London in 1717, there were no "high degrees." The system was a two-degree system, with a third degree introduced in the 1730s. Collectively, these three degrees of "craft" Masonry became known as Blue Masonry.

In 1737 Chevalier Andrew Ramsey, an exiled Scotsman living in France, was the Grand Orator of the French Freemasons. That year he delivered a Masonic address that was full of Scottish references and was destined to change Freemasonry forever. Historians and academics agree that his lecture, delivered against the backdrop of political and religious unrest across Europe, was mostly mythological in nature. The reason for the mythological and Scottish elements seems to have been that he wanted to give Freemasonry a noble and chivalric lineage, which perhaps was lacking in the "craft" aspect of the British three degrees. The French loved the fact that the *hauts grades*, or Freemasonic "high degrees," of chivalry (including Templar and Rosicrucian degrees) began to appear.

Ramsay's boldest claim was the suggestion that Freemasonry was actually founded at the time of the Crusades, as you can see from the following extract from his oration, taken from *The Quest for the Celtic Key*, by Karen Ralls-Macleod and Ian Robertson:

> At the time of the Crusades in Palestine, many princes, lords, and citizens associated themselves, and vowed to restore the Temple of the Christians in the Holy Land, and to employ themselves in bringing back their architecture to its first institution. They agreed upon several ancient signs and symbolic words drawn from the well of religion in order to recognize themselves amongst the heathen and Saracens. These signs and words were only communicated to those who promised solemnly, and even sometimes at the foot of the altar, never to reveal them. This sacred promise was therefore not an execrable oath, as it has been called, but a respectable bond to unite Christians of all nationalities in one confraternity. Some time afterwards our Order formed an intimate union with the Knights of St. John of Jerusalem. From that time our Lodges took the name of Lodges of St. John.

Ramsay went on to say:

> The kings, princes, and lords returned from Palestine to their own lands, and there established diverse Lodges. At the time of the last Crusades many Lodges were already erected in Germany, Italy, Spain, France, and from thence in Scotland, because of the close alliance between the French and the Scotch.
>
> James, Lord Steward of Scotland, was Grand Master of a Lodge established at Kilwinning, in the West of Scotland, MCCLXXXVI [AD 1286], shortly after the death of Alexander III, King of Scotland, and one year before John Baliol mounted the throne. This lord received as Freemasons into his Lodge the Earls of Gloucester and Ulster, the one English, the other Irish.

By degrees our Lodges and our rites were neglected in most places.
This is why of so many historians only those of Great Britain speak
of our Order. Nevertheless it preserved its splendor among those
Scotsmen to whom the Kings of France confided during many centu-
ries the safeguard of their royal persons.

Ramsay did not suggest creating new Rites, but this is exactly what
his lecture inspired, and very soon Scots Masonry was born. The term
Scottish, Scots, Scotch, or *Ecosse* became a brand name for what were
seen as "elitist" Knightly and Templar-styled Orders. In 1738 Pope
Clement XII issued a papal bull, or decree, prohibiting Catholics from
becoming Freemasons. Interestingly, the first lodge affected by the
bull was a lodge in Rome composed of Jacobites, supporters of the
exiled Scottish Stuart monarchy. Although most French Freemasons
were Roman Catholics, this did nothing to dissuade them, and they
embraced this new craze.

From France, Freemasonry spread quickly across Europe and America. Over the next century, more than 1,100 degrees appeared, forming more than a hundred rites. Many of the rites soon faded from use,
but from these early developments, we find the birth of the Royal
Order of Scotland the rose croix degree, the Rectified Scottish Rite,
and the Ancient and Accepted Scottish Rite.

In 1761 Stephen Morin was given the authority to take a twenty-
five degree system, known as the Rite of Perfection, to the Western
Hemisphere. Starting in the West Indies, this form of Freemasonry
spread to the American mainland. The newly emerging York Rite
containing Royal Arch Chapters, Cryptic Councils, and the Com-
mandery of Knight Templar was also taking root at the same time on
the American continent.

A change from the twenty-five degree Rite of Perfection into a
new thirty-three degree system took place under the Constitution of
1786. The thirty-three degrees were a number settled on in allusion
to the thirty-three years of the life of Christ. By 1802, the Supreme
Council of the thirty-third degree was the name adopted, but this was

changed to the Ancient and Accepted Scottish Rite in 1804, in agreement with the Supreme Council in France. Interestingly, the Scottish Rite was not established in Scotland until as late as 1846.

The full creation of what we have today as Scottish Rite came about when Albert Pike, Confederate general and Freemason, became the Sovereign Grand Commander of the Southern Jurisdiction in 1859, a position he held until his death in 1891. Famously, he rewrote and developed the rituals and produced a book that some refer to as the Bible of the Scottish Rite: *The Morals and Dogma of the Ancient and Accepted Scottish Rite of Freemasonry*, published in 1871. Pike promoted the Rite as the supreme sanctuary for Freemasonry, containing within its degrees the wisdom of Kabbalah, Hermeticism, alchemy, and the philosophical teachings of the Rosicrucians. There's a scene in *The Lost Symbol* where Robert Langdon is racing up a marble staircase in the House of the Temple and finds himself face-to-face with a bronze bust of Pike—Dan Brown's nod to the origins of the Scottish Rite.

It is stated throughout Freemasonry that there are no degrees higher than the Blue Degrees, which include apprentice, fellow craft and master Mason. This said, the exclusivity of the thirty-third makes it one of the most prized degrees. The so-called higher degrees are meant to give more detail and instruction to help members reflect on the teachings of Blue Masonry. The symbolism is very much added to and embellished throughout the Scottish Rite.

The double-headed eagle, or phoenix, is the badge of the final degrees of the Rite and is said to be an alchemical interpretation similar to the "chemical wedding" referred to in the Rosicrucian chapter. To quote Brother G. Peters, a thirty-second degree Freemason: "As Scottish Rite Masons, may we each undertake the task of so analyzing and purifying our natures, that we too may be as proud, noble, august, and bold as the Eagle which is our symbol, showing our minds the direct path of the ascent into the Heavens, carrying our souls aloft to the very throne of All Creation."

As an emblem, it is ancient in origin and is called by many the "Double Headed Eagle of Lagash," Lagash being an ancient Sumerian city. It has been used for centuries by rulers such as Charlemagne, who adopted it around AD 800, when he became Emperor of the Romans; the two heads represented the union of Rome and Germany. It seems to have entered Freemasonry around 1758, with the French Rite of Perfection, and was the emblem of the Council of Emperors of the East and West in Paris. The successors of that council became the Supreme Councils of the thirty-third degree throughout the world. It was said that the founder of the Scottish Rite was actually King Frederick II (the Great) of Prussia, whose heraldic arms bore the double-headed eagle, but although he was known to be a Freemason, this claim for the Rite is believed to be a fable, propagated by Albert Pike and another Masonic writer from the nineteenth century, Albert Mackey, to give a splendid pedigree to their beloved Order.

Having made so much of the thirty-three degrees, there are, to be technical, only twenty-nine. The first three are the craft degrees; degrees four through thirty-two are the degrees proper; and the thirty-third degree is an honor bestowed for outstanding service to Freemasonry. As members are informed,

> *Sublime Princes of the Royal Secret of the Thirty-second Degree, not less than thirty-three years of age, at an annual session of the Supreme Council, may be elected Sovereign Grand Inspectors General of the Thirty-third and Last Degree, Honorary Members of the Supreme Council, by unanimous vote taken by secret ballot. This honour is conferred because of "outstanding service to the Fraternity or for service to others which reflects credit upon the Order." Honorary Members have the right to be present at all sessions of the Supreme Council, except executive sessions, and to a voice therein, but no vote. Sovereign Grand Inspectors General of the Thirty-third and Last Degree may be elected Active Members of the Supreme Council at the Annual Meetings thereof.*

The Mother Supreme Council of the World, as it is called, which is basically the Grand Lodge of the Rite as mentioned in *The Lost Symbol*, is the House of the Temple. The degree structure that it oper-

SIMON COX

ates (and it should be noted that there are slightly different names within the Northern Jurisdiction of the United States and other jurisdictions) is as follows:

Fourth degree	Secret Master
Fifth degree	Perfect Master
Sixth degree	Intimate Secretary
Seventh degree	Provost and Judge
Eighth degree	Intendant of the Building
Ninth degree	Elu of the Nine
Tenth degree	Elu of the Fifteen
Eleventh degree	Elu of the Twelve
Twelfth degree	Master Architect
Thirteenth degree	Royal Arch of Solomon
Fourteenth degree	Perfect Elu
Fifteenth degree	Knight of the East, or Knight of the Sword, or Knight of the Eagle
Sixteenth degree	Prince of Jerusalem
Seventeenth degree	Knight of the East and West
Eighteenth degree	Knight Rose Croix
Nineteenth degree	Grand Pontiff
Twentieth degree	Master of the Symbolic Lodge
Twenty-first degree	Noachite, or Prussian Knight
Twenty-second degree	Knight of the Royal Axe, or Prince of Libanus
Twenty-third degree	Chief of the Tabernacle
Twenty-fourth degree	Prince of the Tabernacle
Twenty-fifth degree	Knight of the Brazen Serpent
Twenty-sixth degree	Prince of Mercy, or Scottish Trinitarian
Twenty-seventh degree	Knight of the Sun, or Prince Adept
Twenty-eighth degree	Knight Commander of the Temple
Twenty-ninth degree	Scottish Knight of Saint Andrew
Thirtieth degree	Knight Kadosh, or Knight of the White and Black Eagle

Thirty-first degree	Inspector Inquisitor
Thirty-second degree	Master of the Royal Secret
Thirty-third degree	Inspector General

Robert Langdon suggests that members of the Rite know the House of the Temple as Heredom, which is also the name given to the journal of the annual transactions of the Scottish Rite Research Society.

However, Heredom is linked most famously to the Royal Order of Scotland, headquartered at the Grand Lodge in Edinburgh, Scotland. It dates to around the 1740s and still works its eighteenth-century ritual virtually intact. The Royal Order comprises two degrees: the Heredom of Kilwinning and the Knighthood of the Rosy Cross. In 1877 the Masonic authority Kenneth Mackenzie wrote the following about Heredom: "Heredom—a word of doubtful significance in Masonry. It has successively been associated with the Royal Order of Heredom in Scotland, with the word Heroden as a Scottish mountain, and from the Greek words for Holy and House; thus the title of the Rose Croix of Heredom would convey the meaning Rosy Cross of the Holy House."

The House of the Rosy Cross perhaps fits extremely well with what is being portrayed in the story. The building, which according to Langdon rivals Scotland's Rosslyn Chapel architecturally, was completed in 1915. It is an amazing replica of one of the seven wonders of the ancient world: the Mausoleum of King Mausolus at Halicarnassus. It is from that very tomb that we get the word *mausoleum*, meaning "for dead remains."

Incidentally, the House of the Temple *is* a mausoleum in addition to a Grand Masonic Temple. In 1944 Congress granted permission for the remains of Albert Pike to be placed in a vault on one side of the light well. Nine years later, another past sovereign grand commander, John Henry Cowles, was buried there too.

One final note regarding *The Lost Symbol* and high-grade Freemasonry: secret vaults and the lost word have always been features of Freemasonry. In the Walt Disney movie *National Treasure*, a material treasure is hidden. The Declaration of Independence acts like a pirate map in which the hidden message is no more esoteric than "X marks the spot." In *The Lost Symbol*, at least Dan Brown seems to have grasped the message and, indeed, the mystery of the ancient traditions that Freemasonry claims as its own. The secret is that the great treasure is not lost, and is *not* material; it is hidden or sleeping within each of us, waiting to be recovered.

See also: *Freemasonry, Heredom, House of the Temple.*

Seal of Solomon/Star of David

Having taken the first fundamental steps toward deciphering the pyramid and capstone, Katherine Solomon and Robert Langdon grab a cab and head away from the Thomas Jefferson Building. In an apparent eureka moment, Katherine Solomon realizes that the motto *Jeova sanctus unus*—"one true God"—was summed up in the sacred symbol of the Hebrews: the Seal of Solomon, also known as the Star of David. As she excitedly tells Langdon, the Seal of Solomon is a highly significant Masonic symbol. She pulls a dollar bill out of her pocket and proceeds to draw the Star of David over the Great Seal of the United States, revealing the word *Mason*. The Seal of Solomon consists of two equilateral triangles, one pointing upward and the other inverted. It may be shown as a solid shape or, more commonly, as an outline, with the triangles intertwined to form a six-pointed star. This symbol is known variously as the Seal of Solomon, Star of David, or Shield of David, the latter term thought to derive from the metal structure used to strengthen King David's battle shield. The symbol's origins are obscure, but since 1897, it has been used as a

Zionist nationalist symbol, and it is now closely identified with the state of Israel. However, despite its identification with Judaism, the Seal of Solomon/Star of David does not have any specific Judaic religious significance and is not solely a Judaic symbol.

Nevertheless, within Jewish tradition, it appears that the Seal of Solomon's earliest use was as an amulet against evil. Talmudic texts from the medieval period make reference to the Seal of Solomon engraved upon a magical ring, a divine gift to King Solomon that provided not only protection against demons but a means of commanding them. It would appear that sometime after the eleventh century, the Seal of Solomon began to be called the Star of David, although as for why is uncertain. By the twelfth century, references to the Seal of Solomon/Star of David motif start showing up in Jewish biblical commentaries. One notable example is *Eshkol ha-Kofer* by the Jewish scholar Judah ben Elijah Hadassi, who observes that the Shield of David acts as a form of protection in connection with the *mezuzah*—a small parchment scroll containing verses from the Torah. It slips into a slim case, which is affixed to the door frame in Jewish homes. Bearing in mind the Star of David's connection with a shield, it is not surprising that its early use appears to have been on amulets and mezuzahs.

The hexagram is found extensively in Islamic tradition, with the six-pointed star engraved on the bottom of cups and various artifacts, and as architectural decoration in mosques and other structures. Islamic literature also links the symbol specifically to King Solomon and his magical seal ring. In fact, it is thought that the Judaic tradition of the Seal of Solomon/Star of David hexagram evolved from an Arabic source that was then "converted" to Judaism by Islamic decorative arts within kabbalistic literature.

According to the Jewish scholar Gershom Scholem, thirteenth-century copies of Jewish religious books bearing the symbol had been translated in Islamic countries, then found their way to Spain and Germany. However, Raphael Patai, author of *The Jewish Alchemists*, questions this assumption, citing the case of Maria Hebraea (Maria the Hebrew), an alchemist who lived in Egypt during the third century. From the writings of her student Zosimus the Panopolitan, Patai concludes that Maria Hebraea was aware of the kabbalistic form and properties of the hexagram.

As in the Islamic tradition, the Seal of Solomon/Star of David was also used as a decorative motif in synagogues. The book *The Hiram Key*, by Christopher Knight and Robert Lomas, contains the following quotation from Alfred Gotte, a nineteenth-century synagogue builder: "As its geometrical shape lent itself easily to all structural and ornamental purposes, it has now been . . . an established fact, already hallowed by tradition, that the *mogen david* for the Jews is the same kind of holy symbol that the Cross and the Crescent are for the monotheistic faiths."

Indeed, a stone from a late-third-century synagogue in Galilee, Israel, is engraved with the Shield of David. Considering that the stone came from an entrance arch, its association with the mezuzah equally underlines the hexagram's early use as a symbol of protection. When Sultan Süleyman the Magnificent rebuilt most of the Temple Mount in Jerusalem in 1536, he decorated the walls around the city with the Seals of Solomon as a means of protection.

Whatever its origins, the Seal of Solomon has great significance in the Kabbalah, the Jewish mystical tradition. Although the hexagram is associated with a number of meanings, primarily it symbolizes the number 7. Its six points represent the directions up, down, north, south, east, and west, illustrating the universal and omnipotent dominion of God, while the central hexagon containing the Tree of Life signifies harmony and grace. The two triangles suggest good and evil, God and mankind, heaven and earth. The upward triangle also represents fire and is symbolic of mankind's desire to return to God. The downward-pointing triangle represents water and the descent of the Divine into the physical. Additionally, the kabbalistic hexagram can be used to illustrate the ten *sefirot* (the attributes and emanations of God), with the Tree of Life in the center and the nine remaining *sefirot* at each point and outer angle of the hexagram. As an astrological association, the twelve signs of zodiac are incorporated into the kabbalistic hexagram within the six points.

As in the Kabbalah, the hexagram is used in alchemy to represent fire and water. In addition, when a horizontal line is drawn across both triangles (fire and water), earth and air are also represented, thus illustrating the four elements. In alchemy, the hexagram is therefore the sign of transmutation; Herbert Silberer's book *Hidden Symbolism of Alchemy and the Occult Arts* calls the Seal of Solomon the philosopher's stone that would bring about a spiritual metamorphosis. In *The Continuum Encyclopedia of Symbols*, Udo Becker notes that the hexagram is "often a symbol of the interpenetration of the visible and invisible worlds" and is the "symbol of the union of all opposites, since it is composed of the basic shapes and signs of the elements."

In Buddhism, the hexagram is the symbol for Anahata, the heart chakra in Tantric yoga. As for Hindu religious practices and tradition, the symbol has enormous importance and meaning, being revered as the sign of the sacred union between the two gods Shiva and Shakti. As such, the two interlocking triangles symbolize the male and female aspects that together represent creation itself. The concept of the male △ "blade" and the female ▽ "chalice" appears to be an ancient one suggesting male procreative power and female reproductive power. This controversial theme featured prominently in Dan Brown's *The Da Vinci Code*. Margaret Starbird, in her book *Magdalene's Lost Legacy*, states that these symbols, united, are "in sacred harmony renewing the cycles of life on the planet.

This "intimate union and partnership" suggested by the sacred union of the two triangles in the form of the hexagram might be the reason why the Great Seal of the United States has thirteen stars, representing the original colonies, displayed in the shape of the Star of David hexagram.

Within Freemasonry, the Seal of Solomon/Star of David symbolizes the union of male and female, as well as opposite forces such as active and passive, dark and light, and good and evil. It is widely used as an insignia for a badge of office, often being placed within a circle, or as a decorative element in Masonic temples.

In paganism, the hexagram is symbolic for harmony and knowledge and represents the concept of "As above so below"—the balance between the macrocosm and the microcosm—while in Satanism, the symbol has taken on a more sinister meaning, often associated with curses (note the phrase "to put a hex on someone") or used to invoke dark forces. The seventeenth-century magical text *The Lesser Key of Solomon*, which lists demons and spirits and their attributes, states that the hexagram is "shown unto the Spirits when they do appear, so that they be compelled to take human shape upon them and be obedient."

Indeed, Aleister Crowley used the "Hexagram of Solomon" in the Ritual of the Beast, no doubt because the symbol is thought to represent 666, the number of the devil, having as it does 6 points, a 6-sided hexagon, and 6 small triangles.

See also: *Alchemy, Aleister Crowley, Freemasonry, Great Seal of the United States.*

Shriners

In *The Lost Symbol*, the character Inoue Sato explains that the Ancient Arabic Order of Nobles of the Mystic Shrine (AAONMS) is generally known as the Shriners and that they are attached to the Masons. Turner Simkins, a CIA agent, identifies the Shriners as "guys who build hospitals for kids," and recalls the distinctive red fezzes that its members wear. All very mysterious.

The Shriners formed in New York City in 1870. An actor named William Florence had attended a party in Marseilles, France, thrown by an Arab diplomat, and he was so taken by the exotic atmosphere that he and a fellow Freemason, Dr. Walter Fleming, decided to start a new fraternity dedicated to fellowship and fun—with a Middle Eastern flavor. The pair dreamed up a ritual, plus costumes and an insignia, and initiated eleven other men.

Today total membership in the Shriners stands at around a half million. In Washington, DC, the Almas Shrine Center temple is located on Franklin Park. The five-story edifice, built in 1929 in a distinctively Middle Eastern style, turns up in *The Lost Symbol* as a possible answer to the clues "order" and "Eight Franklin Square."

Although the Arabian theme is still part of the Shriners' culture, the international fraternity's ritual contains no Islamic elements. There is, in fact, no particularly religious aspect to the Shriners' ceremony. However, since all members must be Masons in order to join, a man must profess a belief in the Supreme Being. From its origins as a largely social group, the Shriners acquired a reputation as essentially a Masonic drinking club. As John Michael Greer explains in *The Element Encyclopedia of Secret Societies and Hidden History*: "For the first half of its existence, if not more, the Shrine existed primarily as an excuse for partying and drinking on a heroic scale. By the early 1880s the annual convention of the Imperial Council, the international governing body of the Shrine, had already earned a reputation as the wildest party in American fraternalism."

Eventually a more public-spirited purpose developed, with fundraising activities including provisions for victims of the 1888 yellow fever epidemic in Florida. In 1930 a plan was launched to build and maintain children's hospitals that would provide their services for free; it was to become the activity most associated with the Shriners.

The Shriners Hospitals for Children is headquartered in Tampa, Florida. Its admission policy stipulates that patients must be under eighteen years of age and capable of receiving treatment. There are now more than twenty of these not-for-profit free hospitals in North America. Each specializes in a particular area of medicine, such as spinal cord injuries and treating burn victims. Patients with chronic conditions are eligible for inpatient and outpatient care up to twenty-one years of age. In addition, the Shriners finance free screening clinics for children under seventeen.

The distinctive hat worn by Shriners, the fez, was chosen as part of their regalia because of its association with the Arab world, even though the popularity of the latter has declined in North Africa. The Shriners have stuck to their tradition of wearing the black-tasseled red fez, to maintain their connection with the past.

Shriner circuses are among the most important and enjoyable attractions staged to raise contributions to their charities. Featuring acrobats, performing horses and dogs, jugglers, and all the other colorful and exciting aspects of a family circus, they attract huge crowds. And their spectacular parades feature drum corps, bagpipers, clowns, and, of course, the obligatory small cars. The Shriners were originally formed to provide fun for its founding members, and today that fun is brought to the wider community.

Although the Shriners is a male organization, members' wives and daughters can join women's groups. Almost inevitably, given the Arab theme of the male fraternity, these women call themselves "Daughters of the Nile." The group formed in 1913.

One of the most famous Shriners was Harold Lloyd, the silent screen actor, comedian, and film producer. He was not just a member, though. Lloyd became Imperial Potentate of North America in 1949; and in 1963, he became president of the Shriners Hospital Corporation and chairman of the board of trustees.

In 2000, membership requirements were changed. No longer did a Shriner have to hold a high degree within the Scottish Rite or the Knight Templar degree of the York Rite of Freemasonry. This was intended to attract more members, although the move has reportedly decreased Scottish Rite membership in some areas.

See also: *Freemasonry, Scottish Rite Freemasonry*.

Joseph Smith and the Book of Mormon

One of the religious practices given as an example of "frightening if taken out of context" in *The Lost Symbol* is the Mormon practice of baptism of the dead. This posthumous baptism into the church is possible for those who died before having a valid baptism, and it enables passage into God's Kingdom for those in the spirit world who accept the Gospel.

The Church of Jesus Christ of Latter-Day Saints, sometimes referred to as the Mormon Church, was founded by their prophet, Joseph Smith, who was born in Sharon, Vermont, in 1805. The family's farm failed, so eventually they moved to New York State. Like many poor families of the day, Joseph and his siblings had to work and, consequently, did not receive much schooling.

Joseph had a vision in 1827 of an angel called Moroni, who had taken him to a hill. Digging there revealed gold plates on which were inscribed the Book of Mormon in "reformed Egyptian," and in addition two stones, Urim and Thummin, by means of which Joseph could translate the Book. In *The Lost Symbol*, Robert Langdon suggests that Joseph used "magic eyeglasses" to translate these plates; and it seems that the two stones are synonymous with the two lenses of a pair of spectacles.

The method of transcription is explained by Richard Van Wagoner and Steven Walker in *Joseph Smith: The Gift of Seeing*, where they quote Michael Morse, who was Smith's brother-in-law, describing how, "The mode of procedure consisted in Joseph's placing the Seer Stone in the crown of a hat, then putting his face into the hat, so as to entirely cover his face."

Joseph Smith told of Jewish families from Old Testament times who traveled from Jerusalem to America. One group, which Smith called the Lamanites, was said to be the ancestors of the American Indians. His translation also showed that Jesus Christ had visited America, after his resurrection, before ascending into heaven. The title of the book is taken from a "prophet-historian," Mormon, said to have compiled the writings on the gold plates. A small group of believers began to lend their support. By 1830, Smith's translation of the Book of Mormon was completed. He found people who were willing to testify that they had seen the gold plates, and their testimony is included in the publication. Eventually the plates, along with Urim and Thummin, were returned to the angel Moroni, who took them away.

The Book of Mormon's publication provoked a storm of protest from the more orthodox churchgoers. Nevertheless, others were attracted by its revelations and came along to be baptized as members of the incipient Mormon Church. Joseph became an eloquent, humorous, and persuasive speaker. An attraction for many of his new followers was that, unlike so many of the hellfire and damnation preachers they were used to, this form of religion promised not only a very comfortable afterlife to those who had lived decent, honest lives, but also that sinners would not face eternal cruel punishment.

Unbelievers, referred to as "gentiles" by the Mormons, were frequently extremely hostile toward Joseph and his followers. As violent opposition grew, many of the faithful followed Joseph westward to seek a place where they could practice their faith more peacefully. In 1839 they established a town in Illinois, called Nauvoo, with their leader as mayor. A few years later, he had become ambitious enough to seek election as president of the United States.

Not everything in Smith's life was successful, though. Many of his closest friends and colleagues quarreled with him and left the church or were thrown out. Joseph's most controversial behavior was his proposing "celestial marriage" to a number of women, many of whom were already married—some to his closest colleagues. These celestial marriages would last for eternity and supersede earthly marriages.

For generations, the Mormons have been strongly criticized for once supporting polygamy. It should be noted that the church officially gave up the practice in 1890 and excommunicates any member who disobeys the proscription. There are, however, some so-called Mormon fundamentalists, mainly in the United States, Canada, and Mexico, who claim that multiple celestial marriages are an essential requirement for admittance to the highest degree of Mormon heaven.

In 1844 dissidents set up a printing press to oppose Joseph Smith, who ordered his followers to destroy it. The governor of the State of Illinois ordered Smith's his arrest on the grounds that he had contravened the First Amendment guaranteeing free speech and freedom of the press. The militia escorted him and some followers, including his older brother, Hyrum, to jail in Carthage, Illinois. They then mounted guard, fearing that a mob of gentiles or, alternatively, a troop of loyal Mormons might attack. As feared, a group of ex-militiamen, disguised with blackened faces, broke into the building. Joseph, who'd been allowed to keep a gun, wounded some attackers as they came toward him on the jail's second floor. When he ran out of ammunition, he ran toward the window and was shot by the insurgents. He fell to ground, and more shots were fired into him. Smith's earthly life was over at age thirty-eight.

The Church of Latter-Day Saints has survived Joseph Smith's death and is a powerful force even in countries distant from the United States. Brigham Young, the "American Moses," was president of the church from 1847 until he died thirty years later. Young was instrumental in establishing Salt Lake City and was the first governor of the territory of Utah. The famous university bearing his name is owned by the Mormon Church.

The *Encyclopaedia Britannica*'s summary of Mormon doctrine gives the following explanation: "Mormon doctrine diverges from the orthodoxy of established Christianity, particularly in its polytheism, in affirming that God has evolved from man and that men might evolve into gods."

No better description could fit the concept that Dan Brown is exploring within the pages of *The Lost Symbol*.

Smithsonian Institution

The Smithsonian Institution plays a crucial role in *The Lost Symbol*. Not only is Peter Solomon its secretary, but Mal'akh, posing as Solomon's assistant, deceives Robert Langdon into leaving Harvard University to travel to Washington, DC, ostensibly to speak at a Smithsonian gala dinner.

The Smithsonian Institution is an educational and research institute administered by the U.S. government. It is also funded partly from public money, in addition to private endowments, donations, and the profits from its media and retail outlets. According to a statement published by the institution, "The Smithsonian develops, maintains, preserves, studies, exhibits, and interprets collections of art, artifacts, natural specimens, living animals and plants, images, archival and library materials, and audiovisual and digital media of unparalleled scope, depth, and quality," while its research aims to "increase and diffuse knowledge the Smithsonian engages in and supports original research in science, art, history, and culture."

With 19 museums, 9 research centers, and Washington's National Zoo, the Smithsonian Institution is the world's largest museum complex; its diverse and unrivaled collections contain a staggering 136 million objects. In addition, 156 affiliate museums worldwide are able to "borrow" the Smithsonian's vast resources and share them with the world. Of the 19 museums, 17 are in the U.S. capital, including the National Museum of the American Indian, National Museum of American History, National Museum of Natural History, National Air and Space Museum, Smithsonian American Art Museum, National Portrait Gallery, the Smithsonian Institution Building, and other museums and galleries. There are also two Smithsonian museums in New York and the National Air and Space Museum's Steven F. Udvar-Hazy Center in Chantilly, Virginia. All of the Smithsonian museums, galleries, and zoo are free to the public.

It was thanks to a bequest by James Smithson that the Smithsonian Institution was founded. Smithson was a celebrated British scientist and mineralogist. Born in 1765 in Paris, France, he was the illegitimate son of Sir Hugh Smithson, Duke of Northumberland, and Elizabeth Hungerford Keate Macie, a wealthy widow and reputed descendant of Henry VII of England. In 1782 James Macie, as he was known until a few years after his mother's death in 1800, entered Pembroke College, part of the University of Oxford, to study chemistry and mineralogy, obtaining a Master of Arts degree in 1786. A year later, at the age of just twenty-two, he became the youngest fellow to be elected to the Royal Society, an academy of science established in London in 1660. James Smithson traveled all over Europe searching for and classifying minerals and crystals, publishing around twenty-seven scientific papers. By the time of his death in Genoa, Italy, in 1829, Smithson had amassed a large personal fortune, through his inheritance of his mother's estate and shrewd investments, which he bequeathed to his nephew and sole heir, Henry James Hungerford. In his will, written in 1826, James Smithson stated that should his nephew die without heirs, legitimate or otherwise, his estate was to go "to the United States of America, to found at Washington, under the name of the Smithsonian Institution, an establishment for the increase and diffusion of knowledge among men."

Bearing in mind that James Smithson never visited the United States and apparently had no contact with anyone living there, his bequest is highly unusual, although some commentators think this could have been either because he admired the United States's spirit of Enlightenment, or that he wished to snub the stringent social code and strictures prevalent in Britain at that time, a code that denied him social status and title due to the stigma of illegitimacy. Interestingly, he appears to have been a detractor of the monarchy, writing in 1792: "May other nations, at the time of their reforms, be wise enough to cast off, at first, the contemptible encumbrance." He also later wrote that he wished for his name to "live in the memory of man when the titles of the Northumberlands and the Percys are extinct and forgotten," suggesting that he was unable to forgive the British class and social system for the penalties imposed upon him.

With Henry Hungerford's death in 1835, Smithson's assets passed to the United States. Surprisingly, there was much debate over whether the bequest should be accepted or not, with South Carolina senator John C. Calhoun arguing that it was "beneath the dignity of the United States to receive presents of this kind from anyone." By 1836, Congress had accepted the bequest, but a lawsuit in London kept the matter tied up in court until 1838. Upon settlement, eleven boxes brimming with 104,960 gold sovereigns were loaded onto the USS *Mediator* and shipped to the United States. There the gold was melted down and minted into coins totaling $508,318. Eight years of further debate followed, focusing on what form the institution should take, where it should be located, its administration and building design, and so on, until the matter was finally settled and the Smithsonian Institution was established August 10, 1846.

SIMON COX

In order to fulfill the Smithsonian's multiple functions, a new building was required. Designed by James Renwick Jr., the Smithsonian Institution Building on Jefferson Drive was completed in 1855, and included a library, chemical laboratory, natural history laboratory, lecture halls, museum, and an art gallery. Built of red sandstone, the building is now more generally known as "the Castle," because of its nine towers and battlements. Most delighted in its architecture, but not everyone; Dorothea Dix, a social reformer and crusader, called it a "monstrous pile of misshapen towers, arches, columns." Today the Smithsonian Institution Building houses administrative offices and an information center. Organizationally, the Smithsonian Institution is divided into four areas: science; history, art, and culture; finance and administration; and Smithsonian Enterprises.

The act of Congress establishing the Smithsonian Institution stated that it was to be administered by a board of regents, which was to be responsible for overseeing and managing the institution on behalf of the federal government, and for carrying out "the responsibilities of the United States as trustee of the Smithson trust." The board meets four times a year and takes its role very seriously. As "The Smithsonian Institution Statement of Values and Code of Ethics" states, "Given this unique and special status, the Smithsonian must be mindful that it is a public trust operating on behalf of the American public and the United States government to carry out its mission to increase and diffuse knowledge."

The high-profile board of regents is made up of seventeen members, consisting of the chief justice of the United States, the vice president of the United States, three members of the House of Representatives, three members of the Senate, and nine citizens. The chief executive officer of the Smithsonian, known as the secretary, is appointed by the board of regents. It was thanks to the vision and tenacity of the Institution's first secretary, the distinguished physicist Joseph Henry, that the Smithsonian grew and developed into the scientific and research organization we know today.

See also: *the Royal Society and the "Invisible College."*

Smithsonian Museum Support Center (SMSC)

A major location for the action in *The Lost Symbol* is a secret laboratory hidden within a large support complex for the Smithsonian Museum.

Due to the Smithsonian's vast collection, only a tiny portion of it is able to be displayed at any given time. In addition, many of the artifacts are invaluable for scientific research, and the Smithsonian needed to be able to give researchers access to elements of the collection while ensuring their survival for future generations.

To address these concerns, a separate facility was constructed. The Smithsonian's Museum Support Center (SMSC) is the vision of Vince Wilcox, director of the massive structure since 1981. Wilcox spent several years planning this state-of-the-art storage facility for one of the nation's most valuable historical collections. Dedicated in May 1983, the SMSC was built using the latest in museum technology.

The facility is located in Silver Hill, Maryland, just outside Washington, DC. It is approximately six miles form the famous National Mall at the heart of the capital. It covers four and a half acres and provides a total of 435,000 square feet of storage space. The SMSC is made up of ample office and laboratory space and five "pods" that house the actual collection.

Each pod is the size of a football field and stands approximately 28 feet high. The units, which have insulated outer walls over a foot and a half thick, are positioned in a zigzag pattern, making future pod additions to the existing building relatively easy. The office and laboratory space and the storage pods are separated by a 20-foot-wide street. Current estimates are that the Smithsonian requires another 3.5 million square feet of storage. Plans are in the works to address these needs over the next two to three decades by adding on to the SMSC.

There are tens of thousands of storage cabinets to hold the more than 54 million items in the collection. Everything from 44-foot-long totem poles to microscopic plants and animals are stored here.

Because the facility is home to such a valuable collection, it is protected by a top-notch security system that couples sophisticated monitoring and detection equipment with security staff. When you enter the facility, the first security checkpoint requires a search through any personal belongings brought into the SMSC, and credentials for building access are issued. Employees are issued pass cards that open doors and record access to specific areas of the facility.

February 2010 will see the completion of the renovations to pod three, also known as the "wet pod" because it contains millions of biological specimens preserved in fluids such as formalin and ethanol. The pod is equipped with several special features, including explosion-proof electrical devices, and special floor drains.

In *The Lost Symbol*, pod three is the setting for the murder of Trish Dunne, whom Mal'akh drowns in a tank filled with ethanol preserving a giant squid. Pods one, two, four, and five are for storing other museum collections of both human and natural origin. Pod four also has a section referred to as the "high bay," which was constructed specifically to house the largest items in the collection such as totem poles, large mammal skeletons, and boats.

In Dan Brown's book *The Lost Symbol*, pod five is home to the special research facility of Katherine Solomon for her work in the Noetic Sciences. It should be noted that there is no evidence that such a facility exists in pod five—or anywhere else in the SMSC, for that matter.

The laboratory facilities all feature the latest in available technology. In addition, this facility is home to the Smithsonian's conservation analytical laboratory (CAL). Occupying 24,000 square feet of the laboratory, this area is used in the technical study, research, restoration, and training of conservation techniques.

Interestingly, there is also a clean room that has been especially constructed for the department of mineral sciences. Its collection of Antarctic meteorites is stored in nitrogen gas, to keep the items free from contamination. The only similar such facility is at the Johnson Space Center in Houston.

The Museum Storage Center was never intended for public viewing. Limiting the number of people who visit the facility minimizes the random factor of human body heat, which has played havoc in other collections around the world. For example, many of the tombs open to the public in Egypt have been severely damaged by the erosion caused by decades of playing host to thousands of daily visitors.

The principal goals for the SMSC involve researching, preserving, and conserving the Smithsonian's collection. A museum by its very nature is a contradiction in purposes; by displaying the items for public viewing, it exposes them to possible damage or contamination. The SMSC is here to minimize the potential danger to the collection and to allow the public at large to marvel at the wonders included here.

See also: *Institute of Noetic Sciences, Smithsonian Institution.*

Solomon's Temple

"Is there no help for the widow's son?"

These words were encoded on the dust jacket of the U.S. edition of *The Da Vinci Code* back in 2003. It was from this dust jacket, all those years ago, that many people first gleaned clues as to the content of what was to become *The Lost Symbol.*

The phrase itself is Masonic in origin and points to a parable-like story that plays a prominent role within Freemasonic rites and rituals: the story of Hiram Abiff, master Mason and chief architect of the legendary, Solomon's Temple in Jerusalem. In *The Lost Symbol,* the story of Abiff's murder is vividly re-created in the Freemasonic initiation ceremony that has been clandestinely filmed by Mal'akh.

This Hiram Abiff seems to be the same person referenced in the Bible, 1 Kings 7:13–14, who was a master bronze worker and craftsman employed by King Solomon on the construction of his temple. Hiram is described as "the son of a widow" and as coming from Tyre in Phoenicia. He is not to be confused with Hiram, king of Tyre, who is mentioned as having sent materials for the construction of the Temple.

Solomon's Temple holds special significance to Freemasons, not only because of their association with Hiram Abiff but also because of some of the symbolic and mysterious elements that the Temple displayed. The Masonic scholar Reverend Dr. George Oliver explained the significance of the Temple to Masons in his 1801 book *Revelations of the Square:*

> *The Society adopted the Temple of Solomon for its symbol, because it was the most stable and the most magnificent structure that ever existed, whether we consider its foundation or superstructure; so that of all the societies men have invented, no one was ever more firmly united, or better planned, than the Masons. . . . The edifices which Freemasons build are nothing more than virtues or vices to be erected or destroyed; and in this case heaven only occupies their minds, which soar above the corrupted world. The Temple of Solomon denotes reason and intelligence.*

King Solomon was the son of the legendary leader of the Jews, King David. David himself had attempted and offered to build the First Temple to God, even going as far as to purchase and prepare the land for the site on Mount Moriah, but God refused him the honor, and the duty fell to his son, Solomon. The main accounts of the building of the Temple are to be found in the Old Testament books of Joshua, Judges, Samuel 1 and 2, and Kings 1 and 2.

The dimensions and size of the original Temple are constantly debated, with many of the measurements being of symbolic importance. At the eastern entrance to the Temple stood the two pillars, Boaz and Jachin; today, in every lodge room in the Masonic world, two pillars also called Boaz and Jachin also stand to remind the initiate of the connection to the Temple of Solomon.

In the story of Hiram Abiff, we are told that he is murdered by three assassins, who try to extract from him the secret password of the master Mason. Hiram refuses to divulge the sacred and secret word and is killed. Masons explain this parable as teaching the initiate that one's word is one's bond, and that the brevity of life should be understood.

According to Masonic author Chris McClintock, the ritual in which an initiate is received into Freemasonry incorporates, in a symbolic way, the method by which Hiram Abiff was murdered. In the ritual, the candidate, as Hiram Abiff, is first symbolically cut across the throat with a Masonic rule, in a simulation of the first blow Hiram received. Then the initiate is struck on the left breast with a heavy Masonic square, which is supposedly how the second assailant attacked Hiram. The final and fatal blow (metaphorically) is with a mallet aimed at the head; again in imitation of the original story. It is in this ritual that Hiram is referred to as "the widow's son." In McClintock's soon-to-be-published book *Sun of God*, several astounding revelations are brought to light regarding not only the symbolic and mysterious origins of such rituals but also the hidden deeper identity of Hiram Abiff as well as other characters involved in Masonic ritual.

Within the holy of holies of Solomon's Temple was placed the legendary Ark of the Covenant. This supernatural vessel was said to contain the two tablets that Moses had brought down from Mount Sinai, etched with the Ten Commandments of God. Interestingly, some Freemasonic lodges also include a reproduction of the holy of holies, in which is placed a copy of the Ark of the Covenant. A fine example of this is to be found in the Royal Arch Chapter Room in the lodge (number 22) of Alexandria, Virginia, at the site of the George Washington Masonic Memorial. It is claimed to be the most beautiful reproduction ever created for Masonic purposes.

Today the site of Solomon's Temple is the center of political intrigue and machinations on a global scale. The Temple Mount, as it is now known, is under the control of a Muslim council, leading the chief rabbi to forbid Orthodox Jews from setting foot on the site. To some fundamental Christians, the Temple Mount is the place where the Second Coming of the Messiah will be heralded and the site where the mythical Third Temple will be built. To the fundamentalists on all sides in the debate, the Temple Mount is a rallying call for dogmatic belief and religious intolerance.

Freemasonry, however, sees Solomon's Temple as a movable feast; a temple to the Great Architect of the Universe that can be replicated in multiple locations. It's an example of the "As Above, So Below" Hermetic principle, with the re-creation of God's house on earth. Solomon's Temple was the First Temple to God, intended to be a microcosm of the greater universe.

See also: *Boaz and Jachin, Freemasonry.*

2012

The world is going to end in 2012. To be precise, it will end on December 22, 2012. So say the burgeoning number of believers who are convinced that this fateful day will be our last.

In *The Lost Symbol* the character Peter Solomon discusses the prophecy of the enlightenment of mankind with a group of students. The prediction by cosmologists of a date for this event is revealed as 2012 according to the Mayan calendar.

While a fairly recent phenomenon, the roots of this prophecy lie in antiquity and in particular hinge upon an ancient Mayan calendar known as the Mesoamerican Long Count. Put simply, the current cycle of this calendar comes to an end after some 5,125 years in December 2012.

The Long Count is divided into various cycles. A *uinal* is composed of 20 days; a *tun* is 18 uinals, or 360 days; a *katun* is 20 *tuns*, or 7,200 days; and 20 *katuns*, or 144,000 days, is known as a *baktun*. We know that the Long Count was begun in August 3114 BC, and so far, we have progressed through well over 12 baktuns. More precisely, in the Long Count, as of September 17, 2009, we stood at 12.19.16.12.9.

Some scholars believe that the arrival of 13 baktuns, or a date of 13.0.0.0.0—the very date that will occur on 12.22.12—is a significant event and, in fact, marks the end of the Long Count itself. The number 13 was indeed very sacred to the ancient Mayans, not least of which because it represented the 13 major joints in the body. It is also the number of times the moon orbits the earth during one of our years. One of the sacred Mayan calendars is the ritual calendar known as the *Tzolkin*, which consists of 260 days. That matches the duration of the average human female pregnancy and was also used to track Earth-Venus conjunctions. In the Tzolkin calendar, the number 13 features again, and 260 days are broken down into 13 "months," each of 20 days.

People put such great store in the Mayan calendars, especially the Long Count calendar, with its ominous pointing toward the year 2012, because the culture that created them was obsessed with marking time and was able to do so with remarkable accuracy. Lawrence E. Joseph highlights this in his book *Apocalypse 2012*:

The Maya love their calendars, see them as visual depictions of the passage of time, which is how life unfolds. They charted the unfolding with not one but twenty calendars, only fifteen of which have been released to the modern world; the remaining five are still kept secret by Mayan Elders. Mayan calendars are pegged to the movements of the Sun, the Moon, and the visible planets, to harvest and insect cycles.

This obsessive attitude toward time led to the Mayans making some incredible measurements; for example, they were able to calculate the orbit of Venus to within one day every one thousand years.

Thirteen of the cycles known as a baktun, or 5,125 of our years, compose an "age" that was known to the Mayans as a Sun. According to their detailed beliefs, we are currently in the fourth Sun, having progressed through three Suns in the past. The fifth Sun—if there is to be a fifth—will start on December 22, 2012, which in the Long Count will be 13.0.0.0.0. Literally year zero.

According to Mayan legends, the beginning of our current age, the fourth Sun, actually began with the birth of Venus in the year 3,114 BC. In *The Mayan Prophecies*, Adrian Gilbert and Maurice Cotterell explain why this is significant in relation to 2012:

> As we approach the doomsday year of 2012 which the ancient Mayans prophesied would be the end of the last age, one can only feel apprehension for the future of our Earth. The start of the last Mayan age was the Birth of Venus, the Quetzalcoatl star, on 12 August 3114 BC. On the last day of the age, 22 December 2012, the cosmic connections between Venus, the sun and the Pleiades, and Orion are once more in evidence. For just as Venus was indeed "born" on the earlier date, its rising just before the dawn being heralded by the Pleiades at the meridian, so it now symbolically "dies."

While this makes for dramatic reading, what is not conclusive is what Venus's "dying" actually means for us and the planet Earth. There are many who would assume that the ending of one age simply leads to the beginning of another. That we are moving out of one Mayan age into another is indisputable. The only unknown is how much blood and agony, if any, will be associated with this "birth."

A number of academics believe that they have found within Mayan inscriptions dates that exist *beyond* 13.0.0.0.0. In fact, dates are mentioned that are thousands of years in our future. For example, an event in the year 4772 is highlighted among the inscriptions found at Palenque, in southern Mexico. So, are these academics correct? Is the turning of the calendar and the arrival of 13.0.0.0.0 nothing more than a magnificent event to be celebrated, just another notch on the great calendar?

If you side with the doomsayers who believe that the world really will end in 2012, then there are currently a lot of world-destroying scenarios from which to choose. Aside from the usual round of nuclear wars, threats of disastrous climate change, and mankind-killing plagues, we also have a number of contenders.

Some theories suggest that what will destroy us all in 2012 is a polar shift. This, it is purported, would lead to a crustal displacement, as first theorized by Charles Hapgood in his 1958 book *Earth's Shifting Crust: A Key to Some Basic Problems*. Both ideas are terrifying, and Hapgood even grabbed the attention of Albert Einstein, who not only corresponded and agreed with Hapgood's research, he even endorsed it by writing a foreword to Hapgood's book. In brief, the theory suggests that every few thousand years the earth's poles suddenly shift, moving large distances. When this happens, it can be accompanied by a crustal displacement, in which the crust of the earth moves across the inner core of the earth, shifting the poles over a vast distance and ultimately moving them nearer the equator. It goes without saying that such a movement alone would destroy most of the civilized world, but massive flooding would wipe out anyone and anything that had managed to survive the initial displacement.

Another popular theory is that the sun will flex her muscles and demonstrate her true power come 2012. Quite simply, the sun is not a stable celestial object. Over time, her power waxes and wanes, subject to cycles that are so complex that we are still trying to map them all. The sun is in constant flux, and the surface is not an even temperature. The surface is said to be an average temperature of 5,800 degrees Celsius. However, areas that are much cooler—some 1,500 degrees Celsius cooler—develop due to strong concentrations of magnetic flux on the surface and appear as large black dots on the sun. These are the areas that we call sunspots. This sunspot activity is linked closely to the sun's cycles, and we progress from one solar maximum (the maximum number of sunspots) to a solar minimum, when sunspot activity is at its lowest.

A group of scientists, including S. K. Solanski from the Max Planck Institute for Solar System Research, in Germany, published a report in the journal *Nature* in 2004 explaining that according to their data, the sun has been unusually active since 1940. "Here we report a reconstruction of the sunspot number covering the past 11,400 years," they wrote. "According to our reconstruction, the level of solar activity during the past 70 years is exceptional, and the previous period of equally high activity occurred more than 8,000 years ago. We find that during the past 11,400 years the Sun spent only on the order of

10% of the time at a similarly high level of magnetic activity and almost all of the earlier high activity periods were shorter than the present episode."

This is indeed a strange coincidence; the sun just happens to be demonstrating much higher than usual activity in the run-up to the Long Count end date of 2012. Does the sun have a surprise in store for us in December of that year? While not conclusive, we have to remember that the culture that devised the Long Count calendar spent a vast amount of time viewing the heavens, and many of its calendars are tied closely to the sun.

The sun isn't the only force of nature capable of wiping us out in 2012. There are also large asteroids to consider. A large impact, similar to the one that landed roughly 65.5 million years ago on the coast of the Yucatán landmass (coincidentally, the same landmass that was home to the Mayans), would certainly wipe out civilized life as we know it.

Then there is the idea that our entire solar system is moving as a single unit through the inner space of our galaxy, the Milky Way. Some scientists hypothesize that our system could be moving into a much more active and unstable region of space. Our sun and her planets, including Earth, could be at risk from these dangerous regions of space, and it goes without saying that we would be totally exposed and utterly defenseless against such natural phenomena. Like gears in some vast and ancient machine, we have no control over where our planet and solar system are headed. That we have passed through such regions in the past is without doubt. Did the Mayans possess knowledge of such celestial regions? Did they know the precise date when we would return through such possibly deadly environs?

There have been mass extinctions all throughout Earth's long history. The one undeniable truth is that one will happen again at some point in our future. However, is it likely that such an event is just a few years away?

Having scared the living daylights out of everyone, it is now time to come back down to Earth and try to look logically at where we are now. All of this began because of a date contained in one ancient calendar. While it is without doubt a significant milestone, we cannot be certain that it marked an end-time. In fact, many New Age writers suggest that rather than portending the end of the world, this date actually marks a rebirth. Authors such as John Major Jenkins propose that the Mayans anticipated a great change in humanity's spiritual potential at the end of the current baktun, or age, and many writers have seized on this idea, predicting that human consciousness will develop further in the light of 2012 and usher in a golden age for mankind. Many other people believe that the calendar will tick over with absolutely no drama at all, that it will be just a day like any other.

The truth is that if we are basing the destruction of the world solely on the complex calendars of Mesoamerica, then we have a problem. So many ancient texts were destroyed following the Spanish conquest of Mexico in 1521, led by Hernando Cortés, that we simply no longer have the full story available to us. While fragments of the Mayan beliefs remain, we are missing a great deal. Therefore, all we can really do is wait until December 22, 2012. If we do wake up that morning, we should make sure that we all celebrate, no matter what our beliefs. Subjects such as 2012 make us realize how fragile the very existence of humanity is, and the truth is that it is a miracle that we are here at all. That our entire civilization exists on the surface of one tiny rock that is subject to all the wilds of the galaxy is cause for wonderment.

Washington, DC

Washington, DC, sits on the bank of the Potomac River like a shining diamond amid the rolling hills of Virginia and Maryland. Indeed, the District of Columbia was originally laid out as a diamond shape, some one hundred miles square, with its corners facing the four cardinal compass points, each side of the square being ten miles in length.

The history of Washington, DC, is emblematic of the history of the

United States of America, a nation that rose majestically from the fire and turmoil of revolution. It was President George Washington himself who laid out the plans for the area that was to become this new city of Washington, and eventually the District of Columbia.

Washington is the backdrop to the twelve-hour story that unfolds within the pages of *The Lost Symbol*, and many of its famous landmarks are featured in the novel.

It was in 1790 that the Residence Act was passed, and a new city was planned on the Potomac. Washington dispatched his top surveyor, Andrew Ellicott, to the site, along with a team of surveyors and a very talented individual by the name of Benjamin Banneker. Banneker, the son of a freed slave, had a deep knowledge of astronomy. He and Ellicott would go on to become important players in the birth of this fledgling city. The ten square miles that they surveyed were marked with posts every mile, some of which survive to this day. Once marked out, a new "federal city" was then planned. The year was 1791.

George Washington employed the services of architect and surveyor Pierre Charles L'Enfant, who was asked to produce a design for the city's layout. However, as has been detailed elsewhere in this book, L'Enfant's tenure was short, and the city that we see today is part L'Enfant and part Ellicott, who stepped in to finish the layout and design of the city when L'Enfant was relieved of his post.

In *The Lost Symbol*, while giving a lecture, symbologist Robert Langdon mentions to his students that Washington, DC, has inherent within its design, star charts, astrological signs, and zodiacs. Indeed, Langdon claims that Washington, DC, has more of these symbolic elements that any other city in the world. So what is the truth behind this and the other theories that Washington, DC, is laid out in a sacred and symbolic manner?

According to author David Ovason, there are some twenty complete zodiacs to be found within Washington. In his groundbreaking book *The Secret Architecture of Our Nation's Capital*, Ovason goes on to explain that not only do these zodiacs exist within the fabric and architecture of the city but also that certain buildings and corner-stone-laying ceremonies were inaugurated on auspicious astrological dates. Specifically, Ovason claims that the constellation of Virgo, the Virgin, plays an important role in the foundation of Washington, DC. It is his theory that these astrological alignments were planned and executed by important Freemasons, responsible for the layout and planning of the city as it grew.

Other researchers and conspiracy theorists claim that the very street layout of Washington, DC, hides deeper symbolic meaning. Again, the Freemasons have been blamed for this. One of these so-called satanic features is the appearance to the north of the White House of what appears to be an inverted pentagram, or five-pointed star, with the main point converging on the White House itself.

This can be discerned on a map or satellite image of the capital and seems to be a geometric feature of the layout. However, there is a slight problem with this theory: where Rhode Island Avenue inter-sects with Connecticut Avenue, it fails to continue onward, meaning that the pentagram is missing this extension to its western point.

Others see within the street layout different symbolic elements. For instance, stretching out in a northwesterly direction from the Capitol building is Pennsylvania Avenue, and in a southwesterly di-rection, Maryland Avenue. This configuration is, some claim, indica-tive of a Masonic compass. However, like the supposed inverted pentagram to the north of the White House, Maryland Avenue does not extend fully to the southwest, and therefore the so-called com-pass is longer on one axis than the other.

On the fringes of conspiracy theory, some researchers even see the outline of an owl within the gardens and grounds of the U.S. Capitol. This owl is claimed to be a representation of the so-called Illuminati god Moloch, in turn a biblical reference, and is also claimed to be on the dollar bill. (See the chapter "Dollar Bill Symbolism" for more information.)

Returning to author David Ovason, he notes that the area of the Federal Triangle is also highly symbolic:

It is almost as though L'Enfant laid upon his virgin parchment the Masonic square as symbol of the spirit of George Washington, and dedicated its three points to the founder of the nation. In the early map of the city, these three points formed a right-angle triangle, with the 90-degree angle on the monument, and the hypotenuse running down Pennsylvania Avenue, joining the White House with the Capitol. The longest edge of the triangle runs down the centre of the Mall.

Ovason goes on to say that the triangle, designed by L'Enfant, "is imprinted into the earth, in much the same way as the three Masons draw a triangle with their shoes when they combine to make the Royal Arch."

It is Ovason's theory that the Federal Triangle, as it has come to be known, is an earthly representation of the heavenly triangle of major stars that enclose the constellation of Virgo: Arcturus, Regulus, and Spica. He explains:

the undeniable fact is that this triangle of stars seems to reflect the central triangle in the plan of Washington, DC. The stars of the Virgoan Triangle correspond with the L'Enfant triad as follows:

- *Arcturus falls on the White House;*

- *Regulus falls on the Capitol;*

- *Spica falls on the Washington Monument.*

As mentioned before, one of the men on Andrew Ellicott's surveying team was Benjamin Banneker, who went on to write almanacs and papers on astronomy. Banneker would be the natural choice when looking for someone who potentially influenced this layout.

It would seem that Washington, DC, is both a sacred and symbolic city with an original layout envisioned by Pierre L'Enfant that had deep esoteric meaning.

In his book *The Sacred Geometry of Washington, D.C.*, author Nicholas R. Mann notes: "The challenge is to find the will and imagination to restore and expand the pattern of the original vision. Yet who today has anything like the vision that Pierre L'Enfant experienced in the spring of 1791, when he imagined Washington in relation to the 'celestial axis,' and began to imprint upon the American landscape a geometric pattern that could perfectly represent the revolutionary principle of a new nation? The city L'Enfant dreamt, designed and passionately believed in was to surpass anything that anyone else could imagine at the time—even the vision of George Washington."

See also: *Pierre L'Enfant, George Washington.*

George Washington

Perhaps the image of George Washington wearing Freemasonic regalia and laying the cornerstone of the Capitol building is not the first picture of this great American to spring to mind. It is, however, significant within the pages of *The Lost Symbol*, where the links between the layout and architecture of the capital city of the United States and its first president are described.

In February 1732, George Washington was born into a wealthy Virginia plantation family whose forebears had their origins in England. Since his father died when George was only eleven, much of his formative life was spent with relatives, Another key figure during Washington's youth was neighbor Lord Fairfax, the only British peer resident in Colonial America. Fairfax had Washington accompany a group to survey his lands in the Shenandoah Valley, which young George clearly enjoyed. He was appointed Culpeper County surveyor in 1749.

While still in his early twenties, George first leased and then inherited a fine estate called Mount Vernon from his older half brother, Lawrence, who died of tuberculosis in 1752. The year before, he and

George sailed to the tropical island of Barbados, in an ultimately futile effort to improve his health. (It was Washington's only trip outside America.) George was not to have the luxury of enjoying his inheritance without interruption.

Washington became an officer in the Virginia militia. He played a part in the French and Indian War (the Seven Years War) of 1754–63, during which the governor of Virginia, Robert Dinwiddie, twice gave him commissions to counter French ambitions in Ohio in support of the British interest. In 1755 he was an aide-de-camp to General Edward Braddock on his march to Fort Duquesne in western Pennsylvania. Despite holding the courtesy title of colonel, Washington resented the way the British treated Colonial officers such as himself, who were automatically subordinate to an officer of the same rank who held the king's commission. Braddock was killed by the French when the British forces reached the Monongahela River, forcing George Washington to take charge. He retrieved the situation bravely and had two horses shot from under him during the fighting. In recognition of his valor, Washington was appointed commander of all Virginia troops. He later led a force under Brigadier General John Forbes and recaptured Fort Duquesne. Having seen off the French, and with the honorary rank of brigadier general, Washington left the army in 1758.

In addition to caring for his growing estates, George Washington sat in the Virginia House of Burgesses in Williamsburg. For many years, he was not known for any political opposition to the way his country was being run. Then in 1765 the British parliament passed the Stamp Act. Its aim was to help fund the costs of having British troops in North America to defend the colonists. With no representation in parliament, they were understandably outraged. Violent protest broke out, and it became apparent that the act was not enforceable. By this time, Washington's attitude toward the British interests in North America had begun to harden as his remark about the British parliament demonstrates. The English government, he asserted, had "no more right to put their hands into my pocket, without my consent, than I have to put my hands into yours for money."

By 1774 he signed the resolutions in Virginia that called for the establishment of the Continental Congress, where the colonies would collectively try to resist the actions of the British parliament. Washington was elected as one of the Virginia representatives to the First Continental Congress. Fifteen years after his previous military service, he was again called upon to take up command, when in 1775 he was appointed commander in chief of the Colonial army around Boston, after the battles of Lexington and Concord. His assiduous enforcement of a siege ensured that the British were made to surrender the city and evacuate it in March 1776.

During the following five years, despite setbacks at times, his forces of American patriots achieved success over the British and their loyalist colonist allies. It was Washington's energy and common sense, and the confidence that the army had in him, that contributed to the victory. The war effectively ended when General Charles Lord Cornwallis was forced to surrender at Yorktown, Virginia, in October 1781. Two years later, Washington resigned his commission and returned to his Mount Vernon estate, where he spent the next four years.

As the political situation moved toward a federal government, Washington went to Philadelphia in 1787 to participate in plans to produce a constitution suitable for the union. He was unanimously welcomed as president of the Constitutional Convention. The representatives widened the scope of their original brief, which was to revise the Articles of Confederation that were then in force. The result was that the Constitution of the United States was born, and in 1789, George Washington was elected the first president of the United States of America in another unanimous vote. His inauguration took place in New York, which was then the seat of government. The country reelected him in 1792, and Washington could have run a third time, but he stepped down at the end of his second term, establishing a practice that has now been enshrined in law. In his farewell address to the people of the United States, he offered the following advice: "I hold the maxim no less applicable to public than to private affairs, that honesty is the best policy."

The capital city of America was not fixed for the first few years of the republic's history, and Congress sat in various places, including Philadelphia and then New York. The location of the capital was a contentious one, with these two great cities being rival claimants. There was also a problem of southern states not wanting the capital to be in the north of the country. It was decided to settle on a compromise location, on the Potomac River. In his diary entry for July 12, 1790, President Washington wrote: "Had two bills presented to me by the joint committee of Congress. The one, an act for establishing the temporary and permanent seat of the Government of the United States."

This became the Residence Act, and the size of the new territory was fixed at one hundred square miles. The act specified that there must be a location for Congress to meet by 1800 in the new city, and the president was given the authority to choose the exact site and appoint a surveyor.

George Washington appointed Andrew Ellicott and by 1791 had selected the current site of the present District of Columbia. Pierre L'Enfant, a French architect, began designing the city plan in collaboration with Washington and Thomas Jefferson. In honor of Washington, the new city was named "the City of Washington in the Territory of Columbia."

George Washington is remembered as the "Father of His Country." Most ancient Roman emperors were voted that title by the senate, and the initials *PP*, standing for *"Pater Patriae"* were proudly inscribed on their coins. In the U.S. Senate, there hangs a painting of Washington, titled *Patriae Pater*, by the artist by Rembrandt Peale. Surrounding the image of Washington is a garland of oak leaves and the head of the god Jupiter.

Rome referred to itself as a republic, but the Republic of the United States prides itself on being a true democracy, governed as it is not by oppression but by agreement. Some disaffected Americans, many of them military officers who claimed they had not been paid properly for their efforts in the war, seeing George Washington's great popularity, sought to change his position to that of king, but he rebuffed them. Colonel Lewis Nicola wrote the May 22, 1782, letter to Washington proposing that he become king and received a categorical reply:

> Be assured Sir, no occurrence in the course of the War, has given me more painful sensations than your information of their being such ideas existing in the Army as you have expressed, and I must view with abhorrence, and reprehend with severity.

In his personal life, George Washington married Martha Dandridge (1732–1802) in 1759. She was the widow of Colonel Daniel Custis and had two small children. It is an endearing feature of Washington's personality that he treated these children very much as if they were his own flesh and blood, and he adopted both of them.

Other stories about George Washington showing him as a simple human being include ones that indicate his willingness to perform manual labor when necessary. His wealth and consequent position did not make him too proud, and he enjoyed playing cards, billiards, and other games which gentlemen of his position at that time enjoyed. He was, though, a man of his time and place in that he owned slaves who worked on his land. Washington ensured that they received the services of a doctor when it was required, however, and he refused to sell them, explaining that he was against trading in human beings. He is reputed to have been assiduous in ensuring that his slaves were well fed and adequately clothed; however, for his own clothes, he wore the best available and placed orders with London tailors.

During his presidency, George Washington lived with his wife and their grandchildren in Philadelphia before returning to Mount Vernon two years before his death, on December 12, 1799. There had been plans to bury George Washington in the crypt of the Capitol building, but he instructed in his will that he was to be buried at Mount Vernon. On either side of the entrance to the tomb stand two Egyptian-style obelisks.

As with many of America's Founding Fathers, there is speculation about what George Washington's religious views were. He himself said in a letter to Sir Edward Newenham, in 1792, "Of all the animosities which have existed among mankind those which are caused by a difference of sentiments in religion appear to be the most inveterate and distressing, and ought most to be deprecated."

Washington attended services in Anglican and Episcopalian churches, such as that of Christ Church in Alexandria, Virginia. This has not prevented speculation that in private his views may have been more inclined to Deism, a system that balances belief in God with the laws of nature. Its adherents tend not to participate in some of the sacraments of organized religion, and, consequently, attention has been drawn to whether or not he took Holy Communion. Discussing this question in *The Faiths of the Founding Fathers*, author David Holmes quotes the Episcopalian bishop William White, who said, "General Washington never received the communion, in the churches of which I am parochial minister." On the other hand, it was the opinion of Washington's granddaughter that, prior to the Revolution, he had taken communion with Martha.

It is possible, of course, that both accounts are correct and that his beliefs and religious observance could have changed throughout his life. Given the central part that George Washington plays in the history of America, the subject of his faith is still being hotly debated.

The landmark memorial erected in Washington, DC, commemorating this great man is built of granite faced with Maryland marble. It stands 555 feet high, echoing the monuments erected by the mightiest pharaohs of ancient Egypt. The Washington Monument takes the form of an obelisk, a symbol of pride reaching into the sky. Masonic ceremonies accompanied the laying of its cornerstone in 1848 as described in its separate entry in this book.

To return to George Washington's association with Freemasonry, the following details are given by the George Washington Masonic Memorial. The first lodge with which Washington was associated was the Fredericksburg Lodge in Virginia, into which he was initiated as an entered apprentice on November 4, 1752. He became a master Mason on August 4, 1753, at the age of twenty-one. Washington also became a member of Alexandria Lodge No. 22 and was the Master of this lodge at the time of his presidential inauguration. From his entry into Freemasonry as a young man and his participation in ceremonial Masonic regalia at events such as the cornerstone laying of the Capitol building, it is clear that Freemasonry was an important and enduring part of his life.

Evidence suggests that many of the great men associated with the American Revolution, including Benjamin Franklin, John Paul Jones, Paul Revere, and George Washington were Freemasons. So were the Marquis de Lafayette and most of George Washington's generals, including many of the senior military commanders. Of the signatories to the Declaration of Independence, nine were members and seven others were at least closely associated with Freemasonry. The forty who signed the Constitution included nine Masons, thirteen men who may well have been, and six others who later joined the craft.

It says a great deal about the character and integrity of George Washington that even his defeated adversary, the stolid British king George III, appreciated his character and sacrifice for his country. The king is said to have remarked that if the commander in chief surrendered his position and returned to private life, he would be "the greatest man in the world."

See also: *Washington Masonic Memorial, Washington Monument.*

Washington Masonic Memorial

When the characters Robert Langdon and Katherine Solomon need to create a diversion to their destination in *The Lost Symbol*, they suggest that they are visiting the George Washington Masonic Memorial. This important Masonic edifice is located in Alexandria, south of Washington, DC, and provides a cover for them to take the Metro transport system, although they ultimately head off elsewhere.

Like many important buildings in the city, the architecture of the classical world inspired the design. The George Washington Masonic

Memorial is based upon a famous lighthouse in Alexandria, Egypt, known as the Pharos, which in its day was considered one of the seven wonders of the ancient world. At the summit of the tower is an Egyptian pyramid and a representation of a flame in reference to the function of the lighthouse. Of course, the city that once housed the famous lighthouse and the location for the memorial share the name Alexandria.

Washington was a member of Alexandria Lodge No. 22, but unlike most Masonic buildings, this memorial is supported by lodges from all fifty-two Grand Lodges in the United States. In 1910 Joseph Eggleston, the Grand Master of Virginia, had invited every Grand Master in the United States to attend a meeting with the intention of planning and building a memorial to George Washington. Items of Washington's Masonic regalia and important documents were being housed in the Alexandria-Washington Lodge, but there were concerns about whether they were sufficiently safe there.

The architect was Harvey W. Corbett, and in addition to the Egyptian influences in the building, he included an entrance inspired by the Greek temple the Parthenon in Athens and adorned the memorial with a mixture of ancient styles.

The building had its cornerstone laid on November 1, 1923, in a Masonic ceremony attended by President Calvin Coolidge and former president William Taft, himself a Freemason. In 1932, two hundred years after George Washington's birth, the memorial was dedicated, again with presidential support; this time Herbert Hoover participated.

Internal work continued until final completion in 1970, although as recently as 1999, the well-known Masonic symbol of the square and compass was installed on the lawn.

On the first floor are the shrine rooms used by the Ancient Arabic Order of Nobles of the Mystic Shrine, or Shriners, who are also referred to in *The Lost Symbol*. In the museum dedicated to George Washington, on the fourth floor of the tower, are displayed various items of his Masonic regalia. These include his apron used in the ceremony of laying the cornerstone of the Capitol building. George Washington held the office of Master of Alexandria Lodge when he was inaugurated as the first president of the United States in 1789, and it was after his death that the lodge was renamed Alexandria-Washington Lodge No. 22.

The location in Alexandria chosen for the memorial had once been suggested by Thomas Jefferson as the site of the U.S. Capitol, and it was close to other sites familiar to George Washington, such as Christ Church, where he used to worship.

In the Royal Arch chapter room, there are wall paintings of Hebrew and Egyptian design and a depiction of the ruins of Solomon's Temple, a key theme in Masonry. There is also a replica of the Arc of the Covenant that was, of course, housed in the Temple of Solomon, according to the Old Testament. The murals are all the work of the artist Allyn Cox, who was also commissioned to complete the frieze in the Capitol building rotunda that was left unfinished upon the death of artist Constantino Brumidi.

See also: *Constantino Brumidi, Freemasonry, Shriners, George Washington.*

Washington Monument

Standing a magnificent 555 feet tall, this imposing monument is the tallest building in Washington, DC, and is the tallest freestanding masonry-built structure in the world, as well as the world's tallest obelisk.

On the spine of the book jacket to the U.S. edition of *The Lost Symbol,* you can see the Washington Monument visible through the keyhole. This hints at the revelation within the book, that it is below this lofty tower that the lost symbol itself is to be found.

Construction of this incredible edifice, which was designed by architect Robert Mills, began in 1848 and was completed in 1884.

However, it was left in an unfinished state for a number of years while the American Civil War raged. In fact, if you should visit the monument, look up about one-third of the way, at approximately 150 feet from the ground, and you'll see a subtle change in the shading of the masonry, revealing the point at which work stopped and then continued after the war's end.

The original design for the Washington Monument called for a neoclassical column some 600 feet in height, and, around its base, a colonnade that would have supported a monument of a chariot and horses. Thankfully, this was soon dropped in favor of the more Egyptian-style obelisk we see today. Interestingly, one of the early design proposals called for a mausoleum modeled on one of the seven wonders of the ancient world: the Mausoleum of King Mausolus at Halicarnassus in modern-day Turkey. Though this design idea was not used for the Washington Monument, it would resurface many years later in the design and construction of the House of the Temple, the headquarters of the Scottish Rite Freemasonry, Southern Jurisdiction, in Washington, DC.

Originally, Congress had voted in 1783 to build a statue of George Washington on horseback, and a site was agreed upon. But by 1800, these plans had been shelved, and the above-mentioned mausoleum was proposed instead, to be built of American granite and marble. This project got as far as a foundation stone being laid in 1804 by President Thomas Jefferson, but the stone sank into the soggy marsh. Funds for the monument then dried up for a significant period of time.

The Washington National Monument Society, formed in 1833, reinitiated the plan for a memorial and launched a competition to choose the ultimate design. The designer of an earlier monument to Washington, in Baltimore, Robert Mills, was the winner. Mills planned an obelisk some 600 feet in height, but his initial design was modified after the intervention of George Perkins Marsh. He was the U.S. minister to Italy from 1861 until his death in 1882. However, Marsh is better known as America's first environmentalist. While in Italy, Marsh undertook a study of the many Egyptian obelisks in Rome (there are more standing obelisks in Rome than in Egypt), and even went so far as to undertake a trip to Egypt to learn more.

From his research, Marsh determined that the Egyptian obelisks were constructed to certain set proportions. He calculated that the height of the Egyptian obelisks were ten times their baseline; that the obelisk walls would converge at a height some twenty times its baseline; that the angle of the pyramidion on top of the obelisk rarely deviated from 73 degrees; that the height of the pyramidion was equal to the baseline; and that the obelisk tapered at about a quarter inch per foot.

"Throw out all the gingerbread of the Mills's design!" was Marsh's advice, and it is his influence that is responsible for the elegant and monumental edifice we see today. Based on his research, Marsh declared that the monument's design should be reduced in height from 600 feet to 555 feet.

Originally intended to stand directly south of the White House and directly west of the Capitol, the Washington Monument was moved to its present location because of the unsuitability of the damp and uneven soil at the original construction point. Today a small granite marker sits at the original site, commemorating the Jefferson Pier, which marked the second prime meridian of the United States. This marker sits some 390 feet west-northwest of the monument.

On July 4, 1848, the cornerstone-laying ceremony took place, with James K. Polk, the eleventh president of the United States, and a Mason, undertaking the honors. Some twenty thousand people came to witness the spectacle. In 1847 Polk had also officiated at the cornerstone-laying ceremony for the Smithsonian Institution.

Originally, the marble used to construct the monument was quarried in Maryland, but after the Civil War, this source dried up, so marble from Massachusetts was used instead. During the Civil War, when work was halted, the grounds around the partially completed obelisk were used as a drill field for the Union army. Writer and humorist Mark Twain remarked on the monument at this time that it "looked like a hollow oversized chimney."

For twenty-five years, the monument stood untouched. Finally, in 1876, responsibility for surveying the entire site was handed over to the U.S. Army Engineers, with Lieutenant Colonel Thomas L. Casey being the officer in charge. Casey went on to perform an amazing job at the site. The fact that the monument not only still stands on such sodden and waterlogged ground but also that it hasn't deviated due to settlement over the years is a great testament to his skills as an engineer.

One of the interesting facts about the monument is that individual blocks, most with inscriptions, were donated to the construction effort from throughout the United States and around the world. Casey managed to include most of these stones on the interior of the tower. One donated stone in particular was to cause quite an incident. In the early 1850s, Pope Pius IX donated a piece of marble to the project. This piece of marble was then stolen and hurled into the Potomac River in 1854 by the anti-Catholic nativist American Party, sometimes known at the time as the Know-Nothings.

On February 22, 1885—the 153rd anniversary of George Washington's birth—up to one thousand people attended the formal dedication ceremony. Thomas L. Casey was one the speakers in attendance, along with President Chester Alan Arthur.

When the monument first opened to the public, in 1888, the steam-powered central elevator was seen as unsafe for women to use, so that ladies and children had to take the 897 steps to the top to admire the view. (They might have gotten there quicker using their feet, as the elevator would take upward of twenty minutes to reach the top.) Upon the obelisk's completion, it became the tallest structure in the world and remained so until the construction of the Eiffel Tower in Paris in 1889.

In *The Lost Symbol*, the Washington Monument is given Masonic symbolic meaning, and the denouement of the story takes place at the site. So, what Masonic connections does the monument have?

We know for certain that architect Robert Mills was a Freemason, as were most of the members of the Washington National Monument

Society. There was also President Polk, who laid the cornerstone. The ceremony was presided over by Benjamin B. French, Grand Master of the Grand Lodge of the District of Columbia, who wore the apron and sash that had belonged to George Washington himself, and that had been worn at the laying of the cornerstone of the Capitol building.

At the cornerstone-laying ceremony of the Washington Monument, a considerable deposit of interesting items was buried in the foundation. Dan Brown alludes to one of these items in the plot of *The Lost Symbol:* namely, a copy of the Holy Bible. Among the numerous items, there are also copies of the U.S. Constitution and the Declaration of Independence; various plans and sketches of the monument's design; a catalog of the Library of Congress; a collection of U.S. coins, from the half dime to the gold eagle; the American flag; and the Washington family coat of arms.

According to author and researcher, David Ovason, "In the original design, near the top of the obelisk, there was to have been an enormous five-pointed star." This star, like those on the American flag, has been claimed to be a Masonic symbol representing the star Sirius.

The capstone on the pyramidion, a piece of pure aluminum weighing 100 ounces, was fixed in place and dedicated in a Masonic ceremony on December 6, 1884. The pyramidion has thirteen courses, mimicking the unfinished pyramid of the Great Seal, seen every day on the dollar bill.

There is, however, a problem with the idea that the Washington Monument was completely Masonic in its execution. Although Robert Mills was a Freemason, his original design was replaced by the revised plan of George Perkins Marsh and Thomas L. Casey, neither of whom has been proven to have belonged to any lodge.

Interestingly, though, when we study the height and proportions of the Washington Monument, it becomes plain that number symbolism does play a significant role at the site. In *The Sacred Geometry of Washington, D.C.*, Nicholas R. Mann states:

It seems very likely that the decision to make the monument 555 feet 5+ inches high was influenced by one or a number of the branches of Freemasonry that existed in the city at that time. These men would have had specific symbolism and meanings in mind that related to the number 5. Why the precise angle of the five-pointed pentacle, or the pentalpha, 72 degrees, was not used for the crowning pyramidion seems therefore to pose us with something of a mystery.

Yet by considering the dimensions of the monument in inches we can solve the mystery. The obelisk's total height in inches is 6665.125+, which can be justifiably rounded up to 6666. The height of its pyramidion in inches is 660. The sides of its base in inches are 661.5 Then it is necessary to consider the angle of slope from the four corners of the base to the tip of the pyramidion. This is exactly 66 degrees 6 seconds, revealing the hidden number 666.

The number symbolism inherent within the monument seems to point to 5 and 6 being the prevalent digits—both numbers of great significance in Freemasonic lore and in the ancient world.

In *The Lost Symbol*, it is revealed that on the eastern face of the aluminum capstone is the Latin phrase *Laus Deo*, meaning, "praise be to God."

This is indeed true, with all four sides of the cap bearing the following inscriptions:

North Face:
Joint Commission
at
Setting of Capstone
Chester A. Arthur
W. W. Corcoran, Chairman
M. E. Bell
Edward Clark
John Newton
Act of August 2, 1876

West Face:
Corner Stone Laid on Bed of Foundation
July 4, 1848
First Stone at Height of 152 Feet Laid
August 7, 1880
Capstone set December 6, 1884

South Face:
Chief Engineer and Architect,
Thos. Lincoln Casey,
Colonel, Corps of Engineers

Assistants:
George W. Davis,
Captain, 14th Infantry
Bernard R. Green,
Civil Engineer
Master Mechanic
P. H. McLaughlin

East Face:
Laus Deo

There has been recent controversy over the display of a replica of the aluminum capstone at the visitor center. With the original capstone 555 feet off the ground, and hence inaccessible, the U.S. National Park Service has a copy on display. The object was displayed so that the side with *Laus Deo* carved into it was set against a wall and therefore not visible. As of 2007, the written material next to the display was also missing the reference to the east side of the capstone—whereas previously it had contained the explanation "The casting was inscribed with the phrase *Laus Deo* (praise be to God)."

A group of those who saw the deliberate elimination of God from this national monument was mobilized to contact the National Park

Service, and the campaign was reported on in the national news. In the face of protests, the capstone was rotated so that the *Laus Deo* inscription can be read and the associated notice adjusted to include details of the inscription.

The Washington Monument stands today as a permanent and enduring symbol of endurance through adversity. Its message, like a lightning bolt from the heavens, is indelibly marked upon the fabric of Washington, DC, and it towers over the city as a fitting tribute to the first leader of the fledgling nation. It has stood through turbulent and tumultuous times, and led President Herbert Hoover to say of it, while in the midst of the stock market crash of 1929, "this apparently is the only stable thing in my administration."

See also: *Dollar Bill Symbolism, Freemasonry, House of the Temple*.

Washington National Cathedral

Having evaded the CIA, Robert Langdon and Katherine Solomon dash to the Washington National Cathedral, where they have been sent by the enigmatic old man, following his suggestion to go to a refuge containing ten stones from Mount Sinai, one from heaven itself, and one with the visage of Luke's dark father.

Set on fifty-seven acres, the magnificent Washington National Cathedral took eighty-three years to complete after the first stone was laid in 1907. The foundation stone was laid by President Theodore Roosevelt, a Freemason, and the stone itself came from Bethlehem in the Holy Land. The $65 million cost of its construction was raised solely by public donation, as is its maintenance and upkeep today. Based on the design by the English architect George Frederick Bodley, a famed proponent of the neo-Gothic revival, the Episcopalian cathedral church is dedicated to Saint Peter and Saint Paul.

Bodley died in 1907—followed ten years later by Henry Vaughan, his supervising architect. At that point, the design of the cathedral came under the auspices of American architect Philip Frohman. He continued in the spirit of Bodley's master plan, making additions and changes where required. Today the Washington National Cathedral is the sixth largest cathedral in the world, with seating for four thousand. Its east-to-west central aisle is 517 feet long and spans 104 feet; its two enormous front-facing towers are 232 feet tall; and its central tower stand thirty stories high. If you take into account the fact that the ground the building sits on is 676 feet above sea level, the central tower marks the highest point in Washington, DC (although not the tallest structure; that distinction belongs to the Washington Monument). The two symmetrical towers of the west-facing façade dedicated to saints Peter and Paul are decorated with no fewer than 288 angels. Rising out of the mid-nave crossing, the enormous Gloria in Excelsis Tower houses 53 carillon bells and 10 peal bells, the only complete set of both bells in the United States. Built in a unique, Gothic-inspired style, the Washington National Cathedral has all the conventional Gothic elements of flying buttresses, soaring arches and vaulted ceilings, carved stones, and large stained glass and rose windows.

As with any Gothic cathedral, gargoyles and grotesques are important architectural elements, of which the Washington National Cathedral boasts 112. Gargoyles are carved stone waterspouts, usually in the form of unusual or evil-looking humans or animals, whose purpose it is to direct rainwater away from the structure. Grotesques, on the other hand, while having the same purpose, do not contain waterspouts—rainwater simply bounces off them. Examples of these can be found on the front and sides of the cathedral and include a curly-haired man reading a book, a cat clinging to the top of a tree, a dragon, a coiled snake, a three-eyed man with a millstone around his neck, the Greek god Pan with his pipes, a devil holding a pitchfork and a basket of fruit, a snake twisting around the skeleton of a winged creature, and a fat, warty toad.

Its most famous and unique gargoyle, however, features the face of Darth Vader. Yes, that Darth Vader. Situated high upon the St. Peter Tower, the *Star Wars* villain took third prize in a competition held in the 1980s to design a new gargoyle. This is the face of Luke's father that is mentioned in *The Lost Symbol*.

Built in Indiana limestone, the cathedral contains many architectural materials from specific sites around the world. The Canterbury pulpit, which depicts the translation of the Bible from Latin into English, was carved from stone from Canterbury Cathedral in England. The bishop's seat, the Glastonbury cathedra, is made from stone from Glastonbury in England, while the stone for the Jerusalem altar came from a quarry close to Jerusalem, and the ten stones in front of the Jerusalem altar—representing the Ten Commandments—came from Mount Sinai.

The front of the cathedral has a creation theme carved above the three doors; the creation of day is depicted above the left door, the creation of mankind above the middle door, and the creation of night above the right door. Between the three main doors, the theme running through the decorations is one of redemption through faith. As such, the statues depict Saint Peter with his fishing net, representing the moment he was called to Christ's ministry; Adam emerging from a stone; and Saint Paul blinded by God, representing the moment of his conversion to Christianity.

Inside the cathedral, the sixteen bays on each side of the wide nave hold statues, carvings, and stained glass windows detailing diverse aspects of the United States's heritage, such as the search for freedom; the 1803 Lewis and Clark expedition; aspects of law; Woodrow Wilson, the twenty-eighth president; an image of Martin Luther King Jr., who preached his last sermon in the cathedral just days before he was assassinated in 1968; images of world peace; the roles of Christian women; a depiction of the 23rd Psalm ("The Lord is my shepherd . . ."); and a bronze statue of Abraham Lincoln. There is also a window dedicated to the Confederate generals Robert E. Lee and Thomas "Stonewall" Jackson, and a space window containing a piece of moon rock, which commemorates the Apollo 11 mission.

In all, the Cathedral has 215 stained glass windows, including three rose windows that feature brightly colored glass. In the middle of the nave is the West Rose Window, which details the creation story, while the North Rose Window relates to the Last Judgment, and the South Rose Window celebrates the Church Triumphant. The 18 windows of the nave clerestory show the preparation for the Messiah.

At the east end of the Cathedral is the high altar, separated from the main nave by an ornately carved rood screen. Behind the high altar is the magnificent Ter Sanctus Reredos, featuring 110 carved figures surrounding the central figure of Jesus. The cathedral has eight chapels: the War Memorial Chapel, the Children's Chapel (built to the scale of a six-year-old), St. John's Chapel and St. Mary's Chapel in the far nave, and the Good Shepherd Chapel, Bethlehem Chapel, Chapel of St. Joseph of Arimathea, and Resurrection Chapel, all situated in the crypt. The four crypt chapels are of a Romanesque design, to imitate the tradition of building Gothic cathedrals over earlier Norman churches.

Once a month, a large canvas labyrinth is placed on the floor of the central nave to enable the public to walk in prayer using the pattern of the famous labyrinth at Chartres Cathedral in France. The Washington National Cathedral, nominated as the National House of Prayer, has hosted the state funerals of four presidents and inaugural services for newly elected presidents. There are 220 people interred there, including President Woodrow Wilson, Helen Keller and her teacher Anne Sullivan, and the Cathedral architects Philip Frohman and Henry Vaughan.

Zohar

The notion that twentieth-century discoveries in physics such as string theory could have been predicted by ancient texts appears astonishing. However, this is the very idea suggested to the noetic scientist Katherine Solomon by her brother, Peter, in *The Lost Symbol*. The remarkable text that seems to contain advanced concepts of the way the universe is constructed is *The Zohar*.

This book of Jewish mystical lore is seen as one of the most important works within the Kabbalah, its name translating literally as "splendor" or "radiance." *The Zohar* became the central text of the Kabbalah, developing in western Europe sometime in the twelfth and thirteenth centuries. It is a collection of texts that are seen as some of the highest expressions of Jewish literary and mystical imagination ever written.

Arthur Green, in his book *A Guide to the Zohar*, has this to say about the sacred text:

> *The Zohar is a work of sacred fantasy. To say this about it is by no means to impugn the truth of its insights or to diminish the religious profundity of its teachings. The Middle Ages were filled with fantasy. Angels and Demons, heavenly principalities, chambers of heaven and rungs within the soul, secret treasures of the spirit that could be seen only by the elect, esoteric domains without end—all of these were found in the writings of Jewish, Christian, and Islamic authors throughout medieval times.*

It should be noted that *The Zohar* is not a single entity but, rather, a series of books. In some modern translations, there are some twenty-three volumes in the set. Today debate rages between two camps over the ultimate origins of *The Zohar*, with one, as noted above, believing that the text was set down in medieval times. The alternative view, as put forward by scholars such as Gershom Scholem, suggests that the text originated around the first or second century AD.

What impresses Katherine within the pages of *The Zohar* are the depictions of the ten Sephiroth. Peter Solomon then notes that these can be interpreted as the ten dimensions of the quantum universe. In effect: string theory.

Within *The Zohar*, there is indeed described the concept known as the Sephiroth, which when translated means "enumerations," of which there are ten through which God reveals himself. These ten emanations are seen as different spiritual aspects of the Godhead, and when laid out on paper, they form the traditional Kabbalah Tree of Life. God, as a concept within *The Zohar*, is seen as embodying both male and female aspects, and even has a female "counterpart" called the Shekinah. This idea of an ancient "Sacred Feminine" is something that Dan Brown has explored before in his previous book, *The Da Vinci Code*.

When the circumpunct symbol is being discussed by Robert Langdon and the dean of Washington National Cathedral, within *The Lost Symbol*, the Kether, the highest Sephiroth is said to have been represented by kabbalists using the circumpunct.

The Zohar is a complex and detailed text that demands deep study and a lifetime of understanding. Its secrets and mysteries are only now beginning to come to light as more and more people in the twenty-first century begin looking for a more spiritual dimension to their lives.

Acknowledgments

Books are only made possible by many people. In the case of books written in double-quick time, this is doubly true. My gratitude and love go out to the following quite amazing people who have helped, encouraged, cajoled, and generally supported me in the effort before you. I thank them all from the bottom of my heart:

For their efforts in making this book appear like magic from nothing, thanks to: Susan Davies and Mark Foster, who have been utterly amazing; Ian Robertson, Freemason, esotericist, Scot, and quite brilliant; Jackie Harvey, for her top-notch (as always) work; Ace Trump: Ace Trump, for efforts above and beyond and for being a true friend throughout everything—and for the photos too; Ed Davies of Ancient World Research, for the extra research and material; William Henry and Mark Gray, for the use of the photographs and quotes. Your book on the Apotheosis is awesome.

M. J. Miller, Joel Schroeder, and Steve Honig, the American connection who have been supportive, kind, and positive throughout everything, thank you. And M.J., it's not all about me anymore! Thanks to John Payne, musical genius, friend, and a great guy. Look out for the Architects of Time CD *Decoding The Lost Symbol* by John and friends. Chris McClintock: I'm sure *Sun of God* will be a big hit. I'd also like to express my appreciation to Bob and Shirley Hicks in Georgia, Henu Productions, and all at www.intotheduat.com and www.decodingthelostsymbol.com for a great thrill ride.

My mum and dad on Gozo have been awesome. With everything you have gone through and for your amazing fighting spirit and support of me, I am in awe.

More thanks: Mark Cox for the words of encouragement. Salah Tawfik and Ahmed Ali in Cairo, great friends—here's to a great future together in friendship and business. Mark and Jill Oxbrow, for your unwavering optimism and friendship. Edgar and Dave at Casa Hayworth for looking after Jenn. Judith at Casa Hayworth for the insights. Michael Paige and Charlotte. Gemma Smith; good luck in Oz, Gemms! The guys in Agalloch for letting me use the music. Greg

Taylor at the *Daily Grail*. Adam Parsons, Kim Nielson-Parsons, Joe Sutton, Marie Tang, and all at MPTF.

In the publishing world, I would like to thank Trish Todd at Touchstone Fireside/Simon & Schuster: you have been a dream to work with, along with Danielle, Martha, Philip, and all your colleagues at the imprint. The Pan Macmillan team in Oz have been great too. The guys at Generate—Jared, Chris, Michael, Matthew—my new management team in L.A., are real superstars, and I'm looking forward to working with them on all my future projects. Additional thanks go out to Laurie Petok, for the Upper Class euphoria and the amazing introduction and friendship; and to Betty and Chip Clymer in New Jersey, for the kindness and hospitality and for a beautiful blue-eyed girl.

To all my Facebook friends and Twitter followers (@FindSimon Cox), many of you have been wonderfully supportive, even though we have never met. A second mention goes out to Mark Foster—this time in his guise as graphic designer and artist: a brilliant cover on the UK edition, matey! Sushi Dan on Sunset has the best white tuna sashimi in the world! Aaron and Emily at Greenblatt's in L.A.: I told you it was a stone! Thanks to Yolanda in Northern Ireland and Viv in Edinburgh for the amazing hospitality. David Ritchie up on Skye for the insights and education; Robert John at Robert John Photography, for the incredible headshots; and Robert and Olivia Temple for the friendship, great conversations, and for writing the best book on the Sphinx ever. Beth Andrews: it's only the beginning.

Oh, yes, to Dan Brown: you keep the Langdon novels coming, I'll keep doing the guides!

Thanks to Claire Cox, Mark and Tina Finnell, Lynn Schroeder, Dennis on Gozo, Richard Ranken, Richard Belfield, Gordon Rutter and all the Edinburgh crew, the Marina Court mob, Jane and Alexander, Neil and Alison (and Joe and Imogene) Roberts, Jon Rappoport, Michael Cremo, and John Major Jenkins.

It's at this point in my books that I usually give a rundown of my musical listening pleasure while writing. Usually it's been a heavy mix, with lots of dark, gothic, heavy material. This time around, though, slightly different: female jazz/blues singers have graced the CD player as much as rock bands, with Melody Gardot, Jackie Allen, Sophie Milman, and Madeleine Peyroux all whispering softly in my ear. On the other side of the coin, Muse, Epica, Kamelot, Amorphis, Agalloch, and Wuthering Heights, to name a few, have let me know I am still alive.

I will have missed people, I'm sure. And for that I am sorry and hope that you will forgive me. It's been a long, hard road to get to this point, and I am indebted to you all. Thank you.

Finally, to Jennifer Elizabeth Clymer: You are my light in the darkness. Thank you for everything. For being you. For your kindness and support. For your love and compassion. I love, respect and adore you. Beren.

Bibliography

AA City Map & Mini Guide: Washington. Cheadle, UK: AA Publishing, 2008.

Anderson, Aaron, and Becca Blond. *Lonely Planet Washington, DC.* Lonely Planet, 2007.

Arcana Mundi: Magic and the Occult in the Greek and Roman Worlds: A Collection of Ancient Texts. Trans. Georg Luck. Baltimore: Johns Hopkins University Press, 2006.

Atkinson, William Walter. *The Secret Doctrine of the Rosicrucians.* Forgotten Books, 2008.

Bacon, Francis. *The Essays.* Gloucestershire, UK: Dodo Press, 2006.

———. *The New Atlantis.* Gloucestershire, UK: Dodo Press, 2006.

Baines, John, and Jaromír Malék. *Atlas of Ancient Egypt.* New York: Facts on File, 1980.

Bartlett, Robert Allen. *Real Alchemy: A Primer of Practical Alchemy.* Lake Worth, FL: Ibis Press, 2009.

Bartrum Giulia. *Albrecht Dürer and His Legacy: The Graphic Work of a Renaissance Artist.* London: British Museum Press, 2007.

Bauer Alain. *Isaac Newton's Freemasonry: The Alchemy of Science and Mysticism.* Trans. Ariel Godwin. Rochester, VT: Inner Traditions, 2007.

Bauval, Robert. *Secret Chamber: The Quest for the Hall of Records.* London: Arrow, 2000.

Bauval, Robert, and Graham Hancock. *Keeper of Genesis: A Quest for the Hidden Legacy of Mankind.* London: Arrow, 1997.

Bayley, Harold. *The Lost Language of Symbolism.* Garden City, NY: Dover Publications, 2006.

Berg, Rav P. S. *The Essential Zohar: The Source of Kabbalistic Wisdom.* New York: Harmony/Bell Tower, 2004.

Bernstein, Richard B. *Thomas Jefferson.* New York: Oxford University Press, 2005.

Bierlein, J. F. *Parallel Myths.* New York: Ballantine Books, 1994.

Black, Jonathan. *The Secret History of the World: As Laid Down by the Secret Societies.* London: Quercus, 2007.

Blanchard, John. *Scottish Rite Masonry.* Vol. 1. Bensenville, IL: Lushena Books, 2001.

Bryan, John Morrill. *Robert Mills: America's First Architect.* New York: Princeton Architectural Press, 2001.

Capt, E. Raymond. *King Solomon's Temple: A Study of Its Symbolism.* Muskogee, OK: Artisan Publishers, 2006.

Churton, Tobias. *The Golden Builders: Alchemists, Rosicrucians, First Freemasons.* Boston: Weiser Books, 2005.

Clark I. Edward. *Hiram Abif, Jubelum and King Solomon's Temple: A Solar Allegory.* Kentucky: Masonic Home Journal, 1929.

Cox, Simon. *Cracking The Da Vinci Code: The Unauthorized Guide to the Facts Behind the Fiction.* London: Michael O'Mara, 2004.

———. *The Dan Brown Companion.* Edinburgh: Mainstream Publishing, 2006.

———. *Illuminating Angels & Demons: The Unauthorized Guide to the Facts Behind Dan Brown's Bestselling Novel.* New York: Sterling Publishing, 2005.

Cox, Simon, and Susan Davies. *An A to Z of Ancient Egypt.* Edinburgh: Mainstream Publishing, 2007.

Cox, Simon, and Mark Foster. *An A to Z of Atlantis.* Edinburgh: Mainstream Publishing, 2008.

———. *An A to Z of the Occult.* Edinburgh: Mainstream Publishing, 2008.

Dell, Pamela. *Benedict Arnold: From Patriot to Traitor.* Minneapolis: Compass Point Books, 2005.

Dobbs, Betty Jo Teeter. *The Foundations of Newton's Alchemy.* Cambridge and New York: Cambridge University Press, 1983.

———. *The Janus Faces of Genius: The Role of Alchemy in Newton's Thought.* Cambridge and New York: Cambridge University Press, 2002.

Drury, Nevill. *The Dictionary of the Esoteric: Over 3000 Entries on the Mystical & Occult Traditions.* London: Watkins Publishing, 2002.

Ellis, Joseph J. *American Creation: Triumphs and Tragedies at the Founding of the Republic.* New York: Knopf, 2007.

———. *His Excellency: George Washington.* New York: Vintage, 2005.

Fara, Patricia. *Newton: The Making of Genius*. New York: Columbia University Press, 2004.

Ferling, John E. *The Ascent of George Washington: The Hidden Political Genius of an American Icon*. New York: Bloomsbury Press, 2009.

Flammel, *Nicholas. Nicholas Flammel's Theory and Practice of the Philosopher's Stone*. Whitefish, MT: Kessinger Publishing, 2005.

Freke, Timothy, and Peter Gandy. *The Hermetica: The Lost Wisdom of the Pharaohs*. New York, Tarcher, 2008.

Gardiner, Philip. *Gnosis: The Secret of Solomon's Temple Revealed*. Franklin Lakes, NJ: New Page Books, 2006.

Gest, Kevin L. *The Secrets of Solomon's Temple: Discover the Hidden Truth That Lies at the Heart of Freemasonry*. Beverly, MA: Fair Winds Press, 2007.

Grabar, Oleg. *The Dome of the Rock*. Cambridge, MA: Belknap Press of Harvard University Press, 2006.

Green, Arthur. *A Guide to the Zohar*. Stanford, CA: Stanford University Press, 2003.

Greer, John Michael. *The Element Encyclopedia of Secret Societies and Hidden History: The Ultimate A-Z of Ancient Mysteries, Lost Civilizations and Forgotten Wisdom*. London: Harper Element, 2006.

Hall, Manly P. *Lectures on Ancient Philosophy*. New York: Tarcher, 2005.

———. *The Secret Destiny of America*. Los Angeles: Philosophical Research Society, 2000.

———. *The Secret Teachings of All Ages*. New York: Tarcher, 2006.

Hamblin, William J., and David Rolph Seely. *Solomon's Temple: Myth and History*. New York: Thames & Hudson, 2007.

Hancock, Graham, and Robert Bauval. *Talisman: Sacred Cities, Secret Faith*. London: Michael Joseph, 2004.

Hauck, Dennis William. *The Complete Idiot's Guide to Alchemy*. New York: Alpha, 2008.

Heaton, Mary Margaret. *The History of the Life of Albrecht Dürer of Nürnberg: With a translation of his letters and journal, and some account of his works*. New York: Adamant Media Corporation, 2005.

Hermetica: The Greek Corpus Hermeticum and the Latin Asclepius in a New English Translation. Notes and Introduction by Brian P. Copenhaver. Cambridge and New York: Cambridge University Press, 1992.

Hieronimus, Robert. *Founding Fathers, Secret Societies: Freemasons, Illuminati, Rosicrucians, and the Decoding of the Great Seal.* Rochester, VT: Destiny Books, 2005.

Higgins, Frank C. *American Masons May Restore Solomon's Temple.* Whitefish, MT: Kessinger Publishing, 2005.

Holmes, David L. *The Faiths of the Founding Fathers.* New York: Oxford University Press, 2006.

Horne, Alexander. *King Solomon's Temple in the Masonic Tradition.* New York: HarperCollins, 1989.

Huie, W. G. *King Solomon's Temple Its Design, Symbolism and Relationship to the Bible* (pamphlet). Whitefish, MT: Kessinger Publishing, 2006.

King, David. *Finding Atlantis: A True Story of Genius, Madness, and an Extraordinary Quest for a Lost World.* New York: Harmony, 2005.

Klein, Mina C., and H. Arthur Klein. *Temple Beyond Time: The Story of the Site of Solomon's Temple* at Jerusalem. New York: Van Nostrand Reinhold, 1970.

Knight, Christopher, and Alan Butler. *Civilization One: The World Is Not as You Thought It Was.* London: Watkins Publishing, 2005.

———. *Solomon's Power Brokers: The Secrets of Freemasonry, the Church, and the Illuminati.* London: Watkins Publishing, 2007.

Knight, Christopher, and Robert Lomas. *The Book of Hiram: Freemasonry, Venus and the Secret Key to the Life of Jesus.* London: Harper Element, 2003.

———. *The Hiram Key: Pharaohs, Freemasonry, and the Discovery of the Secret Scrolls of Jesus.* Beverly, MA: Fair Winds Press, 2001.

———. *Uriel's Machine: The Ancient Origins of Science.* London: Arrow, 2000.

Laitman, Rav Michael. *Introduction to the Book of Zohar.* New York: Bnei Baruch/Laithman Kabbalah Publishers, 2005.

Lomas, Robert. *The Invisible College: The Royal Society, Freemasonry and the Birth of Modern Science.* London: Corgi, 2009.

Mann, Nicholas R. *The Sacred Geometry of Washington, D.C.: The Integrity and Power of the Original Design.* Woolavington, Somerset, UK: Green Magic Publishing/ Barnes & Noble, 2007.

Marrs, Jim. *Rule by Secrecy: The Hidden History That Connects the Trilateral Commission, the Freemasons, and the Great Pyramids.* New York: Harper Paperbacks, 2001.

Marshall, Peter. *The Philosopher's Stone: A Quest for the Secrets of Alchemy.* London: Pan Books, 2002.

Matt, Daniel Chanan. *Zohar: Annotated & Explained.* Woodstock, VT: Skylight Paths Publishing, 2002.

McClenachan, Charles T. *The Book of the Ancient and Accepted Scottish Rite of Freemasonry.* Plano, TX: Stone Guild Publishing, 2009.

McCullough, David. *1776: America and Britain at War.* London: Penguin, 2006.

Mead Walter Russell. *God and Gold: Britain, America and the Making of the Modern World.* London: Atlantic Books, 2007.

Melanson T. *Perfectibilists: The 18th Century Bavarian Order of the Illuminati.* Waltervill, OR: Trine Day, 2009.

Oliver, Rev. George. *A View of Freemasonry from the Deliverance to the Dedication of King Solomon's Temple.* Whitefish, MT: Kessinger Publishing, 2005.

Ovason David. *The History of the Horoscope.* Stroud, Gloucestershire: The History Press, 2006.

———. *The Secret Symbols of the Dollar Bill: A Closer Look at the Hidden Magic and Meaning of the Money You Use Every Day.* New York: HarperCollins, 2004.

———.*The Secret Architecture of Our Nation's Capital: The Masons and the Building of Washington, DC,* New York: HarperCollins, 1999.

———. *The Zelator.* London: Arrow, 1998.

Parry, Jay A. *The Real George Washington.* Malta, ID: National Center for Constitutional Studies, 1991.

Peake, T. De Witt. *Symbolism of King Solomon's Temple.* Whitefish, MT: Kessinger Publishing, 2003.

Pike, Albert. *Morals and Dogma: Of the Ancient and Accepted Scottish Rite of Freemasonry.* Forgotten Books, 2008.

Pottenger, Milton A. *King Solomon's Temple and the Human Body Are One and the Same.* Whitefish, MT: Kessinger Publishing, 2005.

Quinn, D. Michael. *Early Mormonism and the Magic World View.* Salt Lake City: Signature Books, 1998.

Ralls-MacLeod, Karen, and Ian Robertson. *The Quest for the Celtic Key.* Edinburgh: Luath Press, 2005.

Rebisse, Christian. *Rosicrucian History and Mysteries.* Crowborough, UK: The Rosicrucian Collection, 2005.

Regardie Israel. *The Philosopher's Stone: A Modern Comparative Approach to Alchemy from the Psychological and Magical Points of View.* Saint Paul, MN: Llewellyn Publications, 1970.

Ridley, Jasper. *The Freemasons: A History of the World's Most Powerful Secret Society.* New York: Arcade Publishing, 2002.

Robison John. *Proofs of a Conspiracy: Against all the Religions and Governments of Europe, Carried on in the Secret Meetings of Freemasons, Illuminati and Reading Societies.* Forgotten Books, 2008.

Schneider, Michael S. *A Beginner's Guide to Constructing the Universe: Mathematical Archetypes of Nature, Art, and Science.* New York: HarperPerennial, 1995.

Scott, Walter. *Hermetica,* Vol. 1: *The Ancient Greek and Latin Writings Which Contain Religious or Philosophic Teachings Ascribed to Hermes Trismegistus.* Boston, MA: Shambhala, 2001.

Shanks, Hershel. *Jerusalem's Temple Mount: From Solomon to the Golden Dome.* London: Continuum, 2007.

Stavish Mark, *The Path of Alchemy: Energetic Healing and the World of Natural Magic.* Woodbury, MN: Llewellyn Publications, 2006.

Steiner, Rudolf. *Rosicrucian Wisdom.* Forest Row, East Sussex, UK: Rudolf Steiner Press, 2000.

Three Early Modern Utopias: Utopia, New Atlantis, and The Isle of Pines. New York: Oxford University Press, 2009.

Three Initiates. *The Kybalion: A Study of The Hermetic Philosophy of Ancient Egypt and Greece*. Wilder Publications, 2009.

Tompkins, Peter. *The Magic of Obelisks*. New York: Harper & Row, 1981.

Vidal, Gore. *Inventing a Nation: Washington, Adams, Jefferson*. New Haven, CT: Yale University Press, 2003.

Waite, Arthur Edward. *Albert Pike and Freemasonry*. Whitefish, MT: Kessinger Publishing, 2006.

Washington Pocket Map & Guide. New York: Dorling Kindersley, 2007.

The Way of Hermes: New Translations of The Corpus Hermeticum and The Definitions of Hermes Trismegistus to Asclepius. Translated by Clement Salaman, Dorine van Oyen, William D. Wharton, and Jean-Pierre Mahé. Rochester, VT : Inner Traditions, 2004.

Wheelan, Joseph. *Jefferson's Vendetta: The Pursuit of Aaron Burr and the Judiciary*. New York: Carroll & Graf, 2006.

White, Michael. *Isaac Newton: The Last Sorcerer*. Reading, MA: Perseus, 1999.

Williamson, Benedict J., ed. *The Rosicrucian Manuscripts*. Woodbridge VA: Invisible College Press, 2002.

Wilson, Colin. *The Philosopher's Stone*. Los Angeles: Tarcher, 1989.

Yarker, John. *Two Ancient Legends Concerning the First Temple Termed Solomon's Temple*. Whitefish, MT: Kessinger Publishing, 2004.

Yates, Frances A. *Giordano Bruno and the Hermetic Tradition*. University of Chicago Press, 1991.

The Zohar. Pritzker ed. Vol. 1, Vol. 2, Vol. 3, Vol. 4, Vol. 5. Translation and commentary by Daniel C. Matt. Stanford, CA: Stanford University Press, 2003, 2005, 2007. 2009.